Contents

KT-119-199

Acknowledgements

This book is written in the belief that a basic knowledge of economics is an essential ingredient to the portfolio of skills that a leisure manager must possess. Unfortunately, economics has often acquired a poor reputation for being too theoretical and not related to the real world. It also has a reputation for mathematical and diagrammatic technicality, which makes it incomprehensible to many practising managers. We have done our best to present the material in this book in a way that avoids such criticisms. We assume that most of the readers of this book will have no previous knowledge of economics.

Every chapter in the book involves economic concepts but they are applied specifically to leisure. We hope that the end result is a book which shows that economics is a practical and useful discipline, one that is necessary in order to fully understand leisure behaviour on both sides of the leisure market.

We gratefully acknowledge the assistance of Christine Gratton, who slaved over a hot word processor when she had better things to do . . ., and Geoffrey Taylor, for insights into the hotel business.

We take this opportunity to thank all those organisations which have granted us permission to reproduce various figures and tables in this text. The following are Crown Copyright and have been reproduced by permission of the Controller of Her Majesty's Stationery Office: Figures 3.1, 5.1 and 5.2, and Tables 3.4, 3.5, 3.6, 3.7, 3.8, 5.3, 6.1, 6.2, 6.3, 6.4, 6.5 and 6.9. Despite our best endeavours we have been unable to trace Joint Venture Study Group for Table 11.3, or Joint Unit for Research on the Urban Environment for Table 11.4.

Economics of Leisure Services Management

PITMAN
PUBLISHING

in association with
Institute of Leisure and Amenity Management

PITMAN PUBLISHING
128 Long Acre, London WC2E 9AN

A Division of Pearson Professional Limited

First edition 1988
Second edition 1992

© Longman Group UK Limited 1992

A CIP catalogue record for this book can be obtained from the British Library.

ISBN 0 273 61948 9

10 9 8 7 6 5 4 3

Printed and bound in Great Britain by Bell and Bain Ltd, Glasgow

The Publishers' policy is to use paper manufactured from sustainable forests.

Contents

Preface

Recent years have seen the expansion of leisure services throughout Britain, whether they are provided by institutions in the public, commercial or voluntary sectors. Such leisure facilities and services are now recognised as of critical significance in the changing social and economic structure of contemporary Britain. The effectiveness of such provision, however, lies in the hands of leisure officers and managers and it is clear that there is a need to ensure the highest level of professional support for leisure services.

The Institute of Leisure and Amenity Management (ILAM) has been in the forefront of promoting a scheme of professional education and training leading to the qualifications of the ILAM Certificate and Diploma in Leisure Management. These professional qualifications are designed to ensure that leisure managers have a sound base of education and understanding in the operational and technical aspects of day-to-day management of leisure facilities and opportunities. Similarly there is a concern to ensure a thorough knowledge and understanding of the disciplines and skills appropriate to the manager in the leisure business.

The aim of this series is not only to provide texts which will cover constituent elements in the ILAM syllabuses but also to provide for all leisure professionals the opportunities to update and improve their practice and managerial skills. In that sense they will be relevant not only to ILAM courses but also to other educational programmes leading to Higher National Diploma and Degree qualifications as well as reference sources to the working professional.

Each volume deals with a different aspect of professional activity in the leisure fields. As such the texts can be used on an individual basis to enhance skills and understanding in specific aspects of the day-to-day responsibilities of leisure managers. More significantly, however, taken together, the volumes in this series will constitute an integrated support system for professional development which will enhance the efficiency of individual managers and the effectiveness of the services they provide.

This text provides an introduction to economics for managers in leisure services. It presents the economic principles which are relevant to the industry and applies them to leisure management contexts. The authors concentrate on the relevance of applied microeconomics to the management of leisure services within the context of a more general decision-making framework.

Brian S. Duffield   Series Editor

1 Introduction

The twentieth century has seen leisure emerge as a major industry both in Britain and world wide. Many commentators on the leisure industry today regard it as the most important industry of the future. Phrases such as 'the leisure explosion' or 'the leisure boom' appear with regularity in the financial pages of newspapers, and the leisure industry is regarded as one of the major areas of future employment growth in the economy. For a country such as Britain which has historically depended on manufacturing industry to provide its economic strength it is perhaps a little strange to see such economic emphasis placed on leisure.

Some commentators even go so far as to regard Britain as in the first-phases of a post-industrial society where conventional work is relegated to second place in the order of priority. In such societies, the enjoyment of leisure becomes the main priority. This book is about using economic analysis to understand the leisure market and this includes understanding the reasons for this new importance for leisure. Economic analysis though works in a specific context: the culture of a society that has developed through history. We think it appropriate therefore to look back briefly at the history of the development of the leisure market in the context of the British economy.

Development of the leisure market

In pre-industrial times leisure industries hardly existed. Seventeenth century Britain had most of its population living in small rural villages and towns. Agriculture was the main industry and the agricultural production cycle determined the leisure activities of the workers. There would be periods of intensive hard work which left little time for leisure, but then there would be slack periods with little work to do. The main point is that in such agricultural communities work and leisure were not segregated. A lot of drinking, for instance, went on in the fields during working time. Other leisure activities were organised by the workers themselves. There was no recognisable leisure industry.

The Industrial Revolution dramatically changed the nature of people's lives. Manufacturing industries worked long hours, six days a week, with virtually no respite for holidays. Workers moved from the rural areas into cities where opportunities for their conventional leisure activities were restricted. Leisure activities also required both time and money and the new industrial worker had little of either.

Gradually though as the nineteenth century progressed, the working week declined and at the same time real wages were increasing. It was in the latter half of the nineteenth century that recognisable leisure industries began to emerge. In this period the seaside resorts developed into major leisure attractions, first for the old aristocracy, then taken over by the nou-veau-riche middle classes and finally, following the Bank Holiday Act of 1870, they became the destination for the day out at the seaside of the industrial workers on the newly established August holiday.

Also during this period professional football was established because Saturday afternoon working was no longer the norm. Football was a popu-lar recreation in pre-industrial times but it had tended to die out in the new industrial cities due, as much as anything, to lack of space. However, the nature of the game had changed during the nineteenth century as public schools had adopted a new rigid set of rules, and the new game had more spectator potential. By the end of the century, professionalism was well established and the successful teams were attracting large crowds.

It was in the first part of the twentieth century though, particularly in the inter-war years, that leisure became a commercial industry in its own right. The two forces we have already identified, increasing leisure time and increasing real wages, continued to fuel leisure demands, but technology was also changing rapidly and providing a supply-side boost to the leisure industry. One major technical innovation, the cinema, had a dramatic impact on people's leisure-time activities. By 1919, half the British popula-tion were going to the cinema, on average, twice a week. Demand contin-ued to grow so that by 1934 annual admissions had reached 934 million and gross box-office receipts were £41m. At this time the cinema had become the most popular leisure activity of all time and its rate of develop-ment had been unbelievably rapid. The cinema revolution was the first example in the leisure industry of the effect that a new technological devel-opment could have on consumer preferences in leisure. During the rest of the twentieth century, this 'technology effect' was to show itself time and time again.

It was in the immediate post-Second World War period that these new leisure industries reached their peak attendances. In 1946 the annual atten-dance for cinemas in Britain was 1635m. This proved to be the peak, and the long decline set in from there. Similarly, professional football, having experienced growing attendances throughout the earlier twentieth century, achieved record attendances in the 1948–49 season of 41.25m. Again, since that season the industry has experienced a long steady decline in demand. The same has happened with British seaside towns that were the beneficiaries of the first leisure expansion in the late nineteenth century. Resorts such as Blackpool and Scarborough achieved their best ever visitor numbers in the years following the Second World War, but since then visitor numbers have declined.

This picture of decline in demand is not a picture of recession in the leisure industry as a whole. The early post-war period saw a rapid expansion of the leisure industry; this expansion of demand though was into new areas and again technology had an important role to play. One of the most significant technological developments was television. Although the first television broadcast took place before the war, it was only in the post-war period that televisions started to become standard furniture in every home. In fact television became the prime leisure-time activity of a majority of households by the latter half of the twentieth century. It signalled a change of emphasis in the way people used their leisure time.

We have highlighted three industries' growth in the early years of the leisure industry, holiday trips to seaside resorts, professional football and the cinema. All three involved out-of-home activities and it is certainly true that most consumers wanted to get away from both home and work to fully enjoy their leisure time. This is not surprising since in the nineteenth and early twentieth centuries the average worker lived in accommodation that was not an ideal setting for enjoyable leisure-time activities. The three industries we have picked out all have an aspect of escapism attached to them and there certainly was an element of 'getting away from it all', both home and work, in the leisure activities of early industrial Britain.

The arrival of television coincided with a change to greater emphasis on in-home leisure generally. Television is only one of several leisure goods that made the home a centre of leisure activities in the second half of the twentieth century. Hi-fi equipment, videos, computer games, and the like have provided a variety of activities in the home that were not available previously. At the same time housing conditions have improved considerably so that there has been less incentive to get out of the house for entertainment and enjoyment, a fact supported by the boom in the DIY industry, another expanding leisure industry of the post-war period.

Although the home has become much more important in leisure, other developments in technology have taken people further afield than ever before in search of leisure experiences. It was the development of the railways in the nineteenth century that caused the boom in seaside towns. In the twentieth century, the development of air travel and car transport has considerably widened opportunities for holiday travel. Now many families have two holidays abroad each year which involve air travel, and yet at the same time the car will be used for one or two short-break holidays in Britain.

The decline in the three industries we discussed earlier can be explained to some extent by these developments. Whereas people went to the cinema to watch a film, or to the football ground to watch a match, films and sport can now be seen in the home on television and video. The excitement of a day out at the seaside at Blackpool or Brighton has now been replaced by two weeks on a Greek island or a French camp-site. Consumers are now faced by a much wider choice of leisure opportunities.

We have tried to indicate that leisure industries developed rather slowly in the nineteenth century following slow, but steady, changes in the working hours and real wages of manufacturing industry. The pace of development quickened in the inter-war years, with the arrival of new leisure industries. The pace has continued to increase in the post-war period so that the leisure sector is now one of the most dynamic areas of the economy.

There has also been an important change in the structure of the economy. As we have described above, the leisure sector used to follow developments in manufacturing industry. Today the leisure sector is more of a leader than a follower. It is interesting that, whereas the growth of manufacturing industry in the early years of the Industrial Revolution stifled leisure activities, the relative decline of manufacturing in the last twenty years has led to the spotlight turning to leisure industries as the major provider of new jobs. Economics has an important contribution to make in understanding why leisure has become so important.

Economics and the analysis of leisure markets

It is not enough to simply describe what has happened in the leisure industry, we need to know why it has happened, and this is what economic analysis aims to do. It is a mistake to think that economics has all the answers. There are historical, cultural, sociological and psychological forces involved in leisure behaviour. Where economics is particularly useful though is in providing a framework in which these various forces can be analysed. The aim of this book is to introduce leisure practitioners to that framework and to economic principles of relevance to their work.

At the macroeconomic level the economist looks at the underlying forces that determine the size of the leisure sector in the economy as a whole. We have already identified three major forces that have an important effect on leisure: the availability of leisure time, the level of consumers' disposable income, and the state of technical knowledge. Time, money and technology are three major inputs into the process of leisure production. We need to understand how changes in the national economy influence these factors and in turn the leisure market.

Section 1 of the book concentrates, though not exclusively, on the macroeconomic environment within which leisure markets function. We look in Chapter 2 at a simple model of the operation of the national economy which allows us to analyse how the national economy influences the leisure sector and vice versa.

Chapter 3 assesses the economic importance of leisure both descriptively, in looking at the statistics on leisure expenditure, leisure employment and international trade in leisure; and analytically, by examining the methods by which the size and importance of leisure in the economy can be assessed.

Although in a macroeconomic sense we talk about the leisure sector as if it were a homogeneous sector, which together with other such sectors makes up the national economy, in reality it is not homogeneous at all. Rather than a single leisure market there are a whole series of leisure markets. Each of these markets has different characteristics. Some of these are characteristics of market failure, which can result in government interference with the market allocation of resources. Chapter 4 examines the concept of market failure and analyses the sort of government interference, in particular taxation and subsidy policies, that normally result.

Section 1 provides an overview of the leisure sector, which is an important starting point for a better understanding of the more detailed considerations that appear in subsequent sections.

At the microeconomic level the economist tries to analyse the forces that influence the supply and demand of a particular leisure product or service. The general factors which we have mentioned above will obviously influence each individual leisure market, but it is at this market level that we see the great diversity of leisure demands. If all leisure markets were influenced by the same forces they would all grow, or decline together. As we have already seen, some leisure markets will be expanding rapidly, while others will be in equally rapid decline.

Section 2 of the book concentrates on the economic analysis of the demand side of leisure markets. This section looks at a hierarchy of leisure demands, both descriptively and analytically. At the top of the hierarchy is the collective and individual choices of leisure time (Chapter 5) which set a framework within which demands for leisure activities, facilities, goods and travel (Chapter 6) are determined. Finally in this section, in Chapter 7 we look at demand forecasting techniques. This chapter makes a particular effort to put such techniques and the information they yield into a planning context, so that the leisure manager is encouraged to generate appropriate market research information by seeing the practical uses to which such information can be put.

Section 2 then analyses the economic decisions of the consumer. But it goes far beyond that. Analysing consumer decisions, understanding consumer choices, and obtaining and using demand information is crucial to the leisure manager. We indicated earlier in this chapter that Britain's industrial heritage is manufacturing industry and that the leisure industry is a relative newcomer. A firm operating in a manufacturing industry develops a management expertise in production skills and production technology. Leisure though is primarily a service industry. Management expertise and know-how in service industries is essentially marketing expertise. A thorough understanding of the demand side of the market is a crucial ingredient in the development of this expertise.

Section 3 moves to the supply side of the industry to analyse leisure supply decisions, that is the decisions made by managers operating in the leisure industry. Chapter 8 looks at the rationale for the existence of different types of supplier: commercial, public and voluntary. This includes examination of objectives, finance and market structure.

Chapter 9 introduces the formal relationship between inputs and outputs, both in physical and monetary terms. This gives rise to a discussion of issues relevant to a number of management problems in leisure supply, such as identification of capacity and productivity, the balance of fixed and variable costs, and the possibilities of economies of scale in the production of leisure services. Two important management decisions are given a chapter each, because of the extensive treatment afforded to them in economics – pricing (Chapter 10) and investment appraisal (Chapter 11). Both have substantial roots in the earlier demand section (Section 2) since it is impossible to make decisions in these areas without a thorough knowledge of consumer preferences.

Chapters 12 and 13 are concerned with the important recent developments in the leisure market in Britain. Chapter 12 concentrates on the topic of competitive tendering and contracting out and, in particular, considers how the developing field of institutional economics can be applied to the contracting situation in sport and leisure.

Chapter 13 is concerned with an aspect of management which has a more recent pedigree in economics than pricing or investment appraisal, but is assuming great importance, particularly in the public sector, that is value for money criteria. This chapter considers in detail the sort of activity and output indicators that the manager needs in order to make rational supply decisions. The reason for the increased importance of this topic is, of course, the introduction of compulsory competitive tendering for public sector sport and leisure facilities. Performance indicators assume greater significance in the context of contract management.

SECTION 1: NATIONAL ECONOMY AND LEISURE

2 National economy

Macroeconomics and microeconomics

This first section of the book has mainly, though not exclusively, a macroeconomic flavour to it as opposed to the microeconomic approach of the rest of the book. We should be clear initially on the distinction between *microeconomics* and *macroeconomics*. 'Micro' is derived from the Greek word for small and 'macro' from the word for large. At the micro level economists study the behaviour of individual decision-making units, specifically firms and households. Macroeconomics concentrates on the behaviour of entire economies. Thus, whereas microeconomics studies how demand and supply interact in a market to determine the price level of a particular product and the level of output supplied by the firms in the industry, macroeconomics analyses what determines *national* output and employment. Macroeconomics therefore looks at the aggregate results of microeconomic decisions.

Microeconomics is intuitively easier to understand than macroeconomics because as consumers we all make decisions as to how much of a particular product to buy and most of us are familiar with decisions taken by a firm on how many people to employ and how much output to supply. Macroeconomics though is more abstract. We may understand how a firm decides on its level of output, but how can a whole country make a decision on the level of national output? In a centrally planned economy it is feasible for a government to attempt this type of decision (achieving it is another matter!). In a mixed capitalist economy, such as Britain's, the very idea is obscure to say the least.

The way economists try to explain such abstract concepts is to use the notion of a 'model'. An economic model is a simplified version of the reality. The simplification comes in omitting the less important forces and factors causing change in the economy and concentrating on only the major influences. An economic model tries to strike a happy medium between simplicity and reality. If it is too simple the model will give results substantially different from what happens in the real economy. If the model is so realistic it includes all the economic forces that operate in the real world,

then it ceases to be a useful model because the model becomes too complicated to handle. The aim is to simplify yet still retain the major features of
the real world.

The particular model we will use here is referred to as the 'circular flow
model'; it is a useful framework for thinking about macroeconomics.
We will describe the model first and then indicate how leisure can be incorporated into it.

The circular flow of income model

The circular flow model has as its basis the firms and households whose
decisions microeconomics attempts to explain. The model shows the flow
of money from the household sector to the firm sector that is generated
when households buy goods and services from firms. It also shows the flow
of goods and services in the opposite direction, from firms to households.
These are not the only flows between the two sectors though. Households
also sell factor services (eg labour services) to firms and in return receive
income. Figure 2.1 shows these flows with money circulating in an anti-
clockwise direction and real commodities (goods and services and factor
services) circulating in a clockwise direction.

Since all factor services (ie the services of land, labour and capital) are
owned by households then the total amount paid out by firms in factor
payments to households makes up National Income. In the simple model
of Figure 2.1, households spend all this income on the goods and services
produced by firms. Thus Total Expenditure is equal to National Income,
and both correspond to the total value of goods and services produced,
National Product.

The model of Figure 2.1, though simple, is not very realistic. The model
is a bit like a plumbing system such as a central heating system; just as the
amount of water in a central heating system is constant and continues to

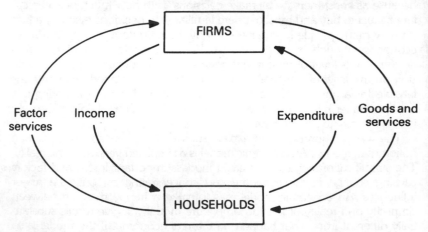

Figure 2.1   Circular flow of income model

circulate hour by hour, day by day, similarly the amount of money in this simple model of the economy is fixed and continually circulates from firms to households and back again. In fact the famous economist A W Phillips built a machine at the London School of Economics in the early 1950s to represent the circular flow model which effectively was a plumbing system with coloured water representing the money flows.

Phillips' machine was more complicated than Figure 2.1. He incorporated valves to allow 'leakages' out of the system and 'injections' into it. In economic terms, leakages represent money that does not continue to circulate. Thus households may decide to save some of their income; they may decide to spend it on goods and services produced by foreign firms; or the government may take income from households in the form of taxation. Saving, import spending, and taxation are all leakages from the circular flow which lead to a reduction in the level of national income, expenditure, and product. On the other hand, other expenditures act as injections into the system and they lead to increases in the level of these three national aggregates. These injections are investment expenditure, government expenditure, and expenditure on exports.

Just as with Phillips' machine, the flow will be increasing, constant, or decreasing depending on the balance of leakages and injections. By incorporating such leakages and injections we now have a model that is more realistic, since national income (and national product and expenditure) can now rise and fall as we know it does in the real world.

The diagram of Figure 2.1 should be adjusted to incorporate other sectors (such as government and foreign countries) and the flows to and from such sectors (the leakages and injections). This is the approach taken by standard economics textbooks. For our purposes though the simple model of Figure 2.1 is adequate. It introduces us to the concepts of national income and national product. These are the national aggregates that have become the prime indicators of a nation's economic health. Before we go on to discuss how leisure fits into the scheme of things it is important to indicate the measurement problems that arise in the estimation of these national aggregates.

Measurement of National Income and National Product

One branch of economics deals with the problems of measuring these macroeconomic aggregates. It is known as National Income Accounting. In many ways it is more similar to accountancy than economics and, at times, it can be quite complicated (as well as rather tedious). It is important though because the results that these procedures give us are used to establish whether the economy is performing well or badly. Statistics on output, income, expenditure and employment are constantly released from government statistical offices and form the basis of government economic policy decisions. At the wider level, comparisons are made between one country and another on the basis of these measurements and judgements made as to relative living standards in different countries.

There are several different ways of carrying out the measurement exercise. The measure of total production in the economy is referred to as Gross National Product (GNP), which is the monetary value at current market prices of all final goods and services produced annually in the national economy. Final goods and services are those that are ready for sale to consumers. Intermediate goods and services are sold to other firms for further processing; these are not included in GNP calculations since their value will eventually be included when they become final goods and services.

In principle then the task is relatively simple. We just need to find all firms that produce only final goods and services and find the value of their annual output. In reality, this proves to be quite difficult. As a result, in general, GNP is measured by looking at what people buy, that is, output is measured by expenditure. We saw in our circular flow model that total output was exactly taken up by total expenditure. Expenditures are easier to measure than outputs and therefore form the basis of GNP measurement.

There is a third way to measure the total level of activity in the economy. We saw earlier that expenditure flowed from households to firms and that income flowed the other way. Since national income and national product are equal, an alternative way is to measure the sum of the different kinds of income earned by households. In principle, the expenditure and income approaches should give us the same answer. In practice, Gross National Product does not equal National Income and several adjustments have to be made to reconcile the two measures. Even then, because both measures come from different statistical sources there is always some additional discrepancy (or residual error) due to errors and omissions in the way the statistics are collected. But instead of dwelling on these problems, we address perhaps the more important question: what does the value of GNP actually tell us?

What it is designed to tell us is the value of all economic activity that takes place in the country. It is for this reason that international comparisons are made between GNP per head to establish international league tables indicating relative affluence. The implication is that increases in GNP are a 'good' thing and that decreases are 'bad'. GNP figures are often taken as a measure of a country's welfare. There are many difficulties in this interpretation.

One major difficulty is that only market activity is included in GNP. The classic example is that of housewives. A woman who stays at home, keeps the house clean, cooks the meals, and looks after the children, makes no contribution in terms of the GNP calculations. Were she to start work, employ a cleaner, cook, and child-minder, her own salary plus that of the cleaner, cook and child-minder would all be included in GNP. The estimated GNP figure would increase but the only net increase in economic activity is the housewife's new salary. The work done by the others was also done before; it was not measured simply because it was not market activity.

Similarly, lots of other economic activity goes unrecorded because the people doing it want it that way. We are referring of course to the 'black economy' or underground economy. Many people do jobs for 'cash-in-the-hand' to avoid paying taxes. Everybody knows it goes on to a considerable extent but by its very nature it does not get measured in GNP. There have been several attempts to estimate the economic importance of the underground economy and one estimate put it at about 10 per cent of GNP, indicating that it is certainly at a significant level.

A third problem that arises with the GNP measure is that it measures 'bads' as well as 'goods'. For example, let us take two countries similar in every respect but one. In country A, nobody smokes; in country B, everybody smokes 60 cigarettes a day, the cigarettes all being produced in its own factories. The GNP figure for country B would be substantially higher because it would include not only all the cigarette production but also all the health care costs that would result from the cigarette consumption. Similarly, economic activities that create pollution or destroy the environment, and disasters such as earthquakes that require economic activity to clear up, are all part of the GNP calculation, even though a country would be better off without the pollution and the disasters (and therefore have a lower GNP figure).

These three examples indicate the problems of using GNP figures for international comparisons of economic well-being. Different countries will have different proportions of the female population active in the labour force, different proportions of economic activity in the underground economy, and different proportions of goods to bads in the GNP figures. Hence comparing one country to another on the basis of GNP per head data is not likely to be an accurate measure of welfare.

There is also another important reason for scepticism at such comparisons and this involves the treatment of leisure in GNP.

Leisure and GNP

As a country gets richer people normally work less hours and enjoy greater leisure time. We show in Chapter 5 that this is basically due to people choosing to trade off increased income in return for more free time. That is, given the choice of high incomes and little leisure time or slightly lower incomes with more leisure time, people in relatively affluent, industrialised (or post-industrialised) societies normally choose the latter. Given that they make this choice it means that they feel better off having more leisure (in economic terms, their welfare is higher) even though they have 'paid' for it in terms of income. Their increased welfare would not be reflected though in measured GNP.

For example, let us compare two countries, A and B, that have identical productive capacity and population. Suppose that the only difference between the two countries is that A has a shorter working week than B and hence more leisure time. From what we have said above A will have higher economic welfare than B. However, B will have higher output, higher expenditure, and higher income, and hence have a higher measured GNP, whichever way it is measured. A's choice for more leisure would actually be interpreted in GNP figures as a reduction in economic well-being.

There is perhaps a more fundamental criticism of the way that leisure is treated in the circular flow model and in GNP calculations. Firms provide leisure goods and leisure services and the value of these will be recorded in GNP. However, the value of these goods and services is only part of the total value of leisure in the economy. Households in fact 'produce' leisure activities by combining their own time with market-purchased inputs (ie goods and services). The time input is often more important than the goods input and hence the tendency of developed economies to have more and more leisure time as affluence increases.

This household production framework is a particularly appropriate one for studying leisure. The 'outputs' produced by households are often referred to as composite commodities. Each composite commodity has a different ratio of goods inputs to time inputs. Hence we refer to goods-intensive commodities (where the time input is relatively small) and time-intensive commodities (where the households time is the main input). For example, in sport, squash would be a fairly goods-intensive commodity since the cost of renting a squash court and buying the required equipment is high relative to the time spent on court. On the other hand, long-distance walking is a fairly time-intensive commodity.

This categorisation of composite commodities helps to explain why households choose to have more leisure time as incomes increase. Time is a finite input into household production. The goods input can be continually expanded as productive capacity grows over time with technological change. Thus time becomes more and more valuable. Yet none of these considerations is taken account of in the standard GNP measurements.

One economist, J I Gershuny, has suggested a modification of the circular flow model that does take account of some of the points made above.

Model incorporating leisure

Gershuny refers to the model in Figure 2.1 as the formal money economy. It is this formal economy that is measured in GNP calculations. The formal economy '*relies on the existence of an informal economy outside the formal one, an economy which, based on the non-money production of services within the household, progressively substitutes for the production of services within the formal economy*' (Gershuny, 1979).

These concepts of formal and informal economies require some modifications to our circular flow diagram. Figure 2.2 redraws Figure 2.1 incorporating the formal economy concept. We replace the firm sector by formal production, a sector which produces the goods and services that are sold for money payments. Households, as well as acting as consumers in making these payments, also supply labour (and other factor services) to the formal economy and in return receive money wages. The sum of these money flows forms the basis of the GNP estimates as we have already seen.

Figure 2.3 introduces the informal economy into the picture. Now the household does not simply consume the goods and services it purchases

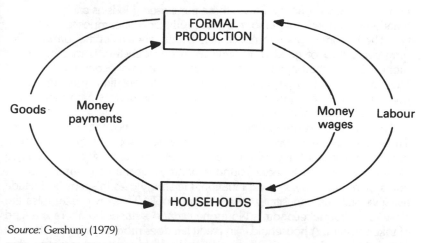

Source: Gershuny (1979)

Figure 2.2 The formal economy

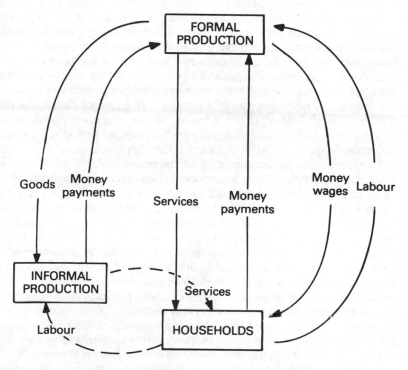

Source: Gershuny (1979)

Figure 2.3 The informal economy

from the formal economy. It uses these purchased goods as capital, in combination with household labour, in the production of composite commodities. The important point to notice here is that whereas in the formal economy every flow of goods and services in one direction is matched by a
money flow in the opposite direction, in the informal economy this is not
the case. No money payments are made for labour time used up in the
household production process and no money exchanges are made in the
final consumption of the composite commodities.

The informal economy does not only consist of household production.
There are two other major components: the black (or underground) economy and what Gershuny calls 'the communal production system'. We have
already discussed the underground economy but the communal production system requires some explanation. Gershuny uses this term to include
activities such as babysitting circles or car pools. These two examples are
close to the formal economy. No money changes hands but there is a kind
of token system. A household is in credit if it does more than its fair share of
communal production (ie it provides babysitters more often than other
households in the circle). However for the communal production system to
survive there must be a balancing out within a reasonably short period of
time such that no household remains in net credit or net debit.

Other aspects of communal production are more removed from the formal economy. In some circumstances the formal economy fails to provide
the particular goods and services that are demanded by households. We
discuss in more detail the reasons for this in Chapter 8, but the effect is that
households that demand such goods and services combine together to provide them. It is similar to household production except it involves more
than one household. What unites these households is a common interest in
the commodity being communally provided. This type of communal production is particularly important in leisure, and is more normally referred to
as voluntary sector activity. Many leisure activities are provided by voluntary clubs. In sport it is the most common form of provision.

Gershuny's model, incorporating the informal economy, is more useful
to us than the simple circular flow model in that we can see explicitly how a
lot of leisure fits into the national economy. It emphasises the extent to
which much of leisure is omitted from the standard statistics on GNP. One
final argument from Gershuny suggests that over time, with economic
development, there is a gradual shift in economic activity from the formal
to the informal economy. The argument rests on different rates of productivity increase in the manufacturing and services sectors of the economy.
The manufacture of goods is a capital-intensive process. As more and more
capital per worker is employed over time, labour productivity increases and
the relative price of manufactured goods decreases. The service sector of
the economy on the other hand is labour intensive, and there is less opportunity to improve productivity by employing more capital per worker. The
result is a relative rise in the cost of services relative to consumer goods.

Households often have a choice of whether to buy services in the formal
economy, or to produce them themselves in household or communal
production. Thus a household can cook its meal at home using food

purchased from the supermarket, the household capital goods of an oven, plates, knives and forks, and the labour time of the household members. Alternatively, the household can buy a meal in a restaurant. Gershuny's argument is that economic development causes the relative price of the restaurant meal to increase relative to the cost of the household capital items required to produce the meal at home. The implication is that more of these services will be provided through household or communal production.

We have seen earlier that official estimates of GNP underestimate the true level of economic activity. Much of this underestimation relates to the importance of household and communal production in the leisure sector. If Gershuny's argument is correct then the extent of underestimation will increase year by year with economic development. Household and communal production in sport is important in money terms, as a later case study, 8.2, demonstrates. In the next chapter we attempt to estimate the economic importance of leisure in the UK economy. For this exercise we are forced to rely on official government statistics. Everything we have said in this chapter should indicate that these statistics will only tell part of the story.

Further reading

Gershuny JI 1979 *The Informal Economy: its role in Post-Industrial Society*. Futures, 1979.

3 The economic importance of leisure

In the nineteenth century, the UK became one of the largest manufacturing nations in the world. In the twentieth century the popular view is that Britain is still primarily a manufacturing nation. This is no longer the case. There has been a profound structural change in the UK economy in the second half of the twentieth century. By the early 1990s manufacturing employment accounted for less than 25 per cent of total employment whereas employment in services was 70 per cent of total employment. The share of services employment in total employment has increased by over a third since 1960 whereas the share of manufacturing employment has decreased by a similar amount. Leisure, though not solely a service industry, has been part of this tremendous rise in the service sector of the economy relative to the manufacturing sector. In this chapter we look firstly at the evidence on the increasing economic importance of the leisure sector and then attempt to analyse the forces that lie behind it. The evidence we present comes from published sources and therefore is open to the criticisms of understatement that were made in the last chapter.

Leisure and the British economy
Consumer expenditure on leisure

For an economist consumer expenditure on leisure goods and services is a major indicator of the economic importance of leisure. However, it is not an easy task to identify leisure expenditure from published statistics on consumer expenditure. Many categories of expenditure (for instance, travel expenditure) includes both leisure and non-leisure items. The UK National Accounts are normally the first place we would look for data on consumer expenditure on leisure, but this data is problematical for the analysis of the leisure market since no distinction is made between leisure and non-leisure elements in the various expenditure categories. Fortunately there are two data sources that identify leisure items specifically.

The first is the statistics produced by the Henley Centre for Forecasting

Table 3.1 Consumer expenditure on leisure, 1984–1989

Trends	1984	1985	1986	1987	1988	1989
Market						
value (£m)	47113	52009	56446	61884	68310	74040
% change	9.6	10.4	8.5	9.6	10.4	8.4
Prices						
(1985 = 100)	94	100	105	111	117	124
% change	5.7	6.4	5.4	5.0	5.4	6.0
Volume (£m)	50114	52011	53548	55896	58516	59843
% change	3.7	3.8	3.0	4.4	4.7	2.3

Source: *Leisure Futures* Henley Centre for Forecasting (February 1991)

in their publication 'Leisure Futures'. These statistics are produced from a combination of official government statistics plus the Henley Centre's own surveys to produce what is probably the best estimate of the overall leisure market in expenditure terms. Table 3.1 indicates the size of the leisure market, estimated by the Henley Centre to be £74b in 1989, or 23 per cent of total consumer expenditure. The table also indicates the rapid growth in the market in the 1980s. In 1985 and 1988 growth was above 10 per cent. After allowing for price changes, volume growth was less than this, but the market still grew by 4.7 per cent in volume terms in 1988, a substantial annual growth rate.

However, 1988 was a year of strong economic growth within the British economy. Since then the economy has slowed down considerably in the late 1980s and early 1990s. Since leisure is mainly discretionary expenditure, it is often among the first to be cut back in a recession. Growth in consumer leisure expenditure in 1989, at 2.3 per cent in volume terms, was well down on 1988. Indications are that growth was further cut back in 1990 and 1991.

Table 3.2 shows the size of individual leisure sectors within the total leisure market, their share of total consumer expenditure and the percentage growth in their share of consumer spending from 1984 to 1989. The largest leisure market is expenditure on eating out, accounting for 4.27 per cent of total consumer expenditure in 1989, followed by expenditure on beer (3.25 per cent of total consumer expenditure), and expenditure on holidays abroad (3.09 per cent of total consumer expenditure). Other major sectors include sports (1.81 per cent) and DIY goods (1.45 per cent). If expenditure on spirits (1.41 per cent) and wine (1.37 per cent) is included then overall expenditure on alcohol is the major single sector of the leisure market.

The fastest growing sectors over the 1984 to 1989 period have been sports, photography, DIY, records and tapes, audio equipment and holidays abroad (see Table 3.2). Interestingly, the largest single market, beer, has hardly grown at all in real terms, and in 1989 accounted for a substantially smaller share of total consumer expenditure than in 1984. The same is also true for the other alcohol sectors, spirits and wine. In fact, out of the 23 sectors in Table 3.2 only 10 of these increased their share of consumer

Table 3.2   Individual leisure sectors: market value, share of consumer spending, and percentage change in share of consumer spending

£m	Market value 1989	Share of consumer spending 1989	Percentage change in share of consumer spending 1984–1989
Audio Equipment etc	2140	0.65	+14
Beer	10677	3.25	–16
Books	1088	0.33	0
Cinema	178	0.05	0
DIY goods	4749	1.45	+18
Eating out	14018	4.27	+2
Foreign visitors	6945	2.11	–9
Gambling	2876	0.88	–11
Gardening	1344	0.41	+5
Holidays abroad	10150	3.09	+11
Holidays in UK	3820	1.16	–22
Home computers	860	0.26	+4
Magazines	825	0.25	0
Newspapers	2124	0.65	–19
Pets	1939	0.59	–2
Photography	1042	0.32	+19
Records and tapes	1175	0.36	+16
Spirits	4641	1.41	–19
Sports	5951	1.81	+28
Television	2570	0.78	–21
Toys and games	1188	0.36	+6
Video	1841	0.56	–11
Wine	4500	1.37	–12

Source: *Leisure Futures* Henley Centre for Forecasting (February 1991)

expenditure over the 1984 to 1989 period although actual consumer expenditure, in both real and money terms, increased in all the sectors.

An alternative source of data on consumer expenditure is the Family Expenditure Survey, which is a household survey in which households keep a record of all their expenditure over a two-week period. Data are reported on the basis of average weekly household expenditure on specific items and those items that can be identified as leisure are reported in Table 3.3. Because of changes in definition some of the data in Table 3.3 are not directly comparable from one year to the next as the footnotes to the table indicate. Holiday expenditure is the major leisure market in 1989 according to these data but this is partly due to the fact that the definition of the alcohol leisure section in this table for 1986 and 1989 is 'alcoholic drink consumed away from home'. The other major sectors in Table 3.3 are meals consumed out, television, radio and musical instruments, books, newspapers and magazines and DIY materials. What is interesting from Table 3.3 is the relatively small amount of expenditure on 'subscriptions and admission charges to participant sports'. The reason again is that participant sport is a composite commodity and only part of the true value is recorded in expenditure estimates. There is much time and effort expended

Table 3.3 Household expenditure on selected leisure items

United Kingdom	£ and percentages		
	1981	1986	1989
Average weekly household expenditure (£)			
Alcoholic drink consumed away			
from home	5.39[2]	5.93	6.92
Meals consumed out[1]	–	4.38	5.51
Books, newspapers,			
magazines, etc	2.00	2.73	3.31
Television, radio and			
musical instruments	3.26	4.85	5.65
Purchase of materials for			
home repairs, etc	1.57	3.06	2.89
Holidays	3.08	5.39	7.76
Hobbies	0.08	0.06	0.09
Cinema admissions	0.14	0.10	0.16
Dance admissions	0.12	0.12	–[4]
Theatre, concert, etc,			
admissions	0.17	0.29	0.35
Subscription and admission charges			
to participant sports	0.43	0.71	0.85
Football match admissions	0.06	0.08 ⎫	0.20
Admissions to other spectator sports	0.02	0.04 ⎭	
Sports goods (excluding clothes)	0.26	0.37	0.62
Other entertainment	0.24	0.41	0.70[4]
Total weekly expenditure on above	16.82[3]	28.52	35.01
Expenditure on above items as a			
percentage of total			
household expenditure	*13.4*	*16.0*	*15.6*

Source: Family Expenditure Survey and *Social Trends* (1991)
Notes:
1 Eaten on the premises, excluding school meals and workplace meals.
2 Including home consumption.
3 The total for 1981 is not comparable with later years since the figure for the category 'Meals consumed out' is not available.
4 For 1989, 'Dance admissions' have been included with 'Other entertainment'.

by the voluntary sector in this area which goes completely unrecorded. Consumer expenditure figures tell us how consumers allocate their money over various leisure activities. They do not tell us how they allocate their time over these activities. For time intensive commodities, such as many sports, time may well be a more important input than money.

There are other categories which have surprisingly low estimates in Table 3.3, for instance hobbies, cinema admissions, dance admissions, and football match admissions. This is because these figures relate to average weekly household expenditure. Not only are weekly amounts of expenditure on these items relatively small but also many households do not spend anything on such items. It illustrates the point that many leisure activities are minority activities. For instance less than 10 per cent of the British population visit a cinema at least once a month. The Family Expenditure Survey averages these expenditures over all households (whether they make an expenditure or not). Hence the small average weekly expenditures recorded in some of the categories. This is also a factor in the participant sports category.

The items in Table 3.3 altogether accounted for 15.6 per cent of total household expenditure in 1989. The main reason for this much lower figure than that of the Henley Centre is that no attempt is made in this table to identify the leisure items of other categories of expenditure which include both leisure and non-leisure expenditures. The Henley Centre figures do include such estimates.

Whichever estimate we use, there is little controversy over one thing: leisure accounts for a substantial part of the economic activity of the British economy. What is also clear is that it is accounting for an increasing share. There is no dramatic boom in leisure expenditure though: some items may experience rapid growth in demand but others will be in decline. Over the long term, leisure expenditure as a whole increases slightly faster than total consumer expenditure.

Leisure employment

We indicated earlier that there has been a major structural change in British employment, with service employment dominating total employment. Leisure employment includes both service and manufacturing employment and the aim of this section is to analyse the importance of leisure employment in total employment, since this represents another indicator of the relative importance of leisure in the economy. Department of Employment data are used to identify the changes in leisure employment that have occurred in the 1980s and what type of employment is benefiting from any growth in leisure markets.

The data sets are confined to post-1983 because of a change in the categorisation of industries at this time (to the 1980 Standard Industrial Classification). This means being confined to five main sets of leisure manufacturing industries; electronic goods, alcoholic and soft drinks, printing and publishing, and 'other manufacturing' (which includes sports equipment, toys, games, photographic processing and jewellery). For leisure services there are two broad categories; hotels and catering, and recreation and culture (which includes film production, radio, television, theatres, libraries, museums, art galleries, and sport and recreation services).

Table 3.4 summarises employment in those leisure industries for which data are available. Over the period of 1983 to 1990, most leisure manufacturing industries show no overall growth, although a couple demonstrate some growth in the mid-1980s, but then a decline in the late 1980s. Clearly leisure goods manufacturing is not exploiting the potential offered by the growth of certain leisure markets. Part of the reason for this relates to the changing industrial structure in Britain as a whole, from manufacturing

Table 3.4 Leisure industries' employment 1983–1990

(SIC 80)	1983	1984	1985	1986	1987	1988	1989	1990
				(September data)	(thousands)			
Manufacturing								
Electronic and Electrical								
Males	119	124	126	123	125	121	112	110
Females	81	82	73	70	68	67	79	80
(part-time)	(16)	(18)	(11)	(10)	(10)	(8)	(11)	(14)
Alcohol and soft drink								
Males	95*	90*	73	70	68	65	66*	62*
Females	40*	36*	26	25	25	25	27*	26*
(part-time)	(6)	(6)	(4)	(4)	(4)	(4)	(4)	(4)
Printing and Publishing								
Males	228	229	231	222	217	211	214	214
Females	113	116	122	125	127	130	142	147
(part-time)	(31)	(31)	(28)	(28)	(28)	(29)	(28)	(31)
Toys, sports goods, photos, etc								
Males	41	39	44	47	49	53	40	39
Females	38	37	39	39	38	39	42	44
(part-time)	(4)	(3)	(10)	(12)	(14)	(15)	(12)	(12)
Services								
Hotels and Catering								
Males	342	355	351	358	376	382	394	403
Females	642	660	692	703	734	773	722	756
(part-time)	(461)	(481)	(466)	(467)	(486)	(504)	(490)	(510)
Recreation and Culture								
Males	208	198	250	270	271	286	256	260
Females	221	225	235	227	239	242	270	284
(part-time)	(128)	(129)	(121)	(115)	(122)	(120)	(141)	(151)

Source: *Employment Gazette* Department of Employment   Note: *Also includes tobacco manufacturing

industries to service industries, but much of the reason lies with Britain's poor international competitiveness in the goods market.

In leisure services a different picture emerges. Both hotels and catering, and sport and recreation services, demonstrate strong growth over the 1980s with some signs of slowdown in the last two years. Imports have less effect in these markets. Sport and recreation services have very little international trade whilst the British hotel and catering industry is very competitive on the world stage.

One distinguishing feature in Table 3.4 is the growing importance of women in the leisure labour market. In all but one leisure manufacturing industry female employment either stays constant or increases. In both leisure services sectors female employment grows strongly. Much of the growth in female employment is part-time. A total of 39 per cent of leisure services employment is female part-time. This compares with equivalent figures of 26 per cent for services generally and 20 per cent for the whole labour force. It is important to realise that part-time work may be the preferred choice of not only employers but also women themselves. A survey conducted by the Department of Employment suggested that only a tenth of part-time workers would prefer a full-time job.

Table 3.5 compares leisure employment with employment generally in the British economy. In leisure manufacturing the decline in employment in the period covered by the data was just over 4 per cent, compared with a 7.5 per cent decline for manufacturing generally. The growth in leisure services employment was at the same rate as for services generally. The leisure sectors represented in these data account for 11.5 per cent of total employment in manufacturing and services.

Finally, Table 3.6 provides evidence that any growth in local authorities

Table 3.5   Overall leisure and GB employment 1983–1990

(SIC 80)	1983	1984	1985	1986	1987	1988	1989	1990
			(September data)		(thousands)			
All manufacturing								
Male	3965	3946	3738	3622	3550	3503	3588	3526
Female	1582	1569	1570	1544	1519	1522	1599	1603
(part-time)	(366)	(363)	(311)	(290)	(294)	(285)	(330)	(337)
Leisure manufacturing								
Male	483	482	474	462	459	450	432	425
Female	272	271	260	259	258	261	290	297
(part-time)	(56)	(58)	(53)	(54)	(56)	(56)	(55)	(61)
All services								
Male	6117	6204	6373	6508	6623	6748	6675	6750
Female	7164	7310	7488	7690	7928	8170	8729	8691
(part-time)	(3548)	(3703)	(3528)	(3720)	(3854)	(3971)	(3963)	(4134)
Leisure services								
Male	550	553	601	628	647	668	650	663
Female	863	885	927	930	973	1015	992	1040
(part-time)	(589)	(610)	(587)	(582)	(608)	(624)	(631)	(661)

Source: Employment Gazette Department of Employment

Table 3.6 Local authority leisure services employment 1976–1990

	1976	1980	1985	1990
		(thousands)		
Libraries and museums				
full-time	28.1	27.3	27.6	28.4
part-time	16.2	17.5	19.6	22.1
Recreation, parks, baths				
full-time	83.7	83.3	82.4	80.9
part-time	20.5	24.1	27.9	35.8
Leisure as % of total LA				
full-time	6.7	6.3	6.6	6
part-time	3.8	4.3	4.8	5.2

Source: *Employment Gazette* Department of Employment

leisure services during the 1980s has benefited part-time jobs rather than full-time jobs.

Overall employment in leisure industries, both service and manufacturing, accounts for a substantially smaller share of total employment than the share of consumer expenditure on leisure in total consumer expenditure. The reason is that consumers spend a large share of their leisure budget on leisure goods and services produced in other countries, which we now go on to analyse.

International trade in leisure

In the last chapter we discussed a simple circular flow model of the economy. A more complete model would include an international sector with money flows from this sector to and from the national economy. Such flows are recorded statistically in the Balance of Payments. The Balance of Payments is divided into three sections: the current account records trade in goods and services; the capital account covers long-term capital movements and investment flows; official financing covers monetary transactions between the UK government and other governments, and international monetary organisations such as the International Monetary Fund. Here we are mainly concerned with the current account. There is a further split in the current account into visibles (goods) and invisibles (services).

In the Balance of Payments positive signs are used to represent money flows into the country, which correspond to flows of goods and services out of the country (ie exports). Negative signs refer to money flows out of the country, which correspond to flows of goods and services into the country (ie imports).

In the post-war period there has been a long term decline in the share of the British consumer goods market that is supplied by home producers. Imports of manufactured goods have increased steadily. What is often not realised is the huge swing that took place in the UK Balance of Payments between the late 1970s and the early 1980s. Also, the services component in the Balance of Payments is often overlooked because many feel that services, by their very nature are not traded over international boundaries. In reality the UK Balance of Payments has become more and more reliant on services.

In 1977, manufactured goods contributed a £5886m surplus to the UK's Balance of Payments compared to a £3038m surplus in services. By 1984 the manufacturing trade surplus has disappeared altogether and there was a £3785 deficit. On the other hand, services not only maintained the surplus but increased it to £3985.

How is it that services can be traded between nations? We all understand that a car can be produced in one country and sold to another. It is easy to send the product overseas for the foreign buyer. But how can a hotelier in Stratford-upon-Avon sell his hotel room to someone in America? The answer is to bring the American over here to Stratford. When a foreign tourist visits this country all his expenditure in this country will count as a British export. The service is provided in Britain, but it is sold to a foreigner and it is just the same as a foreigner buying a British car. Similarly when a British tourist goes abroad, all his expenditure counts as an import.

In fact virtually all of the international trade in leisure services is accounted for by holidays and tourism – ie holidays abroad by the British and holidays in Britain by foreigners. We might expect then, given the strength of leisure services in total employment in leisure, that we would have a healthy balance of payments surplus on this account. In fact Table 3.7 shows that there are quite sharp fluctuations in the Travel Balance of Payments. This table summarises all expenditure by foreign visitors to this country (CREDITS), and all expenditure by British visitors abroad (DEBITS). This expenditure is split into that of business visitors and that by tourists (LEISURE). It is clear from Table 3.7 that the latter is by far the more important. The table shows that only in two years in the 1980s, 1980 and 1985, was the UK in surplus on the travel balance of payments. For all the other years there was a deficit. That is, British tourists spent more in foreign countries than foreign tourists spent in Britain. Moreover, the deficit is increasing. The overall deficit doubled from just over £1b in 1987 to just over £2b in 1988. It moved further into the red, to £2.4b in 1989. The table splits the travel balance of payments into that due to leisure travel and that due to business travel. This split shows clearly that the overall deficit is due to leisure travel since business travel is consistently in surplus, and in increasing surplus in the late 1980s.

Thus the argument that tourism can save the British economy looks rather weak. The British propensity to travel abroad and spend money in foreign countries means that overall international tourist flows have a negative impact on our balance of payments. However, things could be worse. There was fairly strong growth in UK visits by foreigners throughout the 1980s, except for 1980, 1981 and 1986 and equally strong growth in their expenditure. Without this growth the travel balance of payments would be in a substantially worse state. It is the rapid growth in foreign visits by UK

Table 3.7 Travel balance of payments 1979–1989

	1979	1980	1981	1982	1983	1984	1985	1986	1987	1988	£m 1989
Credits											
Business	600	735	763	794	961	1091	1293	1552	1632	1852	2009
Leisure	2197	2226	2207	2394	3042	3523	4149	4001	4628	4332	4868
Total	2797	2961	2970	3188	4003	4614	5442	5553	6260	6184	6877
Debits											
Business	447	521	610	683	805	984	1075	1131	1317	1448	1597
Leisure	1662	2217	2662	2957	3285	3679	3796	4952	5963	6768	7693
Total	2109	2738	3272	3640	4090	4663	4871	6083	7280	8216	9290
Balances											
Business	153	214	153	111	156	107	218	421	315	404	412
Leisure	535	9	-455	-563	-243	-156	353	-951	-1335	-2436	-2825
Overall balance – travel	688	223	-302	-452	-87	-49	571	-530	-1020	-2032	-2413

Source: The Pink Book 1990 United Kingdom Balance of Payments

B

residents that is the main cause of the deficit in the travel balance of payments.

It is through travel that leisure services are traded between nations. The services do not cross international boundaries, but the consumers do. For leisure goods, there is the more familiar trading pattern; unfortunately, there is also the familiar picture facing many UK goods markets: imports often exceed exports. Figure 3.1 shows the international trade position for the major leisure goods markets. Of the four categories of leisure goods in Figure 3.1 two of them, alcohol and books, periodicals and newspapers, have been consistently showing a balance of trade surplus (British exports of these goods exceed imports) over the late 1970s and throughout the 1980s, and one, electronic consumer goods, has been consistently in deficit (ie imports greater than exports). In the mid-1980s, the overall deficit for electronic consumer goods was so great that overall the total leisure goods sector was in deficit. However, in the late 1980s and 1990 this deficit has been substantially reduced mainly due to the rapid expansion in British exports of television and video recorders, and the reduction in imports of video recorders.

The fourth category of leisure goods in Figure 3.1 is sports goods. From 1971 to 1980, Britain exported more sports goods than it imported. Since then Britain has become increasingly dependent on imports of sports goods so that it now has a substantial balance of payments deficit in this market. The market for sports goods was the most rapidly expanding leisure market in terms of consumer expenditure in Table 3.2. It seems that a large part of this increasing consumer expenditure is on imported sports goods. This further reinforces the main point. Expansion of the leisure market is not necessarily an economic benefit. It depends on whether consumers spend their leisure pounds on British produced goods and services or on foreign goods and services. As indicated in this section, in two of the most rapidly expanding areas of leisure, sport and holidays, it is foreign suppliers who are the major beneficiaries.

The evidence we have presented above presents a rather mixed picture of the importance of leisure in the economy. Expenditures on leisure account for a substantial portion of Gross National Product. However because a high proportion of this expenditure is in foreign holidays and foreign leisure goods, employment in the leisure sector is not as big as we might expect. On the other hand it is increasing, particularly in leisure services, although much of the new employment is in part-time jobs for women, which is not the sort of employment which the government is looking for to replace the increasing number of jobs being lost in manufacturing industry (ie full-time jobs for males).

If this all seems rather confusing, it may help to analyse the same evidence from a different perspective. Firstly we return to the macroeconomic framework we introduced in the last chapter to analyse how macroeconomic movements have influenced the leisure sector. Secondly, we look at the leisure sector itself to see to what extent it can influence the national economy by generating expenditure, employment, and income within the industry, which will have repercussions for the national economy.

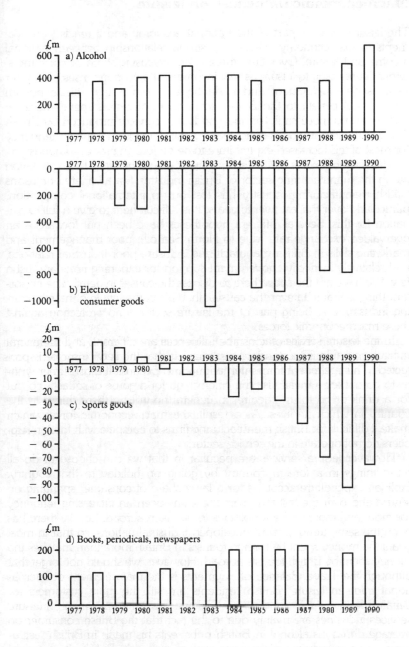

Source: Overseas Trade Statistics

Figure 3.1 Balance of payments in leisure goods, UK, 1977–1990

Macroeconomic influences on leisure

The leisure sector is part of the national economy and it reacts to movements in that economy. There is a strong relationship between national income and leisure. Over time there is an increasing share of consumers' expenditure going to leisure as real income in the economy rises. What our sections on employment and trade have shown is that this is not an unequivocal benefit to the British economy. Consumers spend more on leisure but not necessarily on the goods and services produced by British firms. In the leisure goods sector particularly, there is a long-term tendency for most of this increased expenditure to be on foreign produced goods.

The reason for this has little to do with leisure per se. The explanation lies in the manufacturing sector of British industry. For a variety of reasons British manufacturing industry has lost out to international competition, particularly over the last twenty years. It is difficult here to give a full explanation for this. Several different hypotheses have been put forward – an overvalued exchange rate (due to North Sea oil), poor management and marketing skills in British manufacturing industry, poor industrial relations, and relatively ineffective government support for exporting firms are just a few. We have not the space here to discuss the causes in detail. The important thing is that whatever the causes, they affect the whole of manufacturing industry, and being part of the leisure sector is no protection against these macroeconomic forces.

In the leisure services sector, the influences are different, and in general more favourable. The standard argument is that the service sector is protected to a large extent from international competition. If a consumer wishes to go out for a meal, visit the cinema, go for a game of squash, go out for a drink or go to the theatre, in general he will do these things in the country in which he lives. As a result, the macroeconomic forces which make it difficult for British manufacturing firms to compete with foreign suppliers do not operate in the service sector.

However leisure services are peculiar in that we can choose to do all these things in a foreign country by going on holiday to that country. Holiday expenditure accounts for a large share of consumer spending on leisure and over the last ten years there has been an increasing tendency for more and more of these holidays to be taken abroad. Luckily there has been the same trend in most developed industrial nations, so that in most years the money spent by foreign tourists in Britain more than matches the money spent by British tourists abroad. However, we should not forget that although the Travel Balance of Payments is the main element of international trade in leisure, British residents are still the main customers for Britain's leisure services industries. So large rises in employment in leisure services industries are mainly due to the fact that the British consumer on average drinks his alcohol in British pubs, eats his meals in British restaurants, plays squash in British sports centres, and visits British cinemas and theatres. Leisure services are protected to a large extent from foreign competition since foreign holidays last for a relatively short time.

Thus the macroeconomic forces are tending to increase total leisure spending (in both goods and services) but because of interactions with the international economy, it is increasingly the expenditure on leisure services that feeds through to output and employment in British industries.

This picture paints the leisure sector as a follower of national trends. However, increasingly the leisure sector plays the role as a catalyst which can generate expenditure, employment, output, and income, and it is to this aspect of leisure that we now turn.

The leisure sector and the National Economy

One popular macroeconomic concept, the multiplier, is of increasing relevance to the leisure economist. Keynes popularised 'the multiplier effect' in the context of government intervention in the economy to reduce unemployment. In an underemployed economy, £1 of additional government expenditure will have an effect on national income greater than this. The reason for this is that whereas the initial government expenditure does increase national income by £1, the process does not stop there. The recipients of this income go on to spend it on goods and services and this additional consumer expenditure further increases the national income. The multiplier represents the overall change in national income that results from the additional government expenditure.

Increasingly the multiplier process is being used at the microeconomic rather than the macroeconomic level and it is the multiplier effects of leisure expenditure that is now the focus of interest. Governments were more reluctant in the 1980s to use Keynesian methods to solve unemployment. But the Keynesian multiplier has not died; rather the tourist multiplier has replaced the government expenditure multiplier as job creation through tourism and leisure developments has been put forward as the solution to unemployment in depressed areas.

We have seen in early sections of this chapter the increasing importance of foreign tourists (and in particular American tourists) to the British economy. However it is the impact of tourism and leisure expenditure at the local level, rather than for the economy as a whole, that is attracting the attention of policy makers. Figure 3.2 shows the process of local income generation that results from initial direct tourist expenditure. Suppose an American tourist spends £10 on lunch in a restaurant in Cambridge. The immediate direct effect is to increase the restaurateur's income by £10. What happens next depends on how he spends this £10 (ie the next round in the expenditure process). The amount of this £10 that the restaurateur passes on to his staff and other firms in Cambridge is the indirect effect of the tourist's expenditure. A further effect on the local economy occurs when the local income earned as a result of the direct and indirect effects is spent. The amount of this spending that benefits local businesses is the induced effect of tourist expenditure. The total of the direct, indirect, and induced income, expressed as a proportion of the initial expenditure, is the MULTIPLIER. Such multiplier analysis is the major exercise carried out in assessing the economic impact of tourism and leisure on a local economy.

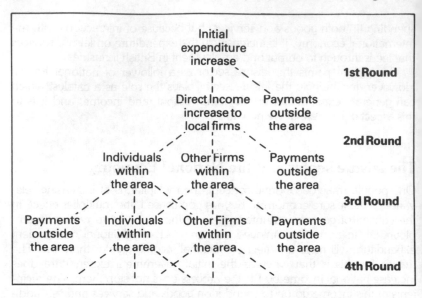

Source: Marion J Jackson (Bristol Polytechnic) Economic Impact Studies: The Methodology Applied to Tourism (*Occasional Research Paper in Economics* 1986)

Figure 3.2   The process of income generation within an economy

Foreign tourist expenditure is particularly important for the British economy as a whole since Table 3.8 shows that foreign tourists in general spend their money on labour intensive service industries. This means that a large proportion of the tourist dollar is directly passed on to British workers, increasing the size of the multiplier effect. Table 3.8 shows the industries that are the main direct beneficiaries of tourism expenditure.

Although foreign tourist expenditure is an unequivocal economic benefit to the British economy, the benefit is unequally distributed over different areas of the country. London is the target for most foreign tourists. Sixty per cent of overseas visitors to the UK spent at least one night in London. Stratford-upon-Avon, Cambridge, Oxford, and Scotland are the other popular destinations for foreign tourists. The economic impact of tourist expen-

Table 3.8   Percentage of tourists' expenditure in the UK by category of expenditure

	Domestic	*Overseas*
Accommodation	31	32
Travel	26	9
Eating/Drinking	25	23
Clothing	3	14
Other shopping	7	13
Entertainment	4	4
Miscellaneous	3	5

Source: Tourism '88 (Department of Employment, 1988)

diture on particular areas is much smaller than for the economy as a whole, since leakages are high and only a small proportion of the tourist dollar is retained within the region, hence reducing the value of the tourist multiplier. Despite this, every local authority in the country is well aware of the potential for increasing income and employment through tourism projects.

It is the policy of both central and local governments to use leisure and tourism projects for economic regeneration of depressed regions. In the 1960s regional unemployment was tackled through the use of Keynesian macroeconomic policies and microeconomic regional policies aimed at attracting manufacturing firms to depressed areas. In the 1990s such policies are no longer in favour. Instead, government grants are targeted at tourism and leisure projects. European Community grants are increasingly focused on tourism projects. A particular example of how one local government used these grants, and its partnership with the private sector, to redevelop one old industrial building for leisure and commercial purposes is given in Chapter 11 (Case Study 11.2 G-MEX).

This new role for leisure in the process of economic regeneration is giving the sector a growing economic importance that has not been fully reflected in the macroeconomic statistics we have reported earlier in the chapter. These statistics tend to look at the leisure industry as a collection of leisure goods and services and as such its economic importance relates to the share leisure takes of the national totals for income, expenditure, output and employment. In the 1980s the leisure industry is seen as a dynamic industry that acts both as a catalyst for economic developments in areas such as housing, retailing and commerce as well as providing an integrating function for such potentially diverse developments. Case Study 3.1 illustrates this process at work in Tobacco Dock, Wapping.

Case Study 3.1 Tobacco Dock, Wapping

Following the success of waterfront redevelopment schemes such as Baltimore in the USA, attention turned in the late 1970s and early 1980s to mixed leisure/retailing/commercial developments for Britain's large areas of disused docklands. Tobacco Dock in Wapping is one example of such developments.

The Tobacco Dock development involved the conversion of nineteenth century waterfront warehouses and vaults into shops, restaurants, bars and other leisure facilities. Originally the buildings were used to house tobacco and spirits brought in from the West Indies and America by boat since the early 1800s. This historical theme is maintained by the mooring at the dock of a full scale replica of a West Indiaman. The Three Sisters is a £1.3m, 103 foot long, three-masted sailing ship which sets the scene for the Tobacco Dock development.

The Tobacco Dock development not only conserves the warehouse for a new commercial role, it also emphasises the important relationship between leisure and shopping. Leisure interconnects with shopping in three different ways. First of all, there is the retailing of leisure goods. Secondly, there is the integration of leisure attractions such as restaurants and bars with shopping. It is the third aspect, though, leisure shopping, ie *shopping as a leisure activity*, that is the concept behind developments such as Tobacco Dock. Quality shopping in an attractive environment is a leisure experience in itself. The waterside location for Tobacco Dock enhances the leisure element; people like to spend their leisure time close to water.

The situation of Tobacco Dock, within only a mile of one of London's prime tourist attractions, the Tower of London, is a particular advantage. The development is expected to attract nearly three million visitors annually by the early 1990s. Such a visitor attraction has knock-on effects for the immediate surrounding area. Other buildings in the area were converted to leisure-related uses such as a rehearsal and recording studio, a small museum, and a small marina with shopping and other leisure facilities.

The Tobacco Dock development alone is expected to generate 800 local jobs but this is only one of many such developments in London Docklands. It has been estimated that current proposals in Docklands could produce something of the order of 14,000 direct jobs alone. These developments show the important part leisure and tourism projects now play in the economic regeneration of areas of cities that have suffered from the decline of Britain's traditional manufacturing role.

In many ways, the decline of Britain's traditional manufacturing industries has provided the ideal environment for such developments. It has left us with a heritage of old Victorian factories and unused docklands. Job losses are not the only result when docks or a factory close down. The environment of unused, run-down buildings creates an attitude of decline. Leisure developments such as Albert Dock in Liverpool, Tobacco Dock in Wapping, and Salford Quays in Manchester aim not only to provide new jobs but also to change this attitude by creating a new pride in the local environment.

In Chapter 1 we showed how the Industrial Revolution attracted people to Britain's cities in the eighteenth and nineteenth centuries and radically changed the nature of leisure in Britain. During that period of manufacturing growth, we built huge factories and mills, impressive transport networks including canals, and had more ports and docklands than any other country in Europe to export the products of our manufacturing industries. It is perhaps ironic that, with the destruction of Britain's manufacturing base through foreign competition, leaving a heritage of redundant industrial buildings and docklands, it is these same buildings that are now the focus of development to create a richer leisure environment. The aim is to attract foreign tourists to spend the money they have earned from their manufacturing success.

Further Reading

Beiolry S, Crookston M, Tyrer B 1988 London Docklands: The leisure element. *Leisure management*, February.

Gratton C, Taylor P 1991 The leisure market, in Hebden R (Ed) *ILAM guide to good practice in leisure management*.

Tibbot R 1986 Leisure development – the heritage factor. *Estates Gazette*, October.

4 Leisure markets, market failure, government policy and government failure

In this chapter we concentrate on the role of government in leisure for an economy such as Britain's. The questions to which we address ourselves here are: to what extent should government intervene in the market allocation of resources? In what circumstances is it appropriate to have government intervention? In what ways should the government intervene? What are the effects of government intervention?

One thing is certain. In Britain, as in all other industrialised western societies, governments certainly do intervene considerably in the market economy. Over the 1960s and 1970s, government expenditure accounted for an increasing share of Gross National Product in most industrialised countries including such capitalist havens as Japan and the United States. This seemingly inexorable rise in the size of government has led in the 1980s to serious questions being asked as to whether this is a desirable trend. The climate of opinion has certainly swung against government intervention and nobody that has lived through three terms of Thatcherite policies in Britain has any doubts as to the new political mood to reduce the level of government expenditure. Britain is not the only country to go along this route. Most industrialised countries have implemented policies aimed at controlling the level of public expenditure in the 1980s and early1990s.

Leisure has not escaped the effects of this new political mood. There is more and more pressure on local authority sports centres to reduce their deficits; it is increasingly difficult to obtain capital for the building of new leisure centres; and perhaps the most worrying aspect of all, many publicly owned sports pitches have been sold off to the private sector for housing and commercial development. Public sector leisure facilities have been subject to compulsory competitive tendering. The new political mood has put the whole question of government's role in leisure into the spotlight.

However, before we go on to analyse specifically the interactions between government and leisure we need to look at the more general issues of the role of government in a market economy. To do this we will briefly review the operation of markets, their advantages as an allocative mechanism, and introduce the concept of market failure.

The market system

We have already introduced markets, both product markets and factor markets, when we discussed the circular flow of income model in Chapter 2. In this section we wish to discuss how markets operate and what functions they serve.

Let us initially return to a simple circular flow model with just two sectors – firms and households. More particularly, we will assume all the firms are relatively small and decisions by both individual firms and households are taken independently. No one firm or household is sufficiently powerful to have any influence on any market. In this economy, there is no government and all the resources are allocated, and all products are distributed, through the market system.

What is the motivation of the firms and households in such an economy? Both are motivated by pure self-interest. Households want to maximise satisfaction; firms want to maximise profits. It is not immediately obvious that an economy such as this, with millions of decisions taken independently by firms and households, all pursuing their own self interest will not end in total chaos. Surely such complete anarchy can only spell disaster? Is there not a need for some overseeing body to coordinate these decisions and prevent selfishness getting out of hand? Apparently not; according to the free marketeers, the market mechanism itself acts as a coordinating mechanism. How does it do this?

The operation of the market system was first analysed by Adam Smith in *The Wealth of Nations* (1776). He showed that the individual decisions of self-interest are coordinated by the invisible hand of the price mechanism to produce a resulting allocation of resources that promotes the common good of all. Each individual acts selfishly and has no particular interest in the welfare of society as a whole, but the price mechanism operates in such a way that social welfare is maximised.

The formal proof of this proposition requires a higher degree of mathematical sophistication than we aspire to in this text. However an intuitive feel for the advantages of a perfectly operating market system can be obtained from a basic understanding of demand and supply.

It is the interaction of demand and supply that determines market price. Economics uses the concepts of demand and supply curves to illustrate the price mechanism. A demand curve is the relationship of quantity demanded and price. Since consumers are aiming to maximise their own benefits, in general the relationship is negative: that is, increases in price cause reductions in the quantity demanded, decreases in price lead consumers to demand more. The supply curve indicates what quantity firms are willing to supply at various prices; in general, the higher the price the greater the quantity supplied since higher prices often mean more profit and firms are aiming to maximise profit.

Equilibrium price (P_E) is the price where quantity demanded and quantity supplied are equal, assuming demand curve DD and supply curve SS in Figure 4.1. At this price the market clears; all consumers who wish to buy the product at this price are able to do so; all firms who are willing to

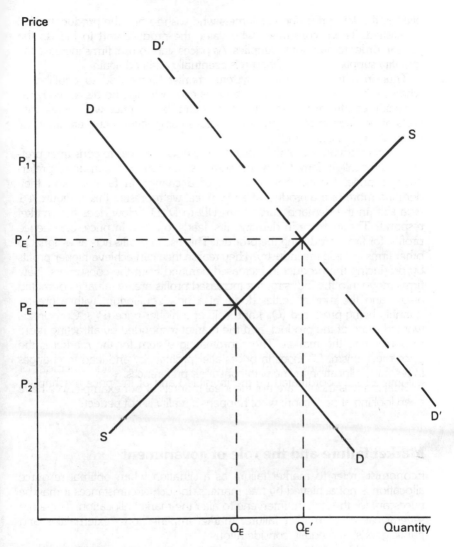

Figure 4.1 A simple supply and demand model

supply the product at this price sell all they supply. Everybody is happy.

What happens if price is above equilibrium (at P_1 in Figure 4.1)? Now quantity supplied by firms is greater than quantity demanded by consumers: there is excess supply and firms cannot sell all they wish at this price. In these circumstances competitive market forces put downward pressure on price. Firms try to sell their product by undercutting other firms' prices. As all firms do this, prices start to fall; as this happens, more is demanded by consumers. Eventually price is driven down to equilibrium.

Similarly if price is below equilibrium (at P_2 in Figure 4.1) a situation of excess demand exists. Quantity demanded is greater than the quantity supplied at this low price and consumers who wish to buy the product are left unsatisfied. Those consumers who value the product start to bid up the price in order to guarantee supplies. As prices start to rise, firms increase the quantity supplied and equilibrium is eventually attained again.

Thus in a freely operating system, market forces lead to equilibrium when all that is produced is sold: there is no waste and no dissatisfied customers. It can further be shown that this equilibrium price will equate with costs of production of the product because competition between firms will eliminate any excess profits.

A further advantage of the market is the power it gives to consumer preferences (usually referred to as consumer sovereignty). If consumer preferences change, for example because of a change in fashion, and they demand more of the product at every price, we represent this in Figure 4.1 as a shift in the demand curve from DD to D' D'. How does the market respond? The increase in demand first leads to a rise in price, and hence profits, for firms producing the product. This rise in profits acts as a signal to other firms outside the industry. They realise they can achieve higher profits by producing the product in increased demand from the consumers. New firms move into the industry, the increased profits are eventually competed away, and the market settles down at a new equilibrium with a greater quantity being produced (Q_E') and sold at a higher price (P_E'). Consumers wanted more of the product, and the market responded by attracting more resources into the market. The coordinating system for the market is the price mechanism. Changes in prices alter profitability and lead to changes in resource allocation in line with consumer preferences.

Real markets though are not the ideal markets of our example. We have been looking at perfection: what happens if reality is not perfect?

Market failure and the role of government

Economists refer to market failure as a situation when optimal resource allocation is not achieved by free markets. In such circumstances it may be necessary for the state to intervene to alter the market allocation. There are several causes of market failure: market imperfections; externalities and public goods; and equity considerations.

Market imperfections

We assumed in our ideal economy that no firm or consumer was big enough to hold any power over the market. Effectively no consumer or firm on their own can have any influence over market price – in economists' terms, everybody is a price-taker. In reality, in any market these conditions are never fully met. The danger normally lies when one firm, or a group of firms, control a large section of the supply of the product. The result is that such a firm will have a significant influence over market price, and the invisible hand of the price mechanism is destroyed. In these circumstances, pure self-interest of the dominating firm can damage the interests of consumers, and other firms. It can be shown in the extreme case of one firm controlling all the supply of a product (ie monopoly) that price would be higher and output lower than under competitive conditions. The monopolist would reduce output in order to keep price high. The argument is not unambiguous as it could be that the sheer size would yield cost savings (see Chapter 9 for a full discussion of the concept of economies of scale), but the argument is persuasive enough to have led most western industrialised nations to introduce some form of monopoly legislation. Such legislation not only outlaws firms as the sole supplier but also allows governments to investigate any situation, where it feels excessive market power (and its possible abuses) could be present.

In the UK, such legislation dates back to 1948 with the Monopolies and Restrictive Practices Act which set up the Monopolies Commission. The Commission was to report on market situations in which one firm, or a group of firms, controlled one third or more of the market and then advise the government on what action to take. Since 1948 there has been a whole series of Acts dealing with market power. The current state of the legislation is that the monopoly definition now relates to situations where at least 25 per cent of the market is controlled by a single buyer or seller and this applies to situations where two companies are about to merge, and when merged, would control over 25 per cent. The government has the power to prevent the merger. The Monopolies Commission has now been renamed the Monopolies and Mergers Commission.

Many leisure markets are characterised by high concentration of supply: that is, a small number of firms account for a large share of the market. There are several cases where such concentration has attracted the attention of the Monopolies and Mergers Commission.

The brewing industry has often been investigated by the Monopolies and Mergers Commission. It is a highly concentrated industry. The biggest brewer, Bass, controls about 22 per cent of the market, just below the 25 per cent monopoly definition. In 1985 the Commission investigated the proposed merger between Scottish and Newcastle and Matthew Brown. In 1986 Elder IXL, brewers of Fosters lager, attempted the take over of Allied Lyons, the next largest brewer to Bass with nearly 14 per cent of the market. The Commission investigated but the bid failed and Elders took over Courage (who had about 8 per cent of the beer market at that time) instead.

One of the worries about monopoly power in the brewing industry relates to the vertically integrated nature of the industry. That is, the major brewers also own a large number of their own public houses (Bass and Allied for instance have over 7000 each). Tied public houses accounted for nearly 60 per cent of all public houses in 1986 (although this percentage is in decline). Thus there is the danger that not only do the producers of beer control the supply of beer to the retailer (the public houses), but also through the tied house system they have a large degree of control of supply to the consumer. In such circumstances there is a danger that consumer sovereignty is substantially curtailed. In the Monopolies and Mergers Commission Report (1989) investigating the tied house it was stated that

89 per cent of managed public houses had just one supplier compared with 29 per cent of free houses. The Commission recommended the enforced introduction of 'guest' beers to give consumers more choice. It also recommended a maximum on the number of tied houses under the control of any one brewery.

There are also elements of vertical integration in the package tour market. Thomsons, for instance, the biggest package tour operator, owns Lunn Poly, a major chain of travel agents with over 200 outlets. They also own Portland Holidays which is the market leader in direct-sell inclusive tours, as well as Britannia, the biggest leisure airline in the world. In 1989, Thomson also took over Horizon to give it then nearly 40 per cent of the package tour market. A Monopolies and Mergers Commission investigation into this takeover found that, despite this high level of concentration, the market remained highly competitive. This was not the major aspect though of the investigation by the Monopolies and Mergers Commission in 1986 which is discussed in Case Study 4.1.

Case Study 4.1 The Monopolies and Mergers Commission investigation into foreign package holidays 1986

A complicated case of possible abuse of monopoly power was looked at by the Monopolies and Mergers Commission in 1986 in its investigation into Foreign Package Holidays. The Commission was asked to investigate whether package tour companies had the right to prevent travel agents competing with each other by offering inducements to the consumer (including reductions in the price of the holiday). In general package holiday companies control the price at which the travel agent sells the holiday to the consumer. The industry is also highly concentrated with Thomson and Intasun dominating the market (at that time). The reference to the Monopolies and Mergers Commission was sparked off by one travel agent, the Ilkeston Consumer Cooperative Society Ltd, offering vouchers worth 10 per cent of the holiday cost for holidays purchased from them. The leading package tour companies took steps to prevent this happening by threatening to withdraw the supply of holidays to the Ilkeston Cooperative Society.

The Monopolies and Mergers Commission found that a complex monopoly situation existed and that tour operators' action of preventing Ilkeston issuing vouchers *'was a step taken for the purpose of exploiting and maintaining the monopoly situation and an action on their part which was attributable to the existence of the monopoly situation ... the public interest would be best served by:*

(a) preserving the ability of the tour operator to control the price of his foreign holidays; and

(b) safeguarding from intervention by tour operators the ability of travel agents to compete with each other by offering pecuniary or other benefits to the public as an inducement' (Monopolies and Mergers Commission 1986).

One aspect of monopoly power that is less obvious and not always open to control is market power across markets. As we will indicate in Chapter 8 there is a tendency for the largest firms in one leisure market to also be involved in other leisure markets. By diversifying into other leisure markets these firms are acquiring more market power in the total leisure sector, but do not attract the eyes of the Monopolies and Mergers legislation since in any one market they remain below 25 per cent (see Case Study 8.1 for an illustration of this). We will discuss more fully the economic forces that lead to this type of firm behaviour in Chapter 8. For now we simply point out that the control of monopoly power is closely tied in with the definitions of the relevant market.

Externalities and public goods

We have seen that the motivations of firms and consumers in the market economy is self-interest. Individuals take decisions on the basis of what is best personally. In economic terms, they choose to do what gives the greatest difference between their own personal benefits and their own personal costs. As long as his actions have no repercussions on any other consumers or firms then all these self-interest decisions can give an optimum level of welfare for society as a whole.

But let us consider a situation where one consumer or firm makes a decision on this basis and as a result of the decision other consumers or firms are substantially worse off. The standard example is that of a firm with a smoky chimney. The cost of emitting smoke and dirt in the atmosphere is virtually nil to the firm; hence it is a very cheap way of getting rid of waste. The people who live in the surrounding neighbourhood have to spend more on cleaning bills for their clothes, houses and cars.

The word 'externalities' describes such situations because there is an extra cost or benefit that is external to the market transaction – these may be external costs as above but external benefits also occur in some circumstances.

There are many examples of externalities in leisure – some beneficial, others detrimental. Participant sport has external benefits associated with it. There are benefits to society over and above the benefits of those taking part. The major one is that exercise contributes to health and therefore the more people that take part in sport, the lower the demands on the National Health Service. On the other hand spectator sport, in particular football spectating, has negative externalities (or external costs) associated with it. The vandalism costs of football hooligans are substantial and they are not normally borne by the club staging the football match.

One of the biggest leisure markets in expenditure terms is the alcohol market. There is increasing evidence that there are substantial external costs involved mainly through over-indulgence in this leisure product. The football vandalism referred to above is generally associated with alcohol abuse. Excessive alcohol consumption leads to health problems which in Britain means that society as a whole must bear the cost of the health treatment (through taxation to pay for the NHS). It is also estimated that 60 per cent of crimes are in some way alcohol related.

How can the government intervene in such circumstances? Essentially the existence of externalities results in the production of too great a quantity of goods with external costs and too small a quantity of goods with external benefits. If it were possible to internalise the externality, by forcing the firm to pay for the external cost resulting from its actions, then no government action would be needed. If for instance the football hooligan was made to pay for any damage he caused inside or outside the football ground then this would be likely to reduce the amount of damage. In any case, any damage would be repaired without the cost being borne by the innocent party. In general it is not normally very easy to internalise the externality (as the above example illustrates), and the government normally tries to correct the market misallocation by taxing those goods with external costs and subsidising those goods with external benefits.

Hence the Sports Council receives grant-in-aid from the government, part of which is specifically directed towards encouraging people to take part in sport. Alcohol is taxed heavily in Britain to discourage excessive consumption.

In some circumstances, external benefits become so large that nearly all consumers receive the benefit. Such goods are often referred to as 'public goods'. Public goods have two characteristics: if one person consumes the product, many others derive the benefit (non-excludable); also one person's consumption does not prevent another from consuming the product (non-rival). In such circumstances the market will underprovide the commodity because of the 'free-rider' problem. Everybody will wait for someone else to buy the good since the benefits are pervasive. In such circumstances, government normally provides the good. The nearest example we have to a public good in the leisure market is large areas of open countryside such as National and Country parks or, in a country such as Britain, the shorelines and coastal paths. In effect these are not pure public goods since it would be possible to exclude (though it may be expensive) and the benefits of such areas become rival when they become congested (ie one person's enjoyment can be decreased by having others too close).

In fact, this problem of congestion is becoming an increasingly important external cost in the leisure and tourism market. The increasing number of tourists, particularly in Europe, over the last 30 years has meant that many tourist areas have become overcrowded in the peak summer season. Residents in tourist areas are complaining about reductions in their quality of life from such congestion and increased criminality associated with tourism. Tourists themselves complain about too many tourists, reductions in the quality of the environment through noise and pollution, and congestion problems at airports, ports, and on roads on their journey to and from the tourist destination. The increasing importance of such negative externalities in tourism means that we are likely to see more government intervention in the 1990s in the tourism market to alleviate such external costs.

Equity

The problems of market imperfections, externalities and public goods are problems of inefficiency in the market economy: that is, the ideal competitive allocation of resources is not achieved. But efficient resource allocation is not the only objective of society. The market may allocate resources and produce products efficiently, but if most of these products are consumed by a small minority of the population (that is, the distribution of income is inequitable) then, in general, society will attempt to change that distribution (normally through the political process). Government often intervenes to alter the market allocation of resources for such equity reasons. Society aims to achieve social justice as well as economic efficiency.

If equity in the distribution of income is an objective of government, we need to ask what distributional policies the government has and what are the means by which these policies can be effected. Answering the first of these questions is not an easy task. There is no clear definition of the concept of equity. Equity does not mean equality of income for all. Rather it means there should be some redistribution from what the free market would give but not so much that all inequalities would be eliminated. The extent of redistribution aimed for would differ from one country to another, and within the same country, from one government to another. This illustrates the point that equity means different things to different people.

How can the government then achieve this rather obscure objective? The simplest way is through a redistributive income tax and income support system. Take money off the rich and give it to the poor. However, often governments wish to ensure that everybody has the opportunity to consume at least a minimum amount of what are regarded as essential goods and services. Health services and education come into this category and in Britain the state provides free access to both. For other commodities, such as housing, the government provides subsidies to encourage consumption.

Leisure services are to some extent regarded as part of the social services and receive subsidies. Government provides and maintains the parks and open spaces where many leisure time activities take place. Sports centres and swimming pools are provided by local government at subsidised prices. The aim is both to encourage sports participation (because of the positive externalities associated with it) and to facilitate access to those on low incomes (for equity reasons).

Arts and cultural activities are subsidised or, as in the case of many museums and art galleries, provided free of charge. Library services are free to the consumer, again primarily for equity reasons.

The difficulty with the equity objective in the delivery of leisure services is in actually ensuring that the lower income groups obtain the benefit of the subsidies, but this is part of the wider discussion of the effectiveness of intervention to which we now turn.

Government failure

The underlying assumption in the discussion above is that government intervention will improve market misallocation in the cases of market failure discussed. We have seen that government could choose to regulate the market system through legislation (for instance in the case of monopoly), or it may choose to tax or subsidise (eg in the case of externalities), or alternatively it may choose direct provision (as in the case of public goods). But will any of these actions improve things? Up until the 1970s, there was a general consensus that it would. Since then there has been growing disillusionment with the benefits generated by government interference with the market mechanism. Markets may fail, but so may governments. Tullock puts it in rather a nice way: *'there is a legend of a Roman Emperor who, being asked to judge a contest between two singers, heard only the first and gave the prize to the second, assuming he could not be worse. This is not an optimal selection procedure'* (quoted in Wynarczyk 1987).

The question is whether government interference makes matters better or worse? We have examined the arguments above for the beneficial effects of government intervention. What is the detrimental side of such intervention? It has been argued that government intervention is inefficient, restricts individual freedom, and, in most cases of market intervention, does little to improve equality.

The efficiency argument against state intervention has several aspects to it. We have seen that perfect market systems achieve efficiency through competition. If a firm is inefficient it will either go bankrupt or it will be taken over by a more efficient firm. In this way prices are competed down to the level of the cost of production. What guarantees efficiency in a public sector institution (such as the library service) providing services at a zero price? None of the market forces operate. There is no competition, no possibility of bankruptcy, there is no price to indicate relative costs of production, and in most cases there is no measurable output. In these circumstances it is very difficult (though not impossible) to monitor if a service is operating efficiently.

Not only is it difficult to measure efficient performance, but also public sector institutions normally lack the financial rewards that exist in the private sector that act as an incentive to efficiency. There is no profit motive in the public sector. The lack of monetary incentives to reward good performance is often cited as a major contributor to poor morale in public sector workforces; this lack is also likely to undermine the efficient operation of the institution.

In our discussion of market failure we assumed that government institutions would operate to correct the misallocation of resources that result from market imperfections. That is certainly the aim of government intervention. However, public institutions are made up of politicians and bureaucrats and it is quite possible that these people have their own, completely different objectives. It has been argued that though politicians are concerned with social welfare, they may be more concerned with maximising their chances of re-election. Bureaucrats on the other hand, are said to be mainly concerned with the size of their budgets. Bureaucrats must deliver the goods that the politicians put to the electorate, politicians have ultimate control of the size of the bureaucrats' budget. It is not perhaps too surprising that the final actions that result may be somewhat different from those that would maximise social welfare.

Another criticism relates to how decisions about resource allocation are made in public institutions. We saw earlier how consumer preferences acting through the price mechanism provide market incentives that lead resource allocation to change in line with those preferences. In a public institution votes, rather than demand, become the vehicle for expression of preferences. However, there are normally long periods between elections. How can public sector decision-makers find out what the consumers want from the public institution between elections? More problematically, if such information is obtained, how can the decision-makers make a decision that satisfies consumer preferences? It can be shown that even if politicians and bureaucrats both aim to maximise social welfare, it is virtually impossible to devise a collective choice mechanism which would allow public decisions to reflect individual preferences.

These arguments emphasise the efficiency problems associated with government intervention. A second line of attack is the argument that government intervention restricts individual freedom. We have already pointed out that one major argument in favour of markets is consumer sovereignty: individuals have the freedom to choose how to spend their income and the market will respond to these expressed preferences by supplying an appropriate collection of goods and services. Consumer choice is only one aspect of the freedom of the market system. Individuals also have the right to choose how much income to earn by supplying their factor services to firms; they, it is argued, can decide how many hours to work and how many to take as leisure. All decision-making is decentralised: each individual makes his own decisions as to how much to work, hence how much income to earn, and then how to spend this income.

Government intervention interferes with this process and centralises decision-making. Government taxation constrains the freedom of the consumer. He is 'deprived' of his income and government makes the decision of how it should be spent.

In reality of course markets do not allow such unbridled freedom of choice, certainly not in the labour market, but we will return to this issue in the next chapter. For the moment, we simply note that the curtailment of freedom is another of the arguments against government intervention in the market system.

It is possible though that reductions in efficiency and freedom are necessary in order to obtain a more equitable distribution of income. Social justice may require sacrifices to economic efficiency. Anti-interventionists argue that most government policies aimed at redistribution have failed. They argue that if society wishes to redistribute income then this should be done through cash transfers rather than by redistribution of goods and services (ie interfering with the market allocation). If people are poor, government can give them more money, but let the poor decide how to spend it. If they decide to spend it on beer rather than on food, clothing, and shelter then so be it; that is their preference. It is a mistake, they argue, to try to force people to consume products 'for their own good', if they do not wish to do so, by redistributing services in kind.

It is not difficult to find counter arguments to this point of view. There are many benefits to be gained from a free health service and a free education system. The problem though is that up to relatively recently everybody assumed that the provision of these services was freely improving equity.

Le Grand (1982) made a comprehensive study of distributional impact of public expenditure. He concluded:

> *Public expenditure on health care, education, housing and transport systematically favour the better off, and thereby contributes to inequality in final income. It has not created equality of cost (or equality of 'access') and indeed in some cases has made cost differences worse; there persist substantial inequalities in outcomes. For several of the services there has not been even a reduction in the relevant inequalities over time. Nor does there seem to be more prospect of retrieving the situation through any piecemeal reform.*

Le Grand's general conclusion also applies to leisure. A large proportion of public subsidies to leisure in Britain go to sports centres and swimming pools; this has certainly been the area of increased provision in the 1970s and early 1980s. All the evidence indicates that such facilities are used disproportionately by professional and non-manual workers. Amongst manual workers, it is only the skilled, normally the higher paid, who use the centres to any great extent.

Similarly, in the arts the major share of the subsidies go to institutions such as Covent Garden, whose main customers are the better off. Achieving equity in the delivery of leisure services is not a particularly easy task.

Conclusions

In this chapter we started with a discussion of the advantages of the market system. We then indicated some of its failings. Finally, we looked at the difficulties of correcting for these failings through government intervention, which perhaps makes one ask whether the market is best left to its own devices.

We have looked at the arguments; but in many ways it is almost a discussion of twentieth century economic thought. In the early 1900s, the *laissez faire* philosophy was still dominant. It was the inability of the market system to correct for long-term mass unemployment that led to the adoption of Keynesian interventionist policies at the macroeconomic level. The post-war Labour government set up the modern welfare state machinery and hence established substantial government intervention with the market allocation of services. It is the disenchantment with the effects of such intervention in the 1970s and 1980s that we have discussed in the last section.

The net results of the arguments of the last section are that in Britain in the 1980s major nationalised industries have been privatised (British Telecom, British Gas, etc); there has been serious consideration and some introduction of charges for goods that were previously publicly provided free of charge; and the policy of most relevance for leisure services, the introduction of competitive tendering by private organisations for services that were formally provided by the public sector.

There is a further aspect though in which government is wielding its power and influence in the leisure market; that is in the deregulation and relaxation of constraints to market activity in leisure which have developed over the years. This form of government interference in leisure markets is much less costly than those we have discussed earlier; no permanent administrative body needs to be set up; and such action is fully in line with the other policies discussed above. Examples include the deregulation of air travel and the relaxation of licensing laws and Sunday trading constraints. The arguments of the free marketeers, for the moment, seem to be winning out. This means that leisure managers must be well informed on their understanding of the operation of markets and of the particular forces that operate in leisure markets. This involves a detailed analysis of demand and supply factors in leisure. The rest of this book is devoted to such an analysis.

Further reading

Gratton C 1984 Efficiency and equity aspects of public subsidies to sport and recreation. *Local Government Studies* **10**: 53–74.

Heald D 1983 *Public Expenditure*. Martin Robertson.

Le Grand J 1982 *The strategy of equality: redistribution and the social services*. Allen and Unwin.

Monopolies and Mergers Commission 1986 *Foreign Package Holidays* Cmnd 9879 HMSO.

Monopolies and Mergers Commission 1989 *The Supply of Beer* Cmnd 651 HMSO.

Monopolies and Mergers Commission 1989 *Thomson Travel Group and Horizon Travel Ltd* Cmnd 554 HMSO.

Roper B, Snowdon B 1987 The fall and rise of laissez faire. In Roper B, Snowdon B *Markets, intervention and planning*. Longman.

Wynarczyk P 1987 Is a pure market system feasible. In Roper B, Snowdon B *Markets, intervention and planning*. Longman.

5 The demand for leisure time

Leisure time is often seen by individuals, academics and policy makers as a residual; something left over after all the important things are finished, like work, eating and shopping. However in this chapter we wish to show that leisure time is all about *choices* that people make, and these choices involve a set of trade-offs between alternative uses of time. It is not always the work and essential chores that win either. In fact leisure time in its various forms is steadily increasing, which means that other uses of time are decreasing. As leisure time expands, so it mirrors and feeds the increasing importance of leisure in the national economy, as we have seen in the first section. By examining the choice mechanisms that create the increases in leisure time we can also point to important management and policy implications, such as the persistence of the peak load problem.

Leisure time choices

In this early part of the chapter we use a very simple and broad definition of leisure time, which is any time not spent in paid work. This is far too loose a definition of course, but it is an essential first stage in the explanation of how leisure time demands are made. Later we refine the concept of leisure time to give a more precise definition.

The income/leisure trade-off

The most basic choice that influences the amount of leisure time an individual or society has involves how much paid work to undertake. The simple trade-off here is between the benefit (or utility, as economists call it) derived from leisure time on the one hand and income on the other. Obviously this is a simplistic representation of the values underlying this trade-off, since leisure time does not always yield utility (people often get bored by too much) and market work often gives other benefits besides income (such as comradeship, status and self-fulfilment). Nevertheless, economic analysis starts by stripping away the complications to reveal the heart of the issue, and financial necessity is at the heart of the income/leisure trade-off choice.

Any time spent in leisure or other non-paid work activities means losing potential earnings, so the opportunity cost, or *price of leisure* is the foregone earnings. If people behave rationally, they will only enter the labour market and continue to work as long as the benefits from income outweigh the benefits from leisure time. There will come a point, though, when enough time is spent in work and enough money is earned. At this point the person reaches an optimum trade-off between time spent at work and time spent in leisure.

This choice mechanism covers individual choices concerning whether or not to work, to take part-time or full-time employment, to work more hours in a week (overtime) or even to take a second job (moonlighting). In many cases individuals will feel they are not making such choices, that they *have* to work a given amount because of financial necessity. But at the root of the problem in each case the individual has a decision to make about the personal allocation of time between work and non-work.

Over time a fundamental influence on this income/leisure trade-off is the change that occurs in rates of pay in the labour market. Apart from the occasional year or two, real rates of pay (ie pay after the rising cost of living has been allowed for) are steadily increasing. This means in effect that the price of leisure is rising over time. How does this affect the income/leisure choice? There are two contrasting influences, which we call the substitution and income effects. First, because the price of leisure time is rising there is an inducement to take less leisure time and devote more time to work. This is a normal demand relationship – as the relative price of leisure rises, the inclination is to use less of it. This is the substitution effect. At its most extreme, it can cause people to take second jobs, which accounted for 4 per cent of jobs in Britain in 1991.

Second, because rates of pay for all *existing* work are higher, total income will rise even if the amount of time spent at work does not change. Some of this extra income may be used to 'buy' more leisure time, by working less time. If leisure is a 'normal good', which in economics means that the demand for it rises as incomes rise (see Chapter 6), then we would expect demand for leisure time to rise as rates of pay rise. This is the income effect.

So we have two effects pulling in opposite directions and the net effect on the demand for leisure time is difficult to predict. What then are the outcomes of such choices? Do they follow the implications of Chapter 3, and show that leisure time is expanding as leisure becomes more important in the national economy? Changes in leisure-time demands can be measured in a variety of ways – hours of work, overtime working, the number of people in the labour force, and holidays being the main ones. These indicators do not always tell the same story, nor do they present a clearcut picture of substitution and income effects. As is often the case we have to examine other factors in order to get a meaningful picture.

Hours of work in a typical week have fallen in the two decades 1971 to 1991, as Figure 5.1 shows. But the overall decline is small and in the 1980s the average working week actually rose slightly. For men and also for many

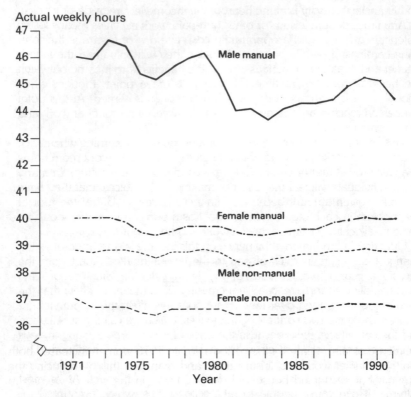

Actual weekly hours

Source: New Earnings Survey

Figure 5.1   Changes in hours of work 1971–1991

non-manual workers this is largely because of an increase in the amount of overtime worked. For example, over half the male manual workers in Britain work an average of about ten hours a week overtime. In the expanding services sector of the economy it is likely that a lot of 'unpaid' overtime is worked but, unfortunately, most goes unrecorded in the official statistics since it is worked by salaried staff and therefore is not paid for directly.

Overtime is also complicated because it only offers a one way choice – work more for higher pay. Furthermore, it may be that overtime is *expected* of many workers; in such cases it is more a choice of the *employers* than the workers.

Table 5.1 shows that the percentage of males, of the right age, who are actually in the labour force (called the activity rate) is steadily declining and the equivalent labour force activity rate for women is steadily increasing. The simple interpretation of such evidence is that the income effect is dominating for men and the substitution effect is dominating for women. However, it is necessary to qualify both conclusions.

Table 5.1 Labour force activity rates (percentage)

	16–19 yrs	20–24 yrs	25–44yrs	45–59 yrs	60–64 yrs	All, 16+
Males						
1971	69.4	87.7	95.4	94.8	82.9	80.5
1981	72.4	85.1	95.7	93.0	69.3	76.5
1990	74.2	86.3	94.5	88.2	54.4	74.2
Females						
				45–54 yrs	55–59 yrs	
1971	65.0	60.2	52.4	62.0	50.9	43.9
1981	70.4	68.8	61.7	68.0	53.4	47.6
1990	70.7	74.8	73.1	72.8	54.9	52.8

Source: Social Trends and Department of Employment

The labour force activity rate of men is falling because of sharp decreases in the oldest age groups, as shown in Table 5.1. This is primarily because of early retirement, but this can only partly be attributed to an increase in the demand for leisure time. Many of the early retirers do so because of ill health – three-quarters according to a recent survey. But also many are induced to do so by attractive financial incentives, so a different income/leisure trade-off is operating.

Female labour force activity rates are rising, but this is not always at the expense of leisure time. In the period 1961 to 1975 women increased both labour market work *and* leisure time, and managed this by reducing the time spent on unpaid household work. Clearly, in the case of women in particular the simple two way trade-off is inadequate and analysis should consider a three way income/household work/leisure choice. Table 5.2 shows that in the 1980s employed women did lose 'free time' but more because of increased commitments to 'essential activities' than because of working longer hours in their jobs.

It will offend some people that we include unemployment as a consideration in the income/leisure trade-off. But it is necessary to do so, not least

Table 5.2 Free time availability 'typical week'

Hours per week:	Employed full-time				Housewife		Retired	
	Men		Women					
	1982	1990	1982	1990	1982	1990	1982	1990
Paid work, inc. travel	45.3	48.2	40.7	41.1				
Essential activities	23.7	23.7	33.5	35.9	57.7	45.6	36.1	31.4
Sleep*	49	49	49	49	49	49	49	49
Free time	50	50	44.8	42	61.3	73.4	82.9	87.6

Source: Leisure Futures The Henley Centre for Forecasting
Note: *Sleep assumed to be 7 hours a night

because there is a lot of academic and policy debate about the effect of unemployment and social security benefit levels on the duration of unemployment. The theory is that higher benefit levels distort the normal income/leisure trade-off and cause people to take too much leisure in the form of unemployment.

Notice that the argument is not principally about the effect of such benefits on the number of people *becoming* unemployed. Rather it is about the incentive of a high benefit/wage ratio (called the replacement ratio) to stay unemployed for *longer*. The first few weeks of unemployment, for instance, are often typified by a 'holiday' feeling, so any extension of this by greater financial support will increase the average duration of unemployment. However, it must be reported that the evidence about the effects of changes in the replacement ratio on the duration of unemployment is very contradictory – as yet there is no clearcut proof that this distortion to the income/leisure trade-off exists. Later in this chapter we also question the qualitative judgement that unemployment is a form of leisure time.

The economic theory of income/leisure trade-off outlined above is framed in terms of certain simplifying assumptions about the way in which people behave and the institutional environment in which they make choices. Such assumptions are necessary to understand the basics of what causes certain economic behaviour to occur. In this case the main assumptions used are that the decision makers are individuals, that they are rational and informed, they have a continuous choice and the opportunities to vary their choices exist, and that the changes in demands are quick and easy.

Of course in the real world these conditions are unlikely. In many instances it is the *household* that is the unit of decision making, not the individual. People may not behave rationally (they may not have enough information to do so), the choice may be very 'lumpy' – such as a 40 hour week or nothing – and the move into and out of employment is anything but quick and easy! However, it is possible to introduce these real world complications one at a time to see how important they are to the basic model of how decisions are made. Household decision making, for instance, involves a set of *household* trade-offs which are more complicated than the simple trade-off for individuals described above, but which concern the same kind of choices between income and leisure.

Because on average, and over time, people do tend to behave in a rational manner and *do* have a fairly flexible choice of years and hours of work, the income/leisure trade-off is still considered to have fundamental validity.

Other forms of leisure time demand

Some leisure time demands do not involve an explicit choice of leisure rather than income. Paid holidays are the best example and Table 5.3 shows that this is one of the most rapidly increasing forms of leisure time. Non-manual workers' holiday entitlements have also increased significantly, with 53 per cent of male non manuals and 43 per cent of female non-manuals enjoying five weeks or more holiday in 1987.

Table 5.3   Holiday entitlements (manual workers, 1951–1991)

	Under 2 weeks	2 weeks	2–3 weeks	3 weeks	3–4 Weeks	4 weeks	4–5 weeks	5 weeks & over
	Percentage of workers having basic holiday entitlement of:							
1951	31%	66%	2%		1%			
1960		97%	1%		2%			
1971		28%	5%	63%	4%			
1980				2%	24%	19%	55%	
1991						6%	78%	16%

Source: Employment Gazette

This expansion of holiday time feeds directly the growth in markets such as package holidays abroad and short-break holidays in Britain. Over a quarter of the British population now take two or more holidays a year, and the short break boom is, of course, predominantly benefiting British venues. Paid holiday entitlement is more of a group choice than an individual choice, but there is an element of income/leisure trade-off about the negotiation of holiday entitlements. They are, after all, part of labour costs for the employer, so more holidays must mean that pay will not increase as fast as it otherwise would.

Other forms of leisure-time demand which do not involve a sacrifice of income, and are not often recognised as leisure, include paid sick leave and other absenteeism, and even slack working practices such as extended tea-breaks, knocking off early, and slow production lines. There is evidence of a long term rise in absenteeism, which may indicate more illness, or more willingness to take time off work under the excuse of illness.

Regarding slack working practices, it is possible that rather than just reflecting poor management, they reflect the fact that on occasions: *'Workers and managers do not seek the greatest possible income; they seek instead an adequate or satisfactory level of income. They prefer tea breaks and long executive lunches, slower assembly lines and longer weekends to strenuous effort for higher incomes'* (B D Nossiter *Sunday Times* 10 September 1978).

In other words there is the possibility of a much more subtle, indirect, income/leisure trade-off. By adopting low productivity work habits, higher pay is sacrificed for the sake of a more leisurely work situation. Such behaviour mirrors the situation before the Industrial Revolution, discussed in Chapter 1, when work and leisure were less easily distinguished. It does appear, however, that the situation is changing. Since the late 1970s in Britain there has been a remarkable growth in industrial productivity, which might be indicative of a different attitude towards 'leisure at work' by both sides of industry.

Another way in which demand for leisure time is manifested, or at least affected, is the growth in flexible working schedules. In Case Study 5.1 we feature the main characteristics and implications of this rapidly expanding feature of working life (and therefore also leisure life) in Britain.

Case Study 5.1 Flexible working arrangements

Flexible working arrangements have obvious implications for leisure lifestyles. They help to break down the traditional patterns of work and leisure – patterns that pervade each day, week, year and indeed lifetime. These traditional work patterns, it must be remembered, are not necessarily the most preferred patterns for workers.

What do we mean by flexible working arrangements? Definitions vary but usually include flexible working hours, early retirement, job sharing, part-time working, home working, self-employment and temporary jobs. Evidence suggests that these flexible working arrangements affect a large and increasing minority of the workforce.

Over eight million workers, some 35 per cent of the employed labour force, are estimated to be in jobs that are not of the traditional, full-time employee status. This compares with 30 per cent in 1981. Table 5.4 gives further details of the scale of part-time, self-employment and temporary working, and the overlap between these categories.

In addition to the evidence in Table 5.4, according to the Department of Employment's Labour Force Survey, over 9 per cent of the workforce are on *flexitime*, ie flexible working hours. This means that around a 'core time', which they are obliged to work, they can work the rest of their time when they choose, and so build up 'credits', which are typically taken as extra half or full days off. Over 6 per cent of the work force are working to 'annualised hours', ie a set number of hours for the year rather than each week; a further 4 per cent work a 'compressed work week', with the standard hours concentrated into less than a five day week.

Unfortunately long term trend data is not available for all flexible job types. However, the ones for which data are available show that flexibility has been on the increase for the whole of the post-war period. For example, one of the largest categories of flexible working, part-time work, accounted for only 4 per cent of workers in 1951, rising to 9 per cent by 1961, 16 per cent in 1971 and 23 per cent in 1991.

A major influence on the increase in flexible working is probably the increase in the proportion of women joining the labour force, charted in Table 5.1 above. It is important to stress that part-time working is often a choice of women in the labour force, because of domestic responsibilities and the role of secondary incomes. According to the Labour Force Survey, nearly two thirds of part-time workers do not want a full-time job. In the same survey 38 per cent of temporary workers did not want a permanent job.

Table 5.4 Flexible Working in Britain, 1986

Type of Worker	Thousands of Workers
Total employed	23,829
Permanent, full time employees	15,592
Others	8,237
The 'Others' comprise:	
Temporary full-time	625
Permanent part-time	3914
Temporary part-time	784
Self-employed, full-time	2189
Self-employed, part-time	326
Self-employed, temporary	97
Self-employed, temporary and part-time	115
Others not specified	187
Total	8237

Source: Hakim (1987)

So workforce attitudes are generally in favour of more flexible working schedules. This impression is reinforced by another survey in which 55 per cent of British workers interviewed were in favour of getting away from a rigid five-day week, and instead being given the choice of dividing the equivalent working hours flexibly over each month or year.

Flexibility in working arrangements has benefits for both workers and employers. Households with flexible working arrangements can organise work around leisure plans and so enhance the quality and productivity of leisure time. They will not be confined to either peak or traditional leisure times. It is also probable that variety in work schedules increases the utility from work in the same way that variety in leisure is a source of greater utility. We explore this notion in the context of leisure more fully in the next chapter.

Flexibility in work causes flexibility in leisure, and this obviously has consequence for leisure industries. As flexible working continues to grow, the scale of the peak load problem (see main text) may diminish. It is ironic, though, that as flexible work arrangements develop in the economy as a whole, leisure industries are in the forefront of many forms of flexible working, particularly part-time working.

It is almost certain that flexible work arrangements will continue to grow in importance in the British economy, and with this growth the quality of leisure time will improve and leisure industries will prosper.

The quality of leisure time

Some working arrangements do not improve the quality of leisure time, and so they have to be compensated by income enhancements. Such is the case with unsocial hours and shiftworking. Figure 5.2 shows the steady increases that have occurred in shiftworking in Britain. This work arrangement has some advantages and some disadvantages as far as the quality of

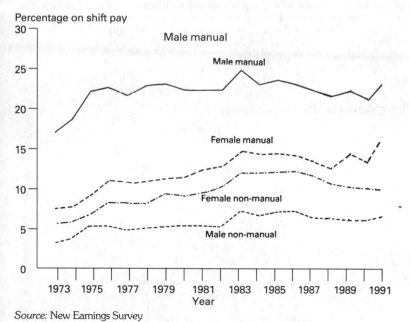

Percentage on shift pay

Male manual

Female manual

Female non-manual

Male non-manual

1973 1975 1977 1979 1981 1983 1985 1987 1989 1991
Year

Source: New Earnings Survey

Figure 5.2   Shiftworking 1973–1991

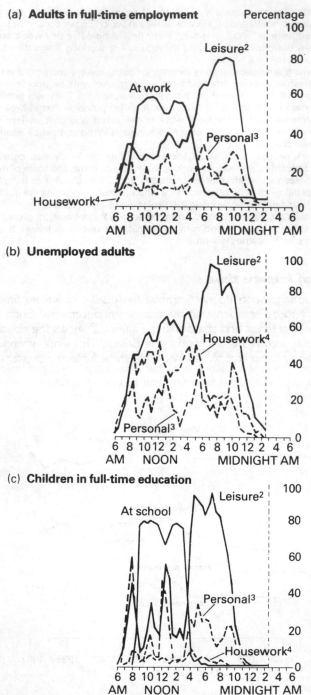

Figure 5.3   Daily patterns in the use of time, Summer 1983

Source: Henley Centre for Forecasting, *Social Trends*

leisure time is concerned. On the one hand access to leisure facilities will be improved at off-peak times, when congestion and price are likely to be lower.

On the other hand the more forceful argument concerning shiftwork, used to back up claims for higher rates of pay, is that it spoils leisure time since it reduces the opportunities for social interaction with people who work normal hours. Figure 5.3 shows just how fixed is the timing of leisure time in the daily habits of employed and unemployed adults, and children, with peak leisure time occurring between 6pm and midnight.

Figure 5.3 demonstrates that the inflexibility of *when* leisure time is taken called *timedating*, is just as apparent for people not in the labour market as those at work, which is testimony to the social function of leisure and the household nature of leisure decisions.

Other working arrangements provide an opportunity to *improve* the quality of leisure time. Flexitime and other flexible working arrangements are obvious examples, and attitudes of working people are certainly in favour of more flexibility in working patterns, as Case Study 5.1 shows.

Another qualitative aspect that needs to be addressed in the context of leisure time is unemployment. The unemployed may be said to be suffering from an excess of leisure time, in so far as they are involuntarily unemployed. But is it really leisure? Two approaches may be taken to answer the question. First we can examine the leisure behaviour of the unemployed, from surveys such as the General Household Survey. We might expect that with an excess of time and a shortage of money this would be reflected in leisure behaviour. The little evidence available does suggest that the unemployed tend towards more time intensive and less goods intensive leisure activities, although this leisure behaviour is not only due to their unemployment, but also their social class (mainly D and E).

The second approach to analysing the relationship between unemployment and leisure time is to examine the social and psychological characteristics of the unemployed. Typically, the results of such studies are to reject the association of unemployment with leisure, on the grounds that the unemployed tend to isolate themselves from conventional, socialising leisure experiences. This is as much because they feel that they have not earned the right to such leisure as because they cannot afford it. It would seem to be wrong to use high unemployment figures as an indicator of increased leisure time. It does not really reflect a demand for leisure time, but rather an excess supply.

Information, consumption skills and leisure time demands

One of the key assumptions underlying the economic analysis of the demand for leisure time is that the individuals who choose do so with the right information. We believe that this is a fundamentally important assumption, since there are potential deficiencies in relevant information which will cause distortions in leisure-time demands.

What information does an individual need in order to make a rational and informed choice of how much time to devote to paid work, essential chores, and leisure time? Obviously labour market information is important, and this includes not only information about what jobs are available at what rates of pay and where, but also the skills that are necessary to do the job. Our education and training systems are geared towards providing labour market skills, so that every opportunity is available (in theory) to make the right choices about employment, using these skills.

But apart from labour market information and skills, there is a need for a balancing amount of *consumer* market information and skills. Advertising plays an important role here, in providing awareness of the consumption options available. What is missing, however, is a systematic opportunity to learn *consumption skills*. Now this may seem an odd concept at first. Consumption skills may conjure up visions of learning how to eat an ice-cream sundae, or how to operate the controls of a modern hi-fi system. In fact the concept goes much further than this. Just as production skills enable an individual to become more productive in paid work, so consumption skills enable individuals to become more productive in their use of leisure time.

Here the principle of household production, which we introduced in Chapter 2, comes into its own. Basically every decision made in a household leads to the creation of a household product. This product may be a meal, a clean house, or an hour of fun in a pure leisure product such as a game of 'Trivial Pursuits'. But just as the firm is interested in acquiring and making the most of the skills of its workforce, so the household can acquire consumption skills and improve the utility to be gained from household activities. Many leisure activities are quite demanding in terms of the skills required to enjoy them to the full – skiing, needlework, DIY and gardening to name just four. If households as consumers have not been introduced to such skills, it increases the probability that these consumers will not find leisure time very productive.

Leisure time can in fact become boring if, without sufficient consumption skills, people are confining their use of leisure time to low skill activities such as watching TV and drinking. The net result is that the demand for leisure time will not be as great as it would be if these consumers had more leisure skills. In certain groups of the population the lack of consumption skills can have more damaging effects. How many times have you heard bored teenagers complain that there is 'nothing to do'? This may be partly the result of a lack of facilities but it is also symptomatic of a lack of consumption skills. A consequence is that too many resort to crime and vandalism, for the excitement they generate.

Management and policy implications

Now we take the analysis above and draw explicit implications for the management of leisure facilities and policies for leisure. It is one thing to understand the processes which condition the amount, the form, the timedating and the quality of leisure time which is demanded. But for decision makers on the supply side of the leisure market it is important to translate this understanding into positive supply decisions. We comment on four representative areas of decision or policy making which are rooted in knowledge of developments in the demand for leisure time. These cover the initial choice of what type of leisure products to offer, coping with the peaking of demand for leisure at certain times, educating consumers with leisure skills, and organising flexible work in leisure services.

Entrepreneurial opportunities

The leisure time preferences that people express reveal clear patterns of growth in different forms of leisure time, as we have shown above. These patterns represent potential for growth in certain types of leisure product. The most obvious example is the growth in the short break market in Britain. Given the evidence we have reviewed above, it is more likely that this market is benefiting from greater holiday allowances and flexible working arrangements, rather than any change in the working week. Hotels, holiday villages, and even local authorities intent on expanding their tourism appeal, have all quickly recognised the commercial potential arising from these changes in leisure time. They demonstrate the importance of designing leisure products to match leisure time developments.

Other important examples of market growth emanate from leisure time trends. The rise in demand for time-saving activities and products, both in the essential chores market and in the leisure market, reflects the increasing relative price of time. Incomes can and do rise steadily, while time has finite limits (ie 24 hours a day!). So time is becoming more expensive relative to market goods. In this circumstance there is a continued incentive to purchase time-saving and goods-using commodities. Short duration sports activities such as aerobics, squash and weight-training are good examples, as are microwave ovens, food processors, tumble driers and package holidays using air transport. Such time-saving markets will continue to provide promising opportunities for entrepreneurs.

The peak load problem

A familiar problem to managers of leisure facilities is the lack of clients from 9am to 5pm during the week and an excess of clients at other times. This is the peak load problem which has serious implications for management. The roots to this problem lie in the timedating of work and leisure activities, noted above and graphically demonstrated in Figure 5.3. This structural problem is compounded by the fact that most leisure firms produce services, which unlike manufactured goods are completely 'perishable' and cannot be stored for peak periods.

A major issue of relevance to leisure managers is whether or not the peak load is a *'firm'* one, resisting all attempts to persuade clients to move from peak to off-peak times, or a *'shifting peak'*, whereby such moves are

c

possible. Given the evidence in Figure 5.3 above, the problem would appear to be a 'firm' one for leisure managers, although Case Study 5.1 does demonstrate that flexibility in work schedules is increasing, so leisure schedules may mirror such changes.

We take up the management problems posed by the peak load in Chapter 10, and consider the extent to which pricing and promotion policies can deal with them. The peak load problem has implications beyond the single leisure facility or service. Recent debates about Sunday trading, licensing hours and the trading hours of shops generally are all rooted in the basic mismatch that occurs between consumers' timedating preferences and the supply of shopping and leisure opportunities. Clearly this policy debate is one that will run and run, but in strict *economics* terms the arguments are indisputably in favour of supply being allowed to respond to demand.

Education for leisure

If we are correct in diagnosing that information and skills for leisure are underdeveloped, which thus distorts work/leisure preferences against leisure, then the management and policy answer is to provide more explicit training for leisure. There are already clear examples of this philosophy in particular leisure markets. In skiing it is very rare for anyone to introduce themselves to the sport. The custom is for any resort to provide extensive and intensive teaching arrangements, which most skiers utilise for the first few skiing holidays at least. This is not an optional extra in the minds of the skiers; it is an essential requirement for understanding and enjoying the sport. A less extreme example is the broadcasting of American Football on Channel 4 television. In order to secure a following in Britain the commentary was not just a description of the game. It was an education in the intricacies of a complicated sport, and this educational emphasis attracted a massive following.

Our point is that these examples are valid for many leisure markets and more importantly they are relevant to any government intent on improving the quality of life and encouraging constructive and fulfilling leisure behaviour. More time is now spent away from paid work than at paid work, for the first time since before the Industrial Revolution. As this trend towards greater leisure time continues, so education for consumption skills becomes more and more important. It is also important if, as many forecasters suggest, new technology causes unemployment to remain at a high level.

Employment conditions in leisure industries

All the analysis and management implications so far have been looking at work and leisure-time choices from the point of view of the economy, the consumer, or the supplier of leisure products. However, it is important to remember that leisure industries are major *employers* too. In this context there are some important implications arising from evolving leisure time demands.

The increasing flexibility and diversity of leisure time demands is mirrored by a similar diversity in the working schedules demanded of leisure services' employees. Unfortunately, the consequences of this requirement are most commonly conditions of employment which are harmful to the leisure life-styles of employees. They suffer, in short, from the worst faults of shiftworking and peak load employment, with low pay, low productivity, high turnover of staff, unsocial hours and poor working conditions. The catering industry typifies this profile.

So, what is good for the consumer is not necessarily good for the employee and this is why trade unions in the service sector are either in two minds about, or directly opposed to, increasing the flexibility of supply via extended licensing and trading hours. Clearly it is important for leisure service industries to organise flexible working arrangements without the detrimental characteristics so often attached to them in practice. Given that a large proportion of those on flexible working arrangements prefer this condition, there is a sound basis for improvements.

Conclusions

Leisure time demands are developing such that the form, the timing and the quality of leisure time are all in a state of continual change. Certain key factors continue to be basic influences on these changes, such as the trade-off between financial needs and leisure time demands, the relative prices of time and goods, the life-cycle of domestic household responsibilities, the development of new technology, and the availability of information and leisure consumption skills. In addition, certain constraints prevent the changes in leisure time demands from being fully realised, these constraints being institutional or merely the habits formed in working practices and domestic leisure consumption.

Policies can attempt to modify leisure time demands, but whereas some are in the control of leisure managers, pricing for example, others such as flexible working arrangements are outside such control. The role of the leisure manager is therefore not only to mould leisure time demands, but also more importantly to anticipate changes in these demands and use this knowledge to provide effective responses. In the supply section to this book we pick up on a number of the management issues raised in this chapter, but before then it is necessary to look more closely at the other leisure demands accompanying the ever increasing demand for leisure time.

Further reading

Employment Gazette, monthly, Department of Employment, NB regular statistical series and articles on work related issues, HMSO.

Gershuny JI, Thomas GS 1980 *Changing patterns of time use.* University of Sussex, Science Policy Research Unit, Brighton.

Gratton C, Taylor P 1985 *Sport and recreation: an economic analysis.* E and FN Spon, London.

Hakim C 1987 Trends in the Flexible Workforce. *Employment Gazette* November: 549–60.

New Earnings Survey, annual, Department of Employment, HMSO (main results reported in *Employment Gazette*).

Owen JD 1979 *Working hours: an economic analysis.* Lexington Books, Lexington, Massachusetts.

Scitovsky T 1976 *The joyless economy* Oxford University Press, New York.

Smith MA, Simpkins AF 1980 *Unemployment and leisure: a review and some proposals for research.* University of Salford, Centre for Leisure Studies, Salford.

Social Trends, annual, Employment and Leisure chapters, HMSO.

6 The demand for leisure commodities

This is the core chapter of this demand section. In it we explain the way economists approach the analysis of demand and introduce some basic economic measurements of demand such as elasticity.

Leisure is a very diverse sector and there are several different components of demand. In earlier chapters we have identified two components: leisure goods and leisure services. Leisure goods include sports equipment, alcohol, books, newspapers, and television sets. With the exception of alcohol all of these are durable goods: that is, they are not completely used up immediately after purchase. Thus a television set provides enjoyment over a period of time. Such durable goods have additional considerations that influence consumer demand over and above those that determine the demand for a non-durable, where the total enjoyment is given in one single act of consumption. Leisure services are identical to non-durable leisure goods in this respect. They are different though in that leisure services normally equate with leisure facilities. Thus a sports centre is a leisure service in that it provides the building in which indoor sports can take place; a cinema provides the location at which consumers can watch a film. The relevant demand considerations for leisure services that make them different from those for leisure goods is this facility aspect. When we attend a leisure facility we normally have to travel to get there. Much of the overall demand for travel is for leisure purposes.

Many leisure activities though involve all three of these elements. A leisure demand is not a demand for a leisure good or a leisure service or leisure travel, it is a demand for a composite commodity that involves all three. The composite commodity is the leisure activity itself and in addition to the three components we have already mentioned, there will be a fourth essential ingredient, time. In fact time is a prerequisite for any leisure activity and that is why we have looked at the demand for leisure time first. In this chapter we will concentrate on the three elements, goods, facilities, and travel, that make up the composite commodities, the leisure activities.

Let us take, for example, the demand for squash. We can talk about the demand for this activity and even provide national statistics on the charac-

Table 6.1   Demand characteristics for squash 1987

| | *Percentage of adults participating in the 4 weeks prior to the interview* | | |
	Male	*Female*	*Total*
Sex	4	1	
Seasonality			
Jan-Mar			2
Apr-Jun			3
Jul-Sept			2
Oct-Dec			3
Socio-economic groups			
Professional	9	11	
Employer/Manager	5	2	
Non-manual, intermediate			
and junior	6	1	
Manual, skilled	3	1	
Manual, semi-skilled	2	0	
Manual, unskilled	1	0	
Age group			
16–19	8	4	
20–24	9	3	
25–29	8	3	
30–44	6	1	
45–59	2	0	
60–69	0	0	
70+	0	0	
Median age	30 years	26 years	

Source: General Household Survey 1987

teristics of this demand as Table 6.1 does. This table shows that people who demand the composite commodity (in other words, play squash) are predominantly male, aged 16 to 44 years. Professionals have the highest participation rates. The table also shows that there is a seasonal pattern to demand. More squash is played in the second and fourth quarters of the year than in the other two.

What the table does not show is how many squash rackets are demanded, in which squash courts these games are played, and how far the players have travelled to get to these courts. Yet to play squash the player has had to purchase goods (racket, balls, clothing and footwear) and travel to facilities. In this example we can regard the structure of demand as hierarchical with the parent demand being the demand for squash. The demand for goods, facilities and travel are derived from this parent demand. We cannot always, however, distinguish such a clear hierarchical pattern. For some leisure activities all the elements of the composite commodity are demanded simultaneously and we cannot distinguish such a parent/derived demand relationship.

A typical example is a package holiday to Greece. The very name 'package holiday' establishes it as a composite commodity: the package includes air travel to and from Greece, transport from the airport to the hotel, and accommodation and meals in the hotel for the duration of the holiday. Some packages include more, others include less. Ski holidays for instance can include ski-hire, purchase of lift pass, and ski-school in the overall package price. When you buy a 'package holiday' you are paying for travel, facilities, and goods all in one go. The package holiday industry puts the essential elements of the composite commodity together and charges a single price. However, this single price is not really the total cost of the holiday. The customer still has to pay for travel to and from home to airport, spending money when abroad and often new clothes to wear when away. The composite commodity is bigger than just the package. In other leisure markets the composite commodity aspect is still there, the consumer normally does the packaging himself.

The analysis of the demand in leisure is therefore a little complicated. To explain it we have adopted the following structure. At first we take a general look at the economics of demand analysis. Secondly we look at how this analysis can be applied to the demand for leisure activities. Next we analyse the demand for leisure goods, facilities and travel, attempting to identify the factors that are particularly important in each case. We will conclude by discussing a specific aspect of demand that we feel is unique to the leisure sector, volatility of demand.

The economics of demand analysis

Consumer demand theory takes as its starting point the individual consumer in the market for a specific product. The basic question that is asked is what quantity of that product will be demanded by the consumer. The answer is that it will depend on the price of the product, the income of the consumer, the prices of other goods and services, and the tastes and preferences of the consumer.

Price

Since goods normally give pleasure most consumers want most goods. Economics distinguishes *wants* from *demand* by defining demand as effective demand, that is not only wanting the product but being willing to pay the price necessary to get the product. Thus price becomes a major determinant of demand. Each consumer must weigh up the potential satisfaction he will receive from consuming the product and make a judgement on whether this is worth more or less than the asking price. If satisfaction is high enough, he will purchase the product. If not, he will not.

In general, the lower the price the more he will purchase, the higher the price the less he will purchase. This negative relationship between price and quantity demanded is usually referred to as the law of demand. It is equally true at the market level as it is for the individual consumer.

The market demand for a product is simply the sum of all the demands of consumers who are in the market for a particular product. Market demand increases when price falls for three reasons. When price falls the product is relatively cheaper and the consumer will substitute this good for other relatively more expensive ones. Therefore this price fall in one market has implications in the market for other goods. Secondly the price fall has left the consumer with more money to spend; if he was purchasing the product before and, together with purchases of other products was spending all his money, if he purchases exactly the same quantities as before he will now have some money over (because of the price fall). He may well spend some of this 'extra' money on the product whose price has fallen. The first of these factors we call a substitution effect, the second an income effect. We have already come across these concepts before in Chapter 5. Both normally lead existing consumers to buy more as price falls. A third factor at the market level is that new consumers may enter the market for the first time since they may now think that, at the new lower price, the satisfaction they receive is worth the price asked.

Although all products exhibit this fundamental law of demand, the rate at which quantity demanded expands for a given fall in price varies from product to product. It is important to a firm supplying a market to know how much extra demand will be forthcoming for a given drop in price for two reasons. Firstly it is necessary to calculate whether or not it is *worth* reducing price; it will not be if demand does not increase sufficiently (the relationship between pricing and revenue is discussed more fully in Chapter 10). Secondly, increases in output have to be planned to meet the extra demand. For this reason the concept of the *price elasticity of demand* is an important part of demand analysis.

Price elasticity of demand measures the responsiveness of quantity demanded of a good to a change in the price of that good. The numerical value of the price elasticity shows the percentage change in the quantity demanded of a good for a 1 per cent change in price. All price elasticities are negative, since quantity demanded falls as price rises; elasticities numerically above 1 indicate *elastic* (ie responsive) demand; elasticities numerically below 1 indicate *inelastic* (ie unresponsive) demand.

Income

We have seen that what distinguishes want from effective demand is the willingness and ability to pay the price asked. Often consumers may be willing to pay the asking price but do not have sufficient income to do so. Thus income is a major determinant of the demand for a product. As consumers' incomes increase they will normally increase their consumption of all goods and services.

At the market level we consider the influence on the demand for the product of an increase in the incomes of all consumers. It follows from what we have said above that for most goods as consumers income increases, demand increases. The typical situation is goods for which demand increases as income increases by a lower percentage. Such goods are known as *normal goods*. There are however exceptions. For some goods as incomes increase people switch to a better higher quality alternative, thus increases in income are associated with decreases in the quantity demanded. Such goods are referred to as *inferior* goods. For others, demand increases but by a greater percentage than income – these are *superior* or *luxury* goods.

In the same way as we wish to measure accurately the effect of a price change on the quantity demanded, we also wish to do the same for an income change. For this we have the related measure of *income elasticity of demand* which measures the responsiveness of the quantity demanded to a change in the consumer's income. The numerical value of the income elasticity shows the percentage change in the quantity demanded of a good for a 1 per cent change in price. Negative income elasticities indicate inferior goods; positive income elasticities below 1 indicate normal goods; positive income elasticities above 1 indicate luxury goods.

Income elasticity estimates are useful in determining future patterns of expenditure. Goods and services with income elasticities above 1 will be the growth industries of the future since over time incomes increase. Those goods with negative income elasticities (inferior goods) decline with economic development.

Prices of other goods

The demand for a good is affected by changes in the prices of closely related goods. If we go back to our Greek package holiday example, it might be that sudden changes in demand for such holidays could occur even if consumers prices and incomes remained the same. If the price of a substitute commodity were to fall then, in general, demand for Greek holidays would also fall. A substitute commodity for a Greek package holiday is a Spanish package holiday. Often there are wide changes, from one year to another, in where the majority of British tourists head for in the peak summer months, on the basis of such relative price changes (normally due to exchange rate variations). Two goods are said to be substitutes when an increase in the price of one results in an increase in the demand for the other.

Another type of relationship between goods is that of complementarity; two goods are said to be complements when an increase in the price of one results in a decrease in the demand for the other. The alcohol product, gin, is a complement with the soft drinks product, tonic water. Similarly, squash rackets are complementary with squash shoes. That is, they are pairs of products that tend to be bought together. When the price of one of them increases, it tends to reduce the demand for both.

The responsiveness of the quantity demanded of one good to the price of another good is referred to as the *cross-price elasticity of demand*. This is the percentage change in the quantity demanded of one good as a result of 1 per cent change in the price of another. For complements, cross-price elasticities will be negative; for substitutes, they will be positive. If the cross-price elasticity is zero, no relationship exists between the two goods.

Tastes and preferences

The standard approach in demand analysis is to assume that each consumer has a given set of tastes and preferences and that these preferences remain relatively stable over time. We can then analyse the effect of income and price changes in the way we have discussed above. There is considerable variation across consumers in preferences for leisure commodities. These differences are related to socio-economic variables such as age, sex, educational background, and occupation. Sports participation, for instance, is closely related to age and sex. Sports participants are predominantly male and young. For most activities, participation falls with age.

We should be wary though of expecting such relationships between preferences and such socio-economic characteristics to remain stable over time. We argue in the final section of this chapter that consumer preferences in leisure are particularly prone to change rapidly and if this is the case these relationships may suddenly disappear.

Economics has difficulty in handling changes in tastes and preferences because they are not objectively observable (unlike price and income changes). Similarly, differences in preferences between consumers cannot be clearly quantified. However, despite the fact we cannot measure preference change, the economist must continuously be aware of its influence on demand, particularly in the field of leisure.

We see then that whatever the product, the economist's approach to explaining variations in demand is to look at changes in the price of the good, the incomes of the consumers, the prices of other goods, and the tastes and preferences of customers. Now we turn to look specifically at the demand for leisure activities, goods, facilities, and travel to see to what extent these analytical tools are useful.

Leisure activities

We have already reviewed important evidence on the demand for leisure activities in Chapter 3 when we looked at consumer expenditure on leisure. In this section, rather than looking at how consumers allocate their expenditures across the leisure market, we concentrate on other indicators of demand for leisure activities. We have a pretty good idea from social survey evidence of how people spend their leisure time. The major source of data on leisure participation in Great Britain over the last two decades has been the General Household Survey (GHS). Questions on participation in various leisure activities have been included in the General Household Surveys of 1973, 1977, 1980, 1983, 1986, 1987 and 1990. Table 6.2 gives the participation rates (for the adult population aged 16 and over) in a selection of leisure activities that have been included in the GHS on a consistent basis since 1977. For these social activities and hobbies there has been little change in the overall pattern of participation over the ten year period, although there has been some growth (in particular, in listening to records, and DIY). The activities listed in Table 6.2 are all leisure activities

Table 6.2 Participation in selected leisure activities in the 4 weeks before interview

Persons aged 16 or over	Great Britain				
	1977	1980	1983	1986	1987
	Percentage participating in the 4 weeks before interview				
Watching TV	97	98	98	98	99
Visiting/entertaining friends or relations	91	91	91	94	95
Listening to radio	87	88	87	86	88
Listening to records/tapes	62	64	63	67	73
Reading books	54	57	56	59	60
Gardening	42	43	44	43	46
DIY	35	37	36	39	43
Dressmaking/needlework/ knitting	29	28	27	27	27
Base = 100%	23,171	22,599	19,050	19,209	19,529

Source: General Household Survey (1987)

with high participation rates. Nearly all adults watch television, visit or entertain friends, listen to the radio and listen to records/tapes/CDs at least once over a four week period.

On the other hand, Table 6.3 shows that participation rates in leisure activities in arts and entertainment and visiting galleries, museums, and historic buildings are relatively low. Visiting the cinema is the most popular activity in Table 6.3 with an 11 per cent participation rate, whereas only 1 or 2 per cent of adults go to the opera, ballet, or classical or jazz concerts. The second column of Table 6.3 shows how frequently over a four week period participants take part in these activities. In all cases the frequency lies between 1 and 2 (ie once or twice a month).

Table 6.4 shows how participation in these leisure activities varies with socioeconomic group (SEG). As with many leisure activities, those in the professional group have the highest participation rates and those in the unskilled manual group have the lowest, with participation rates declining steadily down the SEG groups.

The most comprehensive analysis of leisure participation data from the 1987 GHS has been the analysis of the sports participation data, with a separate report produced for these data (Matheson, 1991). Not only are there twelve-monthly as well as four-weekly participation rates for these sports data, but also because there was a change in survey methodology between 1986 and 1987 there was a substantial increase in reported participation for most activities, particularly outdoor activities, in 1987. The approach prior to 1987 seems to have led to some under-recording of sports participation and the 1987 data will provide a new benchmark for all future analysis of sports participation.

Table 6.5 reports the pattern of sports participation (four-weekly and twelve-monthly) and the frequency (over four weeks) for 1987. A total of

Table 6.3   Arts and entertainment, visits to art galleries, museums and
historic buildings
(a) Participation rates in the 4 weeks before interview
(b) Average frequency of participation per participant in the 4 weeks before
interview

Persons aged 16 or over	Great Britain: 1987	
	(a) Percentage of adults participating in the 4 weeks before interview	*(b) Average number of occasions of participation per participant in 4 weeks*
Arts and entertainment		
Films	11	1.6
Plays, pantomimes or musicals	7	1.3
Ballet or modern dance	1	1.5
Operas or operettas	1	1.3
Classical music	2	1.5
Jazz, blues, soul, reggae	2	1.7
Other music shows inc. folk, variety shows etc	7	1.9
Galleries, museums, historic buildings		
Art galleries or museums	8	1.6
Stately homes, castle, cathedrals or other historic buildings	8	1.7
Base = 100%	*19529*	

Source: General Household Survey (1987)

60.7 per cent of adults took part in at least one sporting activity in 1987
within the four weeks before interview and 77.6 per cent over a year. By
far the largest single participation category was walking with a four-weekly
participation rate of 37.9 per cent and an annual participation rate of 61.9
per cent. Other large participation rates were recorded for snooker/bil-
liards/pool (15.1 per cent over four weeks; 22.9 per cent over a year) and
swimming (13.1 per cent over four weeks; 34.6 per cent over a year). Very
quickly, however, moving down Table 6.5, single figure participation rates
for individual sports occur. As in the arts, most participant sports involve
only a small percentage of the adult population.

Certain sports emerged for the first time as important participant sports
in 1987. That is, the 1987 participation rates were substantially higher than
those recorded previously. These include cycling, keep-fit/yoga, other running (including jogging), and weightlifting/weight training. The latter two
were coded separately for the first time in 1987 and emerged immediately
close to the top of the rankings of most popular sports. Keep-fit/yoga is
dominated by women with a 12 per cent female participation rate over
four weeks (compared to 5 per cent in 1986) and 21 per cent over a year.
Cycling, which had a four-weekly participation rate of 1.9 per cent in 1986,
had a four-weekly participation rate of 8.4 per cent and an annual rate of
14.8 per cent in 1987. These major changes do not reflect a sudden surge
in demand for these sports. Rather they illustrate the effects of the new sur-

Table 6.4 Percentage of people seeing arts performances, visiting art galleries, museums and historic buildings in the 4 weeks before interview by socioeconomic group

Persons aged 16 or over	Great Britain: 1987						
	Socioeconomic group						
	Professional	Employers and managers	Intermediate and junior non-manual	Skilled manual and own account	Semi-skilled manual and personal service	Unskilled manual	Total
	Percentage participating in the 4 weeks before interview						
Arts and entertainments							
Films	15	11	12	8	8	5	11
Plays, pantomimes or musicals	13	10	10	4	4	3	7
Ballet or modern dance	1	1	1	0*	0	1	1
Operas or operettas	2	2	1	0*	0*	0*	1
Classical music	6	3	3	1	1	1	2
Jazz, blues, soul, reggae concerts or performances	2	2	2	1	1	0	2
Other music shows, concerts or performances	9	7	8	7	6	5	7
Galleries and historic buildings							
Art galleries or museums	15	11	11	6	5	4	8
Stately homes, castles, cathedrals or other historic buildings	14	11	10	6	5	4	8
Base = 100%	705	2465	6012	4051	3830	1265	19529

Source: General Household Survey (1987)　Note: 0* indicates less than 0.5%

Table 6.5

(a) Participation rates in the 4 weeks before interview
(b) Participation rates in the 12 months before interview
(c) Ratio of annual/4 week participation rates ((b)/(a))
(d) Average number of occasions of participation per participant in 4 weeks

Persons aged 16 or over		Great Britain: 1987		
	(a)	(b)	(c)	(d)
Walking	37.9	60.1	1.6	8
Snooker/billiards/pool	15.1	22.9	1.5	6
Swimming: outdoor	3.5]	34.6]	–]	4
Swimming: indoor	10.5			
Darts	8.8	15.4	1.8	6
Keep fit/yoga	8.6	14.3	1.7	9
Cycling	8.4	14.8	1.8	10
Athletics – track and field	0.5	2.0	4.0	5
Other running (including jogging)	5.2	10.5	2.0	7
Football	4.8	8.9	1.9	4
Weightlifting/weight training	4.5	8.2	1.8	8
Golf	3.9	9.2	2.4	4
Badminton	3.4	8.2	2.4	3
Squash	2.6	6.7	2.6	4
Table tennis	2.4	6.3	2.4	4
Fishing	1.9	5.8	3.1	3
Tennis	1.8	6.6	3.7	4
Tenpin bowls/skittles	1.8	5.7	3.2	2
Lawn/carpet bowls	1.7	3.7	2.2	6
Cricket	1.2	4.2	3.5	3
Water sports (excluding sailing)	1.1	4.7	4.3	3
Horse riding	0.9	2.6	2.9	7
Self defence (excluding boxing)	0.8	1.7	2.1	7
Ice skating	0.8	3.7	4.6	2
Basketball	0.6	1.7	2.8	3
Sailing yachts/dinghies	0.6	2.5	4.2	3
Motor sports	0.4	1.1	2.8	4
Rugby	0.4	1.1	2.8	5
Netball	0.4	1.4	3.5	3
Gymnastics	0.3	0.6	2.0	7
Boxing/wrestling	0.2	0.4	2.0	[7]
Hockey	0.2	0.3	1.5	[5]
Field sports	0.1	0.2	2.0	[7]
Climbing	0.1	0.2	2.0	[4]
Curling	0.0	0.2	–	[9]
Other	0.7	1.5	2.1	3
At least one activity (excluding walking)	44.7	61.9	1.4	–
At least one activity	60.7	77.6	1.3	–
Base = 100%	19529	19529		

Source: General Household Survey (1987)
Note: [   ] Actual number based on less than 50 participants

vey methodology, in particular the interviewer prompting of these activities for the first time in 1987, on the reported participation rates.

Another important feature of Table 6.5 is the relationship between four-weekly and annual participation rates. The latter picks up infrequent participants. It also takes some account of seasonality since the four-weekly rate is an average for the whole year. If there is substantial seasonal variation, as there is in many outdoor sports, the four-weekly rate is reduced by the averaging procedure. Thus in tennis, for instance, the four-weekly participation rate in the third quarter is 4 per cent but less than 0.5 per cent in the first quarter. The average four-weekly rate is 1.8 per cent. The 6.6 per cent annual rate is above the third quarter rate but the ratio of 3.7 of annual to four-weekly is partly due to this seasonality factor. Many other seasonal sports in Table 6.5 have a high ratio of annual to four-weekly participation rates.

The final column of Table 6.5 shows the frequency of participation over the four weeks prior to interview. Sports participants have much higher frequency of participation than do the visitors to arts events recorded in Table 5. The highest frequencies occur in cycling (10 occasions per four week period) and keep-fit/yoga (9 occasions per four week period). Thus participation occurs in these sports on average once every three days. Since these figures represent averages over all participants, some participants will have considerably higher frequencies than this. This high frequency of participation across a large number of sports is an important characteristic of sports participation.

Over the years the General Household Survey has established a clear pattern of association of sports participation with variables such as age, sex and socioeconomic group. In general, sports participation declines with age, is dominated by males, and is higher the higher the socioeconomic group. This pattern is repeated for the 1987 results for both the four-weekly and twelve-monthly participation rates. However, there are significant trends appearing in this overall pattern. In particular women's participation in sport is increasing at a faster rate than men's, particularly in indoor sports. Also, participation is increasing in the older age groups faster than in the young age groups so that the average age of participants is increasing. Finally, participation in sport amongst the retired has increased quite substantially between 1977 and 1987. However, part of this trend is explained by people taking earlier retirement so that the average age of the retired group has declined.

Social surveys have also established a clear positive relationship between participation and income: for most leisure activities the higher one's income the greater the probability of participation. That is, the income elasticity of demand for leisure activities is positive. However, we need to know the actual values of income elasticities for various leisure activities. It is those with values above 1 that will become increasingly popular with increases in real income over time.

The data from social surveys (with the notable exception the Family Expenditure Survey discussed in Chapter 3) do not collect data on people's money expenditures on leisure. Rather the participation rates and frequencies are more a measure of time expenditure rather than money expenditure. This raises the important question of how we estimate the demand elasticities of leisure participation since there is both a money and a time dimension to participation. One study (Blaine and Mohammad, 1991) incorporated both time and money availability into a demand model for leisure-related expenditures. The theoretical model expressed demand for leisure-related goods and services as a function of prices, income, and leisure time budgets. The study found that demand for leisure-related goods and services was highly elastic with respect to income and leisure time, but relatively price inelastic. The results relate to the USA over the post-war period and indicate that, as more women entered the labour force over this period, reducing the availability of household leisure time, households substituted market-purchased goods and services for leisure time.

We have no reliable estimates at the moment for price and cross-price elasticities of demand for leisure activities. One of the main reasons for this is the difficulty we have in identifying a price for a leisure activity. Take, for example, water-skiing. What is the price of a water-skiing trip? The cost to the participant is a complicated mixture of charges for the use of a lake, equipment costs (the boat, skis, wet-suits, etc), travel costs, and time costs. These elements of price will differ for every participant. This makes estimation of price elasticities particularly difficult since each individual faces a different price. It is possible, though costly, to obtain the necessary data but, at the moment, we do not have such data for the UK.

Despite the lack of statistical estimates of the effect of price on the quantity demanded of leisure activities, we can hypothesise that price is likely to have a twofold influence on the demand for leisure activities. It will affect both the probability of taking part in a leisure activity and the frequency of participation. Whether an individual participates or not is dependent on the *aggregate* cost (entrance charge, equipment cost, travel and time costs). However, for the person who has already made the decision to participate, how often he or she participates is dependent on the *marginal* cost. Some activities have very low marginal costs in relation to the aggregate cost. Sailing, for instance, is an expensive leisure pursuit. However, once the participant owns a boat and all the other necessary equipment, the *extra* cost of extra sailing trips may be relatively small, particularly if the participant lives close to water suitable for sailing.

One study has provided some evidence on these different components of price. A Scottish Sports Council project looked at the overall cost of participation in sport and specifically the entry cost to indoor sports facilities within that. On average, for indoor sports, the entry charge makes up less than a third of the total cost of participation. The study showed that when entry charges were increased substantially, there was little reduction in demand. Part of the reason for this is the relatively small share of entry charges in the total cost of participation. Other aspects of the marginal cost of participation, in particular transport costs, were more important than entry price. Fixed costs of participation, in particular equipment costs and club membership fees, account for about one quarter of the total cost of participation in indoor sport.

Given the difficulties in obtaining suitable estimates of the price and income elasticity of demand for a leisure activity, most economic analysis has concentrated on the various components of the composite commodity – leisure goods, leisure facilities and leisure travel.

Leisure goods

Own-price elasticities and income elasticities for leisure goods and services have been estimated and one set of estimates appear in Table 6.6. The table also gives similar estimates for non-leisure goods for comparison.

As we indicated earlier price elasticities with a numerical value above 1 indicate elastic demand; those below 1 are inelastic. Thus, potatoes and vegetables (–0.17), fish (–0.09), and dairy produce (–0.03) have demand that is price inelastic. For these goods quantity demanded hardly changes as price changes. On the other hand, expenditure abroad (–1.63), catering (–2.61), and entertainment (–1.40) are price elastic. Demand reacts considerably to price changes.

On the basis of the goods and services mentioned above it is tempting to conclude that leisure items are price elastic because they are luxuries and can be dispensed with, whereas essentials such as food are price inelastic because people have to buy them whatever the price. In fact this is not

Table 6.6 Price and income elasticities of demand for leisure and non-leisure goods and services

	Price elasticity	Income elasticity
Non-leisure		
Bread/cereals	–0.22	–0.50
Meat/bacon	–0.44	0.29
Fish	–0.09	–0.03
Dairy produce	–0.03	0.53
Potatoes and vegetables	–0.17	0.87
Clothing	–0.72	0.68
Coal	–0.32	–2.02
Electricity	–0.96	3.76
Gas	–2.64	1.74
Leisure		
Wines/spirits	–0.34	2.60
Expenditure abroad	–1.63	1.14
Books/magazines	–0.13	–0.04
Newspapers	–0.34	–0.21
Recreational goods	–0.67	1.99
Catering	–2.61	1.64
Entertainment	–1.40	0.89

Source: Deaton (1975) Elsevier Science Publishers, Physical Sciences and Engineering Division

correct as a closer examination of Table 6.6 reveals. The essential determinant of price elasticity is the availability of substitutes. Whereas there are no suitable alternatives to potatoes and vegetables, consumers have the alternative of holidaying in Britain rather than going abroad. The evidence suggests that when the price of holidays abroad falls (for instance, due to a rise in the value of sterling as in 1979/80) then consumers do switch from holidays at home to foreign holidays. Holiday trips within Britain fell by over 6 per cent between 1978 and 1980 whereas the number of foreign holidays rose by 33 per cent.

The second column of Table 6.6 deals with the income elasticity of demand for the same group of goods and services. Here we do see a major difference between leisure goods and services and non-leisure goods. The table indicates that for a one per cent rise in income, the quantity demanded of recreational goods will rise by 1.99 per cent whereas the quantity demanded of clothing will rise by 0.68 per cent. Most of the items in the leisure category have income elasticities greater than 1, indicating that they are luxury goods. As people get richer they spend a larger proportion of their income on these items. Books, magazines and newspapers are exceptional since they have negative income elasticities: expenditure on these items falls as income rises.

One area that has been completely under-researched in economics is the cross-price elasticities of demand for leisure goods and services, both with other leisure goods and services, and with non-leisure goods and services. At the moment we have little empirical evidence to indicate which leisure goods and services are complements, and which are substitutes. We are also ignorant of the complement/substitute relationships between leisure and non-leisure goods and services.

At the beginning of this chapter we mentioned that the *durable* nature of many leisure goods sets them apart from both non-durable leisure goods and leisure services in the analysis of their demand. Durable leisure goods are particularly subject to fluctuations in consumer demand. If, for example, we consider a consumer taking up running for the first time, they will need running shoes, shorts, vests, sports socks, tracksuit, and various extras such as waterproof running gear. A new runner will have to buy all this equipment in order to take up the sport. Given the surge in running that occurred in the early 1980s, firms that supplied these goods had a huge increase in demand. However, many of these items are durable and last for many years. If demand does not continue to *increase*, but instead flattens out, demand for equipment will not just flatten out, it will actually *fall*. Instead of lots of new runners buying equipment for the first time, demand will fall to a level determined by how quickly the equipment wears out (or, perhaps more likely, how quickly fashion or design changes). The more durable the equipment, the lower the annual demand for replacement equipment from existing participants. This effect creates another area of variation and fluctuation in leisure demand. Furthermore, this source of variation will only directly affect the demand for leisure goods. Leisure services are by their nature non-durable, so they do not suffer from this particular source of instability.

Leisure facilities

There are some problems in estimating own-price elasticities for leisure facilities where several activities are provided for. We can normally establish elasticities for a specific activity at a particular facility, but it is not normally possible to obtain a price elasticity for the facility itself. However certain facility estimates are available for single activity facilities, and these are shown in Table 6.7.

For cinemas, the value of −2 suggests that demand is elastic in response to price changes. In such circumstances, price reductions increase total revenue. The Rank Organisation certainly found demand for cinemas to be price elastic when it cut prices at its Odeon cinemas in 1985 (*see* Chapter 10 for details).

In the case of the other facilities in Table 6.7 demand appears to be price inelastic. For example, a value of −0.2 for football spectating suggests that a 10 per cent decrease in price will lead to only a 2 per cent increase in admissions. Clearly if such estimates are correct, the prescription for raising revenue is to *raise* prices, since demand will fall by proportionately less than the increase in prices.

No reliable estimates of price elasticity of demand exist for public sector sports facilities. One of the problems in estimating such elasticities is the influence of the demand for the sports activity itself. If the demand for the activity is inelastic, this will tend to cause the demand for facilities to be inelastic too. If the major cost of participation to the consumer is not the entrance charge to the facility, but other costs associated with the activity, this will also cause the demand for the facility to be price inelastic. The results of the Scottish Sports Council's pricing experiment discussed above suggests that this is the case.

Similarly, we have no estimates of income elasticities for public sector sports facilities. However, data reproduced in Table 6.8, which relates to users of over 60 sports centres in Britain, show that the demand characteristics of facility users are very similar to the characteristics of sports participants that we noted above. The table shows that, on average, sports facility users are over-represented by the younger age groups, males and higher occupational groups. The occupational distribution of users indicates that it is higher income groups who are most likely to use sports centres, which suggests a clear positive income elasticity at least.

Table 6.7 Price elasticity estimates for leisure facilities

Facility	Price elasticity
Football spectating	−0.2
Cinema	−2
Historic buildings and monuments in rural areas	
a) Dept. of Environment	−0.15 to −0.4
b) National Trust	−0.3 to −0.6

Sources: Bird (1982), Cameron (1987), Bovaird, Tricker and Stoakes (1984)

Table 6.8   Demand characteristics of UK public sector sports centres

	Average percentage of sports centre users	Percentage of population in England and Wales
Age		
15–19 yrs	21	10
20–29 yrs	39	18
30–44 yrs	32	23
45+ yrs	8	49
Sex		
Male	65	49
Female	45	51
Occupation		
Prof/Manager	26	14
Other non-manual	32	31
Skilled manual	29	28
Semi and unskilled manual	13	27

Source: Veal (1981)

Lack of evidence on the cross-price elasticity of demand for facilities prevents us from establishing substitute and complement relationships between leisure facilities.

There is an important aspect to facility demand that is not present in the other categories of leisure demand. In many ways it is the crucial aspect to demand analysis at the facility level – the facility's *spatial* location. One study, for instance, found that 65 per cent of sports centres users travel less than three miles to the facility, and visits per thousand population decline dramatically with distance from the facility. For other leisure facilities, such as countryside recreation sites, catchment areas are much wider. However, visit rates still decline with distance. This emphasises the important aspect of travel in leisure demand, a topic to which we now turn.

Leisure travel

Leisure travel is a composite commodity in itself in that travel expenditures are normally associated with other ancillary expenditures. In this section we will consider the demand for leisure travel under two categories: the demand for holiday travel and the demand for recreational trips.

As we have seen in Chapter 3 holiday travel is one of the largest areas of consumer expenditure on leisure, and there are several specific surveys into holidays and tourism: the British National Travel Survey, the International Passenger Survey and the United Kingdom Tourism Survey. The National Travel Survey data indicate that 41 per cent of adult residents of Great Britain did not take a holiday of four nights or more in 1989 (Social

Trends, 1991). This was exactly the same proportion as in 1971. The proportion not taking a holiday is higher the lower the social class; only 21 per cent of classes A and B did not have a holiday in 1989 but 59 per cent of classes D and E did not have a holiday. This pattern reflects the pattern noted earlier for other aspects of leisure participation; participation declines with social class and income. Another aspect of this pattern is the extent of multi-holiday taking. Sixteen per cent of those in classes A and B had three or more holidays whereas this was true of only 3 per cent of classes D and E (Social Trends, 1991).

Table 6.9 shows the rapid rise in foreign holidays, more than doubling between 1979 and 1989. Most of these holidays are taken in Europe (87 per cent in 1989) with Spain and France the most popular destinations (Social Trends, 1991).

One of the major determinants of the price of foreign travel is the exchange rate value of the pound (normally measured as the dollar value of the pound or its Deutchmark value). When the pound is low in value, as it was in the mid-1970s and in 1982–1985, Britain is a cheap place to visit, and the surge in overseas visitors to Britain in these two periods is testimony to this influence. The strong rise in the pound in 1979–1981 led

Table 6.9 Foreign holidays[1]: by destination

	Percentages and millions				
	1979	1981	1986	1988	1989
Destination of holidays abroad taken by United Kingdom residents (percentages)					
Austria or Switzerland	3	5	5	5	5
Belgium or Luxembourg	2	2	2	2	1
France	16	19	16	14	18
Germany (Fed. Rep.)	3	3	3	2	3
Greece	6	8	9	8	8
Irish Republic[2]	7	4	2	3	3
Italy	8	7	5	4	4
Netherlands	2	3	2	3	3
Spain[3]	28	24	34	32	28
All in Europe	88	86	91	89	87
United States of America	4	6	3	4	6
Other countries	8	8	6	7	7
Total (=100%) (millions)	10	12	17	20	21

Source: International Passenger Survey, Department of Employment and Social Trends (1991)

Notes:
[1] A visit of one or more nights where a holiday is the main purpose. Business trips and visits to friends and relatives are excluded.
[2] Including day trippers to the Irish Republic.
[3] From 1981 includes Balearic and Canary Isles, but in earlier years only includes Balearic Isles.

to a sharp drop in the number of overseas visitors. It seems as though overseas visits to Britain are price elastic.

On the other hand, foreign holidays for the British are more expensive when the pound is low. The sharp rise in sterling in 1979–1981 led to British holidays abroad increasing by over a third. The curious period, therefore, appears to be 1982–1985 when, in the face of a plummeting pound, British residents continued to increase the number of holidays taken abroad. This seems to suggest that foreign travel is price inelastic, whereas the earlier evidence suggests that it is price elastic.

To explain this we need to consider not only the dollar value of the pound, but also the dollar value of currencies like the Spanish peseta. This, after all, is the currency that nearly a third of British holidaymakers have to buy for their foreign holidays. In fact, the peseta also fell sharply in value against the dollar over this period, so that its price against the pound did not change that much. Consequently, Spanish holidays did not become much more expensive.

Turning to leisure travel in Britain, part of the recent decline in the demand for domestic holidays is certainly due to the relative rise in the price of domestic holidays relative to foreign packages. The cross-price elasticity of demand between domestic and foreign holidays certainly seems to be negative. However, even this relationship is not completely clear cut. Though the standard two week holiday abroad is a close substitute for the two week holiday at the British seaside, there is also a complementary relationship between British and foreign holidays. Many people who take one or more foreign holidays a year also take several 'short-break' holidays in Britain. The short-break domestic holiday market has been expanding rapidly during the 1980s. Figure 6.1 shows how such holidays accounted for 48 per cent of all holiday trips in Britain in 1988 although only 21 per cent of holiday nights. Within this short holiday sector, short-breaks spent in hotels and guest-houses account for an increasing share, and a significant share of total holiday spending (11 per cent).

Another major area of domestic leisure travel does not involve staying away from home overnight (ie it is not holiday travel). Most sports require journeys to and from a sports facility. For activities that take place in the countryside the leisure travel component of the total cost is likely to be significant. Table 6.10 summarises recreational activities in the countryside for the period 1984 to 1986. It shows the dominance of informal recreation (eg drives, outings, picnics, visiting friends or relatives) compared to more formal recreation in the countryside (eg participation in organised sport). The pattern of activity has remained fairly stable over the 1984 to 1986 period. However, there was a sharp decline in countryside trip making following the sharp increase in petrol prices in 1979. Three-quarters of UK holiday trips and four-fifths of countryside recreation trips are made by car. The sharp decline in the number of these trips made in the early 1980s suggests that there is a price elastic demand for such trip making. However, by the mid-1980s demand for such trips had risen above its pre-1979 level indicating that the price elasticity of demand for leisure travel is higher in the short term than in the long term.

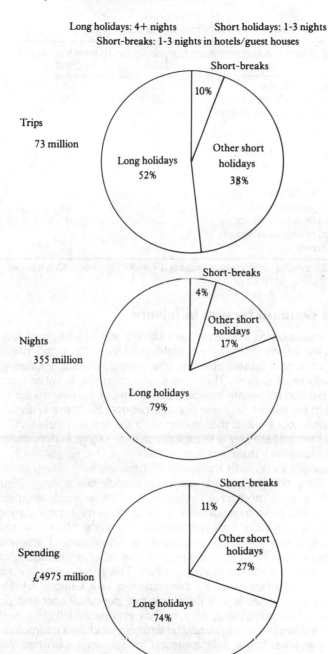

Long holidays: 4+ nights   Short holidays: 1-3 nights
Short-breaks: 1-3 nights in hotels/guest houses

Trips

73 million

Short-breaks 10%

Long holidays 52%

Other short holidays 38%

Nights

355 million

Short-breaks 4%

Other short holidays 17%

Long holidays 79%

Spending

£4975 million

Short-breaks 11%

Other short holidays 27%

Long holidays 74%

Source: British Tourist
Survey (1988) British
Tourist Authority

Figure 6.1   Holidays in Britain by British residents

Table 6.10 Recreational activities in the countryside

Percentage of people taking part in each activity in the 12 month period			
	1984	*1985*	*1986*
Drives, Outings, Picnics	66	55	54
Visiting Friends or Relatives	48	38	38
Historic Buildings, Stately Homes			
or Museums	45	39	40
Sea Coast	45	38	36
Long Walks (at least 2 miles)	41	33	34
Participated in Informal Sport	33	25	25
Country Parks	32	27	27
'Pick Your Own' Farms	32	23	21
Watched Organised Sport	24	19	18
Zoos, Safari or Wildlife Parks	24	19	20
Participated in Organised Sport	17	17	16
Nature Reserves	17	13	14

Source: A Compendium of Recreation Statistics (1984–86) Countryside Commission

Special demand factors in leisure

In the introduction to this book we outlined a brief history of leisure in Britain. One of the features we highlighted was the rapid rise in the demand for certain leisure activities (the cinema, football spectating) and their equally rapid decline. There are similar examples in more recent history (ten pin bowling, skate boarding etc). Some of the reasons for this can be found in the factors we have discussed above. But there is another factor over and above these that is unique to the leisure market. All leisure goods and services are prone to experience wide swings in demand as consumer choice in the leisure sector expands.

It is basically to do with the needs that the leisure industry satisfies. In Chapter 1 we pointed out the escapism aspects of the early leisure industries. In a more modern environment it is not so much escapism, but stimulation, that consumers look for in leisure. This may come through the danger of hang-gliding, mountaineering, skiing, or other risk exercise. Alternatively it can come from the aesthetic stimulation of listening to a symphony or aria. The important point is that what is stimulating for one person is often not stimulating for another. This is related to the stock of consumption skills possessed by the consumer (see Chapter 5). Perhaps more importantly what is stimulating for one person at any one point in time may not be stimulating after he has experienced it time and time again. Thus a beginners' slope may be terrifying (and hence stimulating) for the first year skier. It has little attraction for someone who has skied for many years.

There are two reasons for the volatility of leisure demands. Firstly with increasing affluence, leisure demands become more fragmented. Each individual has the time and money to find that activity that best meets his need for stimulation. Some new leisure products may attract a large demand very quickly simply because they are new, and have a high novelty value (and hence provide stimulation) for a wide audience. The second factor though may present continuing growth of such a market, that is the possibility of repeated leisure experiences to provide less and less stimulation. Where the leisure activity requires a relatively high skill level or provides opportunities for skill learning, the stimulation continues through repeated experiences as the nature of the experience changes as skill levels increase. Thus, although the beginners' slope may not stimulate the experienced skier, there are other runs that are challenging and stimulating. Thus skilled consumption activities provide opportunities for continued stimulation. However, leisure experiences requiring little or no consumption skills depend on the novelty effect for stimulation. With repeated experiences the novelty wears off. This explains how demand for a new leisure product may increase at a rapid rate as everybody tries the product for the first time, but is also likely to decrease equally rapidly unless a means of retaining the novelty effect can be found.

This tendency then for leisure demands to fragment and show high volatility in any one market is a major feature of leisure and sets it aside from other consumer markets. It also, not surprisingly, presents problems for the supply-side of the industry. It is not an easy job for the firm supplying a leisure product to cater to a demand that may well be expanding at record rates in the early years of the firm's life, only to find, when the firm has grown to a sufficient size to meet this demand, that the demand suddenly disappears.

Conclusion

We began this chapter with a discussion of the approach economics adopts in the analysis of demand. We emphasised the importance of measuring the responsiveness of demand to various factors. When we looked at specific aspects of the demand for leisure, however, we found that either appropriate data was not available or the relevant data had not been adequately analysed. The result is that we have only been able to give a partial picture of the demand for leisure.

This is not a very satisfactory state of affairs. The information that is missing is essential to the leisure manager. As we will indicate in Section 3 of the book, leisure supply decisions cannot be made sensibly without an intimate knowledge of the demand factors that we have been discussing in this chapter. There is an urgent need for much more research into the demand for leisure commodities.

Further reading

Bird P 1982 The demand for League football. *Applied Economics* 14(6).

Blaine T W, Mohammad G 1991 An empirical assessment of US consumer expenditures for recreation-related goods and services: 1946–1988. *Leisure Sciences* Vol. 13.

Bovaid AG, Tricker MJ, and Stoakes R 1984 *Recreation Management and Pricing* Gower.

Cameron S 1987 The supply and demand for cinema tickets: some UK evidence. *Journal of Cultural Economics.*

Countryside Commission 1989 *A compendium of recreation statistics: (1984–1986).*

Deaton A 1975 The measurement of income and price elasticities. *European Economic Review 6.*

Matheson J 1991 *General Household Survey 1987: Participation in Sport* HMSO.

Veal AJ 1981 Using Sports Centres. Unpublished report to the Sports Council.

7 Forecasting and planning for leisure demands

Managers of leisure facilities are often too busy with day to day problems to engage in much forecasting of what demand is going to be like in the future. They are indeed often unconcerned to measure the dimensions of current demand. When it comes to planning, this is a rather ad hoc process that relies more on 'gut feelings' about what consumers are looking for, or even paternalistic hopes that customers can be made to realise that what is provided is worth consuming.

It is our view that such an attitude to forecasting and planning for leisure demands is not only short-sighted; it is also foolish and dangerous, because it means that such managers are putting the leisure businesses they run at risk of under-achievement at best and commercial failure at worst. And so, in this chapter we outline the reasons why forecasting and planning for leisure demands are important for the efficiency of leisure businesses. We also identify some of the leisure data that are important for forecasting and planning purposes. Some of these data are published by national agencies, but many of them have to be generated by the managers themselves. In addition we review feasible techniques for demand forecasting and planning for leisure managers.

There are many formal techniques for demand forecasting and planning for leisure provision. Unfortunately, a lot of these are too complicated to be of practical use to the majority of leisure managers. This does not mean, though, that managers need not bother with forecasting and planning at all. It is important to realise that simple means exist by which the nature of demand can be identified. In this way a knowledge of demand now and in the past can be used to back up decisions which will affect demand in the future. So, whereas some of the data and techniques we refer to may seem not to be relevant to forecasting, we must stress that because they increase the *precision* of the manager's knowledge of demand, they help the manager to predict more accurately the way demand will respond to decisions made now and in the future.

Management decisions and demand forecasting

There are no doubt many people, including a lot of managers, who believe that 'good managers are born, not made'. Whether a leisure manager is self-made or rigorously trained, it would be somewhat ambitious to expect her or him to have the power to use a crystal ball to predict the future. Also, and here is the real catch, it would be foolish to expect a manager to make all decisions with no thoughts about what the likely response of consumers will be to those decisions. Even when managers do *not* use formal data and techniques to assess the consequences of their decisions, they do indulge in their own version of forecasting, albeit a subjective judgement about how people will react.

Which management decisions need information about the future? The answer is simple – all decisions! For many of these the required information concerns the way in which consumers, or demand, will behave. In day to day decisions this information will be estimated on the strength of experience. So, for example, how many vegetables to buy into a restaurant will be conditioned by knowledge of how many customers usually arrive at that particular time of the week and year, and in those weather conditions, etc. If the estimate is wrong the restaurant either runs out of vegetables or has to throw some away. Some decisions, though, are made less frequently and have consequences that last longer and are more serious. Pricing and investment decisions are of this type.

Take pricing decisions. Prices of leisure goods and services cannot be varied too frequently – this would upset customers. So a manager is stuck with the consequences of the last decision for some time. Without sufficient information about the way in which customers, both existing and potential, react to price changes there is a danger that a wrong pricing decision will cause a loss of revenue. Moreover, in the case of a price increase, it is possible to lose customers for a long time, no matter what is done to attract them back. The more information there is on the attitudes and behaviour of consumers to price changes – and that includes information on separate client groups, product types, times of day, etc – the more secure will be the decision to change prices.

For investment decisions, demand forecasting is of critical importance. Investing in an expansion of production facilities, or relocation, or starting up a new facility, requires detailed information about the long-term trends in the demand for the product, or the characteristics of demand in alternative locations' catchment areas. Without such information the decision is quite simply more of a gamble. Many a leisure facility has suffered an early financial failure because of inadequate forecasting and planning. It is also only when demand is forecasted accurately that the economic and environmental impact of a new leisure facility or event can be assessed and appropriate policies framed.

Demand types

Before we examine the data that the leisure manager can use for forecasting and planning purposes, it is important to specify precisely the types of demand that are of interest to the manager. The most common form of demand to be measured is 'revealed' demand. This is demand that has been expressed at the current price, so it is the easiest to measure, although where an entrance price does not exist, as in national parks for example, it is not so easy to monitor. For planning and management purposes, though, it is by no means the only important form of demand. *'Latent'* demand is a measure of unrealised or potential demand – ie demand that is unfulfilled because of a lack of opportunity, which could be an absence of facilities or a shortage of programming time at an existing facility. In many ways this is more important for planning purposes, since it is relevant to new investment. It is, of course, usually more difficult to monitor than revealed demand, since it is comprised of people who do not attend existing facilities.

'Induced' or 'generated' demand is new demand stimulated by the provision of new facilities, over and above any latent demand that may be satisfied. The reason this demand appears is simply because the facility is so convenient (and hence cheap, at least in time and travel costs) to some people that they are attracted to visit it. Unlike latent demand this demand does not exist until the facility is provided, and as such it is probably the most unpredictable to forecast. Finally, a new facility, or a new leisure opportunity at an existing facility, will cause some users to switch from other facilities or even other activities in order to take advantage of the new opportunity. Such demand is called *'diverted'* demand if it is a switch from other facilities and *'substitute'* demand if it comes from other activities.

Data for leisure forecasting and planning

Broad indications of market trends are available at the national level, but the individual leisure manager is more likely to be interested primarily in data of a more specific kind – ie relating to *facility* demand or *local market* demand. Managers of existing leisure facilities at the local level will have to generate for themselves much of the information they need about demand. At its simplest this means *accurate* records of the numbers and types of users that use different facilities for different activities at different times of day, and, if it is relevant, the different prices they pay. This is standard market research information and by building it up it is possible to derive a series over a number of years. With such demand information, simple time series techniques can be used to chart the essential characteristics of this demand. We describe these techniques in the next section.

The longer the series, the more reliable a guide it will be to changes in demand under different conditions. Some of these varying conditions, of course, will be under the control of the manager, such as programming time and prices. Others will be largely outside the control of the individual manager, such as the weather and competing leisure attractions. But the important thing is that the more information the manager has on changing demand and the reasons for the changes, the more secure the decisions will be which influence such demand.

Other market demand information, which is usually collected on an occasional or one-off basis at the local level, concerns the attitudes and socio-economic, spatial and demographic origins of existing clients. Such information can be collected by means of sample surveys and will be of use not only in judging the success of past and present policies, but also in forecasting the effects of future policy changes. Case Study 7.1 is a good example of such market research. If the survey technique is used on a local population it will reveal characteristics and attitudes relevant to 'latent' demand, 'induced' demand and 'diverted' demand.

At the national and regional levels of leisure planning it is *market* demand that counts, as opposed to facility demand. There is a wide choice of relevant data available to help forecast market demand. This data ranges from syndicated surveys, the results of which are only available to the sponsors of the survey, through surveys conducted and sold by commercial agencies, to public agency surveys and national government statistics, the main results of which are freely available in many libraries.

An example of a syndicated survey is the British Travel Survey. Whereas the main results are available from agencies like the British Tourist Authority, the detailed results are exclusive to the sponsoring agencies. Many commercial leisure firms sponsor special surveys as part of their market research, and it is not usually possible for others to gain access to the

Table 7.1   Leisure futures forecasts, an example

	Sales volume forecasts percentage change year on year					
	1990	*1991*	*1992*	*1993*	*1994*	*1995*
Audio equipment etc	2.0	2.5	5.5	5.0	4.1	5.3
Beer	–0.8	–0.5	0.7	0.5	0.5	0.9
Books	–0.7	–1.0	0.5	2.5	3.0	2.7
Cinema	3.0	2.4	3.2	3.4	2.9	3.7
DIY goods	0.5	2.0	5.2	4.0	3.0	3.0
Eating out	2.8	1.2	3.0	3.2	3.4	3.7
Foreign visitors	5.0	–1.2	5.1	4.2	3.7	4.0
Gambling	1.1	0.7	1.0	1.5	2.0	2.0
Gardening	–2.0	2.0	2.5	2.4	2.3	2.4
Holidays Abroad	3.0	2.0	4.0	3.5	3.7	3.5
Holidays in UK	1.5	4.0	1.0	2.0	1.0	1.1
Home computers	0.5	5.5	4.9	4.1	3.1	4.1
Magazines	1.7	0.8	1.5	1.8	1.5	2.0
Newspapers	0.0	0.2	0.4	0.3	0.5	0.8
Pets	2.6	1.8	2.6	2.5	2.3	3.0
Photography	2.1	3.1	3.0	3.0	2.3	2.9
Records and tapes	1.5	5.0	6.3	6.4	5.1	5.7
Spirits	–2.3	–2.8	1.0	0.1	0.4	1.3
Sports	1.7	1.9	4.4	3.5	3.4	3.8
Television	–0.5	2.5	3.4	3.2	2.2	2.8
Toys and games	3.1	2.9	4.4	3.9	3.6	4.4
Video	–0.2	2.7	3.2	2.7	2.1	2.6
Wine	1.5	1.4	2.0	1.5	0.7	2.8

Source: Leisure Futures, Henley Centre for Forecasting

results of such research. Regular leisure forecasts are now produced by a variety of commercial market research agencies or consultancies. The Target Group Index, produced by the British Market Research Bureau, is a source of household spending behaviour information which rivals the government's General Household Survey in scale and detail and includes much information relevant to leisure demands.

Two consultancies producing leisure-specific forecasting publications are the Henley Centre for Forecasting, which publishes the quarterly 'Leisure Futures', and Leisure Consultants, who publish regular 'Leisure Forecasts'. Table 7.1 shows one set of forecasts from 'Leisure Futures'. Other standard forecasts in this publication include price changes, market values and shares in consumer spending, for the sectors and time span shown in Table 7.1.

Published government information which can be used for forecasting purposes includes the General Household Survey, the Family Expenditure Survey, the National Travel Survey, the Census and the National Accounts – all of which have been referred to and used in previous chapters. These sources have been produced for many years and so have time series information on leisure expenditures and demographic and behavioural characteristics relevant to leisure markets. Many can yield usable regional information, which will not be published in the main reports, but which is available on request and at a price!

Demand forecasting techniques

Our review of forecasting techniques is confined to three that are considered to be immediately practicable for leisure managers. Two of them – time series and surveys – are discussed principally in the context of forecasting demand at the facility level, although they can both be employed at the market level as well. The third technique, cohort analysis, is probably most suitable for forecasting demand at the market level, but of course this can vary from a local market to regional, national and indeed international markets.

We have deliberately excluded consideration of techniques which are likely to be of less practical use to the majority of leisure managers, particularly at the facility level. So, for such techniques as regression analysis and Clawson demand curves, readers are advised to follow up the further references at the end of the chapter. This advice also applies to those readers interested in the technical details of the methods reviewed. It is not our purpose here to go into such details; rather we are concerned to show the relevance of the results of such forecasting techniques.

Time series

Given that the most likely demand information to be collected by leisure managers is regular records over time of visitors to a leisure facility, this information can be processed so that the manager is aware of the basic trends, seasonal fluctuations and random changes that typically occur at the facility. The means by which this can be done is time series analysis. The results of such analysis will help in making such management decisions as pricing, manning and investment at the facility.

At its simplest, a set of time series data can be plotted on a graph and the trend can be identified and extended into the future by eye. If there has been a steady growth in the number of recorded visits to a leisure facility over a number of years, for example, then it would be fairly easy to identify and extend (or 'extrapolate', to use the technical term) this trend into the future as a forecast. If, though, the past data presented a more erratic profile over time, it would be more difficult to identify and extrapolate a trend.

A more systematic method of time series extrapolation is to use formal time series analysis, for which microcomputer statistical packages are available. In an age when tills are not just the means by which takings can be recorded and cash stored but are also, more importantly, management information storage and retrieval units, facility managers can have access to any level of time series information with which to conduct a formal forecasting exercise.

Time series calculations enable a manager to identify the basic trend in the demand for a service, plus any cyclical effect. They also accurately identify the exact scale, timing and regularity of seasonal fluctuations. When the results are disaggregated into the constituent parts of a service, such as separate facilities, they indicate the extent to which diverted demand is created by facility closures and openings, and they give some idea of the strength of latent and induced demands.

When used in conjunction with catchment area information from user surveys (and possibly household surveys), time series information considerably enhances the planning of new facilities in an area, having built up a record of the way the market reacts to different circumstances over time.

Time series analysis is a technique which can be used at any scale of forecasting, from the individual facility to the regional or national plan. The problem is that it does not explain the *reasons* for the variations in revealed demand. It merely describes the patterns of demand over time and the manager is left to identify the most likely influences on these patterns. At least the manager or planner has something concrete to work on, though, rather than just hunches and gut feelings.

Surveys

Here is not the place to go into depth about the setting up of surveys, but it is important to stress that surveys are important sources of leisure data at the local, regional and national levels, and much of this data is useful to the forecasting of leisure demands and the planning of leisure policies. A local survey, for instance, can help to identify what the local population want to do, or do not want to do, with their leisure time, their attitudes to certain types of leisure provision, and their anticipated responses to changes in leisure policy. In Case Study 7.1 we feature market research undertaken by the Recreation Services department of the London Borough of Waltham Forest in 1984/5, using household surveys.

Case Study 7.1 Leisure market research by the London Borough of Waltham Forest

Between October 1984 and February 1985 the Recreation Services Department of the London Borough of Waltham Forest organised a household survey of just under 1 per cent of the population living within one mile of three of their leisure facilities. The department was interested in two markets in particular – sports and entertainments. The aims of the survey demonstrate very well the links we have emphasised between demand forecasting and leisure management decisions, for example: *'To provide information on the demand for sporting activities and current trends of sports participation shown by the community within the London Borough of Waltham Forest which will form the basis for the Sports Development Priority Programme'* (Sports Market Research). *'To provide information on the demand for entertainments events and current trends in attendance shown by the community within the London Borough of Waltham Forest which will form the basis for the development of future entertainments programmes'* (Entertainments Market Research).

Such aims are based on clearly acknowledged management problems which include a lack of information first, on current patterns of community participation in sporting activities and entertainment events, second, the reasons for non-participation (both at Council facilities and more generally), and third, future demand and community needs.

The focus of the survey was not only on revealed demand at facilities in the London Borough of Waltham Forest, but also on latent demand for Council facilities and any potential diverted demand by Waltham Forest residents from facilities in other areas, or from commercial facilities in the Waltham Forest area. This is explicit recognition that in order to cater for local community demands it is necessary to compete effectively for these demands with commercial providers and other local authorities.

For both the local sports market and the local entertainments market the survey revealed a wealth of information, such as participation rates, disaggregated into age, gender, occupation, venue and area, the reasons for not participating, the reasons for satisfaction or non-satisfaction with the Council's recreation services, consumers' intentions for the future and factors that would influence this future demand. It is highly likely that some of these results could have been predicted by Recreation Services management, but it is only through systematic monitoring of this type that such a detailed and objective picture of demand for services can be built up.

The results of the Waltham Forest survey all led directly to clearly stated management recommendations – some thirty in the case of the sports market research and seventeen in the case of the entertainments market research. Some of these recommendations concern immediate management issues, an example being that more price discrimination between products and client groups would lead to better attendance and revenue. This was based on the finding that price was not found to be a major factor constraining people from attending shows and concerts, and people were willing to pay different amounts for such events.

Many of the recommendations concern long term planning and policy, such as the provision of more sports facilities in one part of the Borough and the targeting of particular ethnic and age groups for particular activities. But a third type of recommendation relates to the need for further management information, such as an examination of the capabilities of other facilities (schools, youth centres, church halls, etc) for alleviating shortfalls in sports provision, and studies of the demand for particular activities with special reference to the effects of pricing, promotion and programming.

D

The recommendations arising from the leisure market research of the London Borough of Waltham Forest were summarised in the form of fourteen policy proposals taken to Committee, and then endorsed by the Council as a whole. The management orientated proposals have since started to be implemented, such as the preparation and implementation of strategies for the development of the most popular sports, the promotion of sports and entertainments to particular target client groups, and delegated powers for managers to modify prices at the facility level. The planning proposals, such as assessing the feasibility of new facilities for sports and entertainments, are due to receive attention in the future, when the resource constraints of a 'capped' authority are less binding . . .

It is important to stress that the Recreation Services Department of the London Borough of Waltham Forest see this market research as one of the first steps in a long-term process of setting up a system of management information, evaluation and review. At the heart of this system is regular information on what customers want and what they think about the service offered by the Council. A knowledge of demand is a prerequisite for the development of the service.

There will always be problems identifying the accuracy of responses in surveys, especially when the questions are attitudinal, or when they pose hypothetical situations and ask for anticipated responses. Nevertheless, to complement information about how people have behaved in the past it is sensible to attempt to find out how they may behave in the future by asking direct survey questions.

Less ambitiously, but still important for forecasting and planning, surveys can reveal basic information about catchment, participation numbers and frequencies, and expenditure patterns. If they were held at regular intervals they would generate time series information, which would be more suitable for forecasting and planning. Unfortunately, many public sector leisure providers and agencies do not indulge in such regular surveys, the main exceptions being the British Tourist Authority and the Countryside Commission.

Cohort analysis

A method of demand forecasting that attempts to explain the reasons for changes in demand is cohort analysis. A cohort is simply a sub-group of a given population. The analysis begins by dividing the relevant population, be it national, regional or local, into cohorts according to variables that are considered vital to the leisure participation rates of the population. Let us assume we are interested in forecasting the numbers of people who go to discos in a particular area. Many leisure activities are heavily influenced by age and gender, so for the sake of simplicity in Table 7.2 we have divided the population of an area into age and gender cohorts.

Estimates of both population and participation rates for each cohort are used to generate a forecast of the number of people in each cohort likely to participate in the disco market by the forecast date. For example, in Table 7.2, out of 12,000 females forecasted to be of the age 11 to 15 years in 1999 in the area under consideration, 30 per cent are estimated to be interested in going to discos, so 30 per cent of 12,000 is 3,600 female disco participants in this age cohort. A similar procedure enables participant numbers to be estimated for all the other cohorts in the table.

Table 7.2 Cohort Analysis: a simple example

| Age | Disco dancing in an urban area | | |
	Estimated 1999 population (000) (1)	Disco participation rate (%) (2)	Forecasted number of participants (000) (3) = (1) × (2)
a) Females			
0–10	14	0	0
11–15	12	30	3.6
16–24	16	42	6.72
25–34	18	12	2.16
35–44	14	11	1.54
45+	52	0	0
b) Males			
0–10	15	0	0
11–15	13	25	3.25
16–24	17	30	5.1
25–34	19	10	1.9
35–44	15	9	1.35
45+	44	0	0

Forecasts for population are fairly easy to generate, from Census data. The Census is held every ten years and sample surveys enable more frequent updates to be made. Many local authority planning departments use Census data to construct population forecasts on a regular basis, using time series analysis.

As for participation rate data, this would have to be derived from sample surveys of the area's population. An alternative would be to take evidence from national surveys which include leisure behaviour, such as the General Household Survey, and assume that local behaviour is similar. In the absence of time series data on participation rates, it could be assumed that they will stay fairly constant over the forecast period, and thus present day participation rates may be used in the cohort analysis.

Table 7.2 demonstrates that a forecast of the number of participants can be constructed not only for any cohort, but also for any level of aggregation of these cohorts, such as all males, all females, all those under 35 years old, etc. Such forecasts can then be used to improve marketing for existing discos and plan investment policies for provision of new discos in the area. The main problem with the forecasts is that they depend on the accuracy of the population and participation rate data used. Any participation rate forecasts must be derived not only from past data but also from expectations about the effects of a whole range of changing influences, such as fashion, income, unemployment and access.

Problems with forecasting

It would be wrong to pretend that if leisure managers were to implement techniques such as those reviewed above then they would have perfect knowledge on which to base future policies. What we do claim is that they will have *better* knowledge of demand, and this is likely to improve their decision making. Nevertheless, it is almost certainly the case that many leisure managers have 'dabbled' with demand forecasting and come away disenchanted. So it is necessary to point to some of the problems with such forecasting, so that readers do not expect too much.

Nearly all forecasting involves using a knowledge of the past to predict the future, and therein lies the root of forecasting problems. As long as patterns of demand have been fairly constant or predictable in the past, then it is fairly safe to assume that they will continue in the same vein. But there are no guarantees. If any of the determinants of demand change unpredictably then forecasts will be wrong. Some factors which are frequently important to leisure demands are also difficult to predict, eg fashion, the weather, and supply of facilities. The case of supply is particularly important, since it demonstrates that any revealed demand in the past has been conditional on existing supply. If supply expands there are likely to be changes in the levels of revealed, latent, induced and possibly diverted demand, all of which may be important for managerial decisions.

Since forecasting is by its very nature involved with changes over time, it is preferable to use time series data as a basis for the forecast. Unfortunately, such data does not always exist, even at the level of individual leisure facilities, so forecasts are sometimes made on the basis of data collected not over time but at a moment in time (say a few months, as in the example of Case Study 7.1), ie cross-section data. This makes forecasting more risky, since demand relationships, eg the effect of age, gender, race, etc, are only known for that moment in time, whereas with time series data any changes occurring in the relationships will have been monitored. To assume that cross-section demand relationships will continue in the future, therefore, introduces an extra error margin into the forecasting exercise. It would be better to build up some time series evidence by repeating surveys at regular intervals. This happens at the market level, but rarely at the facility level.

Errors can also creep into forecasting at the data collection stage, the 'rubbish in – rubbish out' syndrome. This is particularly the case with surveys, especially if they are being administered by unqualified staff with other tasks to perform and no motivation to take the survey seriously. Even machine-based demand data, such as attendance data stored in tills, may be subject to error if the staff are not all following the same procedures.

The point of identifying such problems is not to endorse those managers who do not attempt any demand forecasting! Each problem can be minimised by a rational approach to getting the best possible demand data, and then using this data properly. It may take years to get forecasting right, but with experience and a developed data bank of demand information, management decisions are sure to improve.

Planning implications and techniques

Demand forecasting should be integrally linked with the planning of new developments in leisure policy or facilities. This would be *consumer-orien-*

tated marketing in the best sense, finding out what demand characteristics are and then tailoring leisure provision to these. It is standard practice in the larger commercial leisure firms. When a new social club site is considered by Mecca, for example, not only is the state of competition assessed, but also the state of demand. A careful analysis is undertaken of the spatial distribution of different types of households, through the use of data from such commercial market research agencies as 'Pinpoint'. This ensures that the optimum location is chosen to maximise access to the new facility for those most likely to be interested. In other words supply is matched to demand.

In smaller commercial undertakings, and in the public sector, the planning of new leisure developments is much less likely to be preceded by thorough demand analysis. This may be because of a lack of forecasting skills, a lack of resources to purchase such skills, a lack of faith in the accuracy of forecasts, or just a strong conviction that the right action is being taken. But the end result is that the planning is much more *product-orientated*, ie making a decision and then trying to generate demand to justify the decision. Even with this approach to leisure provision, however, there is a clear role for demand forecasting. Once planning decisions are made, such as the siting of a new facility, together with its programming and pricing, it is then possible to use forecasting to estimate the likely response of demand to the policy decisions. This would provide early warning of any problems, such that decisions may be modified, or supplemented with other appropriate action.

One planning mechanism commonly employed in sports provision is the use of *standards*, ie attempting to reach a level of provision laid down as a national minimum per capita – the standard for indoor swimming pools in Britain, for instance, is five square metres of pool per 1000 population. Standards are easy to understand and simple to aspire to, so they are politically useful. But their use bears little relationship to likely demand for sport in any particular area, so it is a form of product-orientated planning.

A more consumer-orientated planning method is represented by two spatial approaches which are worth reviewing – visit rates and socioeconomic characteristics. One involves identifying the number of visits made to a leisure facility from all the different areas considered to be part of the facility's catchment. Expressing these visits as a proportion of the populations of these areas yields *visit rates*, and knowledge of these visit rates (or better still *changes* in them over time) will enable provision and promotion to be targeted specifically to areas of weakness or strength.

The information on visits can be obtained by survey, but it is easier with membership schemes. In Mecca social clubs, for example, membership cards are used on every visit in a card 'swipe' on entry. By this means Mecca not only record accurately the identity of visitors and the frequency of their visits, but also link this information with all the other information recorded on membership forms, such as address and birthday. This enables target marketing of particular groups, for example according to age, address, or birth sign.

Another spatial planning approach, called *social area analysis,* uses data on demographic, socio-economic and household-type variables to identify

Table 7.3   A simple spatial planning example

Local Authority wards	Unemployment (%)	(rank)	Households with car (%)	(rank)	Pensioners in population (%)	(rank)	Cumulative rankings for the three variables
1	5	5	70	5	12	4	14
2	16	3	53	2	21	2	7
3	25	1	45	1	19	3	5
4	18	2	58	3	23	1	6
5	10	4	60	4	10	5	13

different types of local area. The two main national sources of such data are ACORN and PIN, both of which are conducted by marketing consultancy firms. ACORN uses 1981 census data to classify any Census Enumeration District in the country as one of 38 different neighbourhood types. PIN identifies 60 neighbourhood types. Once areas have been classified in this way, particular areas can be selected as being most suitable for provision and promotion. This is because the area classifications are representative of *potential demand,* in so much as it is influenced by the variables used in the social area analysis.

As an alternative to using the national agencies' data, it is possible to calculate social area analysis for any individual area using census data – but it needs very specific computing and analytical skills. An extremely simplified version can be attempted, though, by choosing census variables that are important to the planning purpose, ranking them for each area being considered, and then summing the rankings (with weights if some variables are considered more important than others). This would yield 'scores' which represent a priority listing of the areas, against which current provision and policy may be compared. A simple example is given in Table 7.3.

In this example, the five local authority wards are ranked according to three indicators of recreational needs: unemployment, car ownership and old age. The cumulative rankings show that ward 3 is the most needy, through to ward 1 the least needy, ie *by these three criteria.* Obviously the choice of variables has to reflect the planning purpose of the provider, for example, planning to meet recreational need is very different from planning to meet recreational demand.

Spatial planning of provision, promotion and other leisure management decisions, would be that much better if *both* types of spatial approaches reviewed above were used – ie identification of visit rates and socio-economic characteristics of catchment areas – since they complement each other.

Another planning approach worth consideration is the Grid Approach. This identifies client groups important to the leisure supplier and these groups' usage of facilities. As always it is the usage data that is difficult to record accurately, particularly if the client groups are socio-economic in type, such as low income, unemployed, elderly, or at the other extreme high income, two-car families, etc. Surveys of users may yield such information or, where appropriate, membership details may give sufficient information on these characteristics. Once the client groups' usage has been identified, planning can take the simple form of membership or usage *targets* for each group, with obvious implications for marketing policies.

Conclusions

In each of the planning techniques reviewed above the objective is to use knowledge of demand to improve the effectiveness of planning. This is the ideal relationship between demand forecasting and planning techniques. Demand forecasting is one of those management aids that is commonly recommended and too infrequently used. Many of the constraints to the use of demand forecasting techniques are not really very valid ones in practice, especially when it is obvious that there are fairly straightforward and cheap methods which can be employed. Market research does not always involve spending a fortune on a national survey!

The adoption of methods to monitor and analyse the changing nature of demand for a leisure product can only help to improve, and thereby reduce the risks of, planning and managerial decisions.

Further reading

Bancroft G 1981 *Maths and statistics for accounting and business studies.* McGraw Hill.

Davies I, Rickett K 1986 *Entertainments Market Research 1986.* London Borough of Waltham Forest, Recreation Services.

Davies I, Rickett K 1986 *Sports Market Research 1986.* London Borough of Waltham Forest, Recreation Services.

Henley Centre for Forecasting *Leisure Futures.* Henley Centre, London, quarterly.

Tourism and Recreation Research Unit 1983 *Recreation site management: methods and techniques for conducting visitor surveys.* E and F N Spon Ltd.

Veal A J 1980 *Trends in leisure participation and problems of forecasting: the state of the art.* Sports Council/SSRC, Sports Council, London.

Veal A J 1982 Planning for leisure: alternative approaches. Papers in *Leisure Studies No 5.* Polytechnic of North London.

Whitehead P, Whitehead G 1984 *Statistics for Business* Pitman

8 The supply of leisure: objectives and structure

Leisure supply is unusual in that it is a mixture of three different types of supplier: commercial, public, and voluntary. We normally assume that each type of supplier has a different set of objectives. The profit motive is the drive behind the commercial sector whereas the public sector exists to provide a social service; the voluntary sector seems to sit somewhere uneasily between the two. Given the diversity of objectives we may well expect the different institutions to operate in completely different ways. In reality efficiency requirements normally mean that there are fewer differences in the methods of operation of these three different types of provider, than many people would imagine, as we will see in later chapters in this section.

In this chapter we will take each of the three sectors in turn, analyse its economic importance in the supply of leisure opportunities, and attempt to specify its objectives. We will then turn to the behaviour of institutions in each sector and analyse the extent to which such behaviour can be related both to the nature of the leisure market and the objectives of the sector to which the institution belongs.

The commercial sector

The commercial sector is the dominant sector in the supply of leisure opportunities. If we look at consumers' expenditure on leisure in Table 3.2 we see that most of this expenditure is revenue to the commercial sector. The growth in leisure spending over the post-war period has made the commercial sector in leisure one of the most buoyant sectors in the private sector of the economy.

It is difficult though to generalise about the sector since it is so diverse: not surprisingly, it reflects the diversity of leisure demands that it seeks to supply. The economist though would say there is a common factor – the profit motive. However, in reality this is no more than a starting point for the analysis of objectives of commercial firms. Empirical investigations have shown that other objectives in many instances are more important than the profit maximisation objective imputed to all commercial firms by economic theory. These other objectives include maximisation of sales revenue, market share, organisational growth, and managerial satisfaction, which may depend on profit to a certain extent, but is also likely to depend on a whole range of other matters, such as the size of the firm, prestigious projects, and the salaries and perks of managers.

Some studies have suggested that it is inappropriate to talk in terms of private commercial firms maximising anything. Instead, they suggest, we should accept that the typical firm ends up aiming for a satisfactory performance for a variety of objectives. This variety is the result of the fact that any firm is composed of a set of managers who all may have different objectives. Profits, then, are just one of a number of aims and as long as they are satisfactory they will not be the main objective.

The growth objective is a particularly interesting one to examine in the leisure field since on the whole the leisure market is expanding and so we would expect a strong growth orientation in private leisure firms. The ways in which growth is achieved can be seen through increased market share and/or diversification into other markets by organic growth or acquisition. We will see that in leisure firms both these strategies are evident in the major markets but long term constraints on growth of market share is increasingly forcing leisure firms to diversify into other markets. It is not only constraints on the supply side though that tend to see leisure firms spread over a selection of different leisure markets. It is also a reaction to the volatility and fragmentation of leisure demands that we highlighted in Chapter 6.

We pointed out in Chapter 4 that many leisure markets are characterised by high concentration on the supply side. That is, a small number of firms account for a large share of the market. It does not necessarily mean that any one firm has succeeded in achieving its objective of maximising market share. In many cases several large firms each control a large share of the market. In the market for beer, for instance, six major brewers account for nearly 80 per cent of the market, with the market leader, Bass, accounting for 22 per cent. The beer market has also been static over the last decade. In these circumstances, it is very difficult for any one firm to continue to grow within the beer market (unless it takes over or merges with one of the other major firms). This situation can become very frustrating for the management team since, in the early years of the firm, growth was probably very fast as the firm established this significant market share position. The solution is often to diversify into other leisure markets. Thus Bass which has the largest share of the beer market, is also a major hotel operator with the Holiday Inn chain, as well as owning Coral (betting and bingo). Scottish and Newcastle also have a diversified range of leisure interests outside brewing including Center Parcs, a Dutch based international holiday company.

The package tour market shows a slightly different aspect of the growth objective. The market is one of the fastest growing of all leisure markets and therefore provides opportunities for rapid growth for all the firms involved in the market. In fact, the growth of the market in the 1980s was accompanied by increasing market share for the market leaders, Thomson and

Intasun, which by 1990 controlled over 55 per cent of the market compared with only 24 per cent in 1982. The collapse of Intasun in 1991 left Thomson dominating the industry with 40 per cent of the market. However, even in a fast growing market such as this there is a constraint on firm growth. Even if demand continues to expand at the same rate, if the larger firms increase market share, their growth will be greater than the growth of demand. In order for such firms to continue to maintain such a growth rate, either industry demand will have to expand faster or the firms will have to expand market share at the same rate. Since market share has a theoretical maximum of 100 per cent, and a realistic (or legally binding) maximum much less than this, then eventually it will become impossible to maintain the firm's growth rate without continual increases in the rate of growth of industry demand. If the firm wishes to maintain its growth it must diversify into other markets. Thus, the International Leisure Group before it went bankrupt had expanded into the airline and travel industries. Thomson is involved heavily in another leisure industry, the publishing industry.

Diversification across leisure markets though is not only the natural corollary to the growth objective. It is also the sensible policy when faced with demands that, though having the potential to increase rapidly, have the equal potential to go into a nose-dive, as happened to the package holiday market in 1985 and in 1990–91. In the longer term we described earlier the rise and fall of the cinema and professional football industries earlier this century. Given this inbuilt volatility of leisure demands for the reasons outlined in Chapter 6, it is not surprising to see leisure firms diversifying into other leisure markets in order to spread the risk over a series of markets. Case Study 8.1 gives a specific example of this by looking at the diversification of the interests of one of the major leisure conglomerates, Rank.

Case Study 8.1: The Rank Group

Rank is probably the most diversified commercial firm operating in the leisure industry. During the 1980s the company became a true 'leisure conglomerate'. Table

Table 8.1   Rank

Holidays and Hotels	Recreation	Leisure	Film and TV
Butlins	Top Rank Clubs	Mecca Nightclubs	Film & TV
Haven Holidays	(101)	Pizza Piazza	Services
Warner	Mecca Social	Sweeney Todds	Precision
Shearings	Clubs (85)	Prima Pasta	Industries
Character Hotels	Rank Amusements	Texacana	
Rank Hotels	(96)	Hard Rock Cafes	
Graisons Catering	Associated Leisure	Rank Ahnert	
Rank Motorway	rental/sales/	Rank Leisure	
Services	gaming	Universal Studios	
	machines	Venture	
	Mecca Casinos		

Source: Collins (1991)

8.1 shows the four core areas of business: holidays and hotels, recreation, leisure, and film and TV. The film and TV services include advertising, audiovisual, film distribution, video services, and Odeon cinemas. The holidays and hotels division contains Butlins, the market leader in holiday camps, Haven, the market leader in caravan parks, as well as Shearings, Rank Hotels, and Rank Motorway Services. Both the recreation division and the leisure division show the importance to Rank's portfolio of activities of the take-over of Mecca Leisure in 1990. In fact, in order to illustrate the process of diversification of leisure firms across leisure markets it is perhaps better to trace the history of another company, Pleasurama, in an attempt to explain, at least partly, how Rank acquired such a diversified structure.

Pleasurama in the early 1980s had its core business in casinos. In the mid-1980, however, it began to diversify into other leisure markets, taking over Associated Leisure (amusement machines, hotels, and holidays) in 1984, Norscot Hotels in 1986, President Entertainments (restaurants) in 1987, and Hard Rock Cafés (restaurants) in 1988. Later, in 1988, Pleasurama itself was taken over by Mecca Leisure. Mecca at that time was already a major leisure company with a diversified portfolio of leisure businesses including keep-fit centres, snooker clubs, dance halls/discos, bingo clubs, holiday camps, public houses, and hotels. In 1990, Mecca Leisure ran into financial difficulties and itself was taken over by Rank. Thus Table 8.1 includes areas of operation that formerly belonged to two other diversified leisure groups. Pleasurama and Mecca. Given that Rank already had a fairly diversified structure of leisure businesses before the Mecca take-over, this take-over made the company one of the largest, most diversified groups in the leisure market.

The diversification will normally be in other leisure markets for two reasons. Firstly, the management team have expertise in providing leisure services and this expertise can be used in another leisure market where similar services are provided. Secondly as we saw in Chapter 3, the proportion of consumers' expenditure going on leisure items is not volatile at all. It is constant over short periods and grows slowly and steadily over long periods. It is highly predictable. It is the way that expenditure is distributed over the various leisure markets that is highly variable. For any firm supplying one of these markets, risk of temporary or permanent adverse changes in demand can be reduced by diversifying within the leisure sector.

Of course if it turns out that the decline in demand for a firm's product is permanent rather than temporary the firm may decide to get out of that market altogether. For instance, in the 1980s, Ladbroke sold off its bingo halls and slot machine arcades, and expanded into the hotel sector. We can envisage the firm collecting a portfolio of leisure products, discarding some as demand goes into long-term decline, and picking up others to replace them. Of course all firms do not have the same perception of market conditions. It is significant that Rank purchased the bingo halls and amusement arcades from Ladbroke. Obviously, different management teams have different perceptions of future profitability.

Despite the diversity of the commercial sector in leisure, it is possible to use economics to analyse how behaviour of firms in the industry is related to the objectives followed and the market environment in which the firm operates.

One other aspect of commercial sector supply can be identified, particularly in the context of sport and the arts – sponsorship. This does not involve the commercial firm in actually supplying leisure opportunities but it is a very real injection of funds. The latest estimates, for 1990, are of

£230m sponsorship for sport and £35m for the arts. In one sense this is commercial sector subsidisation of other suppliers, often in the voluntary sector.

This type of 'subsidisation' seems unusual for the commercial sector. It is behaviour we would perhaps expect of the public sector rather than the commercial sector. However, firms normally expect a commercial return for their sponsorship. Although the commercial benefits are often difficult to measure, the main objective of commercial sponsorship is to market the firm's product and this behaviour is not inconsistent with other aspects of commercial sector behaviour discussed in this section.

The public sector

We saw in Chapter 4 that economic theory gives several reasons why we should expect to see government intervention in the leisure market. The

Table 8.2 Net expenditure on recreation and leisure services, analysed by divisions of service, 1990/91

	£million
Sport	
Swimming pools	81
Sports Halls with pools	144
Sports Halls without pools	46
Community centres, public halls	45
Outdoor pitches	40
Golf courses	(2)*
Urban Parks, open spaces	301
Total sport	655
Arts	
Theatres, halls, arts centres	85
Art galleries, museums	72
Arts activities	12
Grants and contributions	36
Total art	205
Other	
County parks, amenity areas, etc	41
Allotments	4
Grants and contributions	7
Tourism promotion	46
Miscellaneous	51
Central admin (unallocated)	10
Total other	159
Total leisure	£1019

Source: *Leisure and Recreation Statistics Estimates* CIPFA (1990–91)
Note: *Golf courses are in surplus

state though can intervene in several ways and none of the arguments we examined specifically required the government to supply leisure services. Often market failure can be corrected through government regulation, tax or subsidy policies. Government does act as a provider of leisure services in Britain though to a considerable extent.

The largest area of government supply is in local authority leisure services with estimated total net current expenditure in 1990/1991 of £1b in England and Wales alone. This accounted for over 3 per cent of total local authority net current expenditure in England and Wales. Table 8.2 shows the distribution of that expenditure over different types of leisure service.

As the table shows, much of this expenditure is in the provision of facilities for sport and recreation. Swimming pools, sports centres, and parks account for over 60 per cent of total net expenditure. About one third of total net expenditure on leisure goes on the provision of parks and open spaces. This is the historical role of government – providing spaces particularly in urbanised areas – and it has traditionally done so without charge. There has been a significant decrease since the early 1970s in the share of total net expenditure going to this area due to increased investment in indoor facilities. Expenditure on the arts accounts for only 20 per cent of local authority current expenditure on leisure, a considerably smaller share than that going to sport and recreation.

Capital expenditure on leisure started to rise (both in absolute terms and as a proportion of total capital expenditure of local authorities) in the early 1970s. This corresponded to new investment in sports facilities, particularly indoor sports centres and swimming pools. Despite the economic crises of the mid-1970s and the election of the Thatcher government in 1979, capital spending on leisure continued to rise in the early 1980s (particularly as a proportion of total capital spending). The Audit Commission (1989) indicated that capital investment in local authority sports facilities was running at more than £100m a year throughout the 1980s. Again most of this investment was in indoor facilities, swimming pools and sports centres. As new facilities are built, current spending also rises since virtually all of these facilities make a loss.

Although central government funds much of this local authority expenditure indirectly through the Revenue Support Grant (and Urban Programme money), the decisions on the extent of such public leisure provision are made by local government. The result is a wide variation in levels of provision from one authority to another. Subsidy per head of population by local authorities varies in the 1990 estimates, published by the Chartered Institute of Public Finance and Accountancy (CIPFA), from £8.18 in Oxfordshire to £56.08 in West Glamorgan. The degree of subsidy is obviously conditioned by the objectives of the local authorities concerned. It must be said, though, that these objectives are not always made clear or precise in either policy or operations. The Audit Commission has criticised blanket, unreasoned subsidies of any kind in three recent reports on local authority provision for sport, the arts and heritage (1989, 1990 and 1991).

The direct expenditure of central government on leisure is spread over a wide variety of organisations and institutions ranging from quangos such as

Table 8.3   Central government expenditure on leisure: main agencies, 1989/90

	1989/90		
	Gross Expenditure (£m)	Central Government Expenditure (£m)	% subsidy
Broadcasting			
BBC (including external services)	1257.4	125.1	10
Sport			
Sports Council	49.7	41.5	84
Scottish Sports Council	6.1	5.2	85
Sports Council for Wales	6.26	4.39	70
Sports Council for N. Ireland	1.71	1.45	85
Arts			
Arts Council of GB	155.5	155.5	100
Arts Council of N. Ireland	5.9	4.65	79
Crafts Council	3.26	2	61
British Film Institute	22.98	11.8	51
Tourism			
British Tourist Authority	37.9	25.6	68
English Tourist Board	19.15	12.9	67
Scottish Tourist Board	12.225	7.85	64
Wales Tourist Board	13.1	10	76
N. Ireland Tourist Board	3.69	3.69	100
Environment			
Countryside Commission	22.1	22.1	100
Countryside Commission for Scotland	6.358	6.358	100
Nature Conservancy Council	40.9	40.2	98
National Parks	17.1	12.4	73
British Waterways Board	62.964	45.561	72
Heritage			
English Museums and Galleries	198.522	160.407	81
National Museum of Scotland	10.762	9.205	86
National Galleries of Scotland	6.972	6.972	100
National Museum of Wales	17.06	15.9	93
Ulster Museums	6.81	6.59	97
Historic Buildings and Monuments Commission	87	72.9	84
Ancient and Historical Monuments, Wales	0.75	0.75	100
Historical Monuments R.C.	4.4	4.4	100
National Heritage	17.6	3	17
Urban Programme			
Urban Programme Leisure Expenditure[1]	45.5	45.5	100

Sources: Public Bodies 1990; Urban Programme Topic Notes 1989/9, Environment and Social Expenditures; Association of County Councils; Annual Reports and Accounts

Note: [1]1988/89 data

the Sports Council, Arts Council, and the Countryside Commission to national museums and art galleries. The full list is shown in Table 8.3.

A superficial interpretation of Tables 8.2 and 8.3 suggests that the total subsidies from local authorities exceed the subsidies given by central government by over £200,000. The balance of central and local government subsidisation of leisure is changing. In the mid-1980s local authorities' subsidies were more than twice the amount given by central government.

This measure of the balance between central and local government support is something of an illusion since, as indicated earlier, local authorities receive about half their revenue account funding from central government grants. Nevertheless, the balance between central and local government subsidy for leisure has changed markedly in the late 1980s. This period has seen a continued increase in central government subsidies but local authorities' subsidies have declined in real terms for the first time in two decades and for one or two years they have declined in money terms too.

The evidence of Tables 8.2 and 8.3 suggests a very approximate functional breakdown of government subsidisation of leisure in 1989/90 as follows: sport £600m, heritage £370m, arts and entertainment £415m, environment £317m, tourism £106m. Since the mid-1980s the proportion of total subsidies given to sport has declined whilst the proportions going to the arts, heritage and tourism have all increased slightly. Although there is no stated policy intention behind these changes, subsidies to sport are being affected by CCT even though there is no requirement under this legislation to reduce subsidies.

Table 8.4 shows that the cost recovery of various local authority leisure facilities improved over the first half of the 1980s but in many cases it deteriorated slightly in the second half of the 1980s. This may have more to do with different accounting procedures within local authorities than with the ability of local authorities to control costs and generate direct income. In the increasingly stringent local authority financing climate, it is probable that more realistic (ie higher) central administration charges are being allocated to individual services such as leisure. Despite this, three types of facilities in

Table 8.4 Percentage cost recovery for local authority leisure facilities, 1979/80, 1985/86 and 1990/91

	1979/80	1985/6	1990/1
		(% cost recovery)	
Swimming pools	12	33	36
Sports centres	27	47	44
Community centres and public halls	16	30	25
Outdoor pitches	19	27	22
Golf courses	68	93	109
Urban parks and open spaces	4	14	12
Country parks	16	29	18
Theatres and art centres	34	41	40
Art galleries & museums	6	15	16

Source: Leisure and Recreation Statistics Estimates CIPFA

Table 8.4, swimming pools, golf courses and art galleries and museums, managed to continue to improve cost recovery throughout the 1980s.

In the same way as the private, commercial firm has been simplistically represented as a profit maximising organisation, so the public sector supplier of leisure opportunities has often been oversimplified into a branch of the social services. Whereas this may be one important function, public leisure services have shown themselves to be interested in quite conventional commercial objectives too. This is shown in two developments which have occurred in the last twenty years or less. Firstly, there has been a steady incursion by local authorities into trading leisure services, such as sports centres, theatres and arts centres. Such traded services account for 40 per cent of the gross expenditure of local authorities according to the latest CIPFA estimates. Twenty years ago the only major traded public leisure service was swimming. Secondly, the tendency for these services to aim to recover more of their costs through direct income from sales is another indicator of the increasing commercial interests of local authority leisure services.

There is, of course, some concern expressed about the future direction of public leisure services in the face of such developments. Commercialism is seen by some to be a threat to the very existence of public leisure services. These fears have been exacerbated by the introduction of compulsory competitive tendering for public leisure services. In addition it has been argued that if the private, commercial sector 'squeezes out' public sector interest in providing leisure services then the resulting opportunities will be highly standardised and packaged.

Whatever the effects of competitive tendering, public leisure services are most likely to continue their interest in greater financial self-sufficiency, if only as security against the fear of stricter central government controls on local government spending.

The rise of public leisure services in the last twenty years demonstrates that local authorities too are interested in the growth of their services. Whether this is derived from an altruistic desire to serve modern community needs or from a selfish bureaucratic desire to expand, or a mixture of the two, the result is remarkably similar to the growth and diversification of the private, commercial leisure sector in the same period.

The voluntary sector

One of the problems with estimating the importance of the voluntary sector in leisure is the problem we described in Chapter 2: the majority of the resources in the voluntary sector are provided free of charge or at a discount. Since market transactions are not involved, it is virtually impossible to assess the economic contribution made by the voluntary sector. The Henley Centre for Forecasting managed to obtain an economic valuation of the voluntary sector for one sector of the leisure market, the sports market (see Case Study 8.2) but no such estimates exist for the whole leisure sector.

Case Study 8.2: Estimates of the income and expenditure associated with the voluntary sector in sport

The Henley Centre for Forecasting attempted to quantify the monetary flows associated with the voluntary sector in sport in their report: 'The economic impact and importance of sport in the UK' (Sports Council, 1986). Their data was based on a sample of voluntary sports clubs in various sports which was then grossed up using information on the number of clubs in each sport.

Income to the voluntary sector in sport
They found that the principal income to these clubs were players' subscriptions, match fees, raffles, gaming machines' receipts, and revenues from the bar. Table 8.5 shows a detailed breakdown of income to sports clubs. Most of the items in Table 8.5 are self-explanatory. We want to concentrate though on the item labelled 'Voluntary work'. The figure of £81m is arrived at using information on the amount of hours provided by administrators, coaches, and referees. Details appear in Table 8.6. The problem arises of how we value this voluntary labour. The Henley Centre chose an arbitrary 'shadow wage': 50 per cent of average manual workers' earnings. Adjusted to average 1985 prices this amounts to £1.86 per hour.

Table 8.5 Estimates of the income of voluntary sports clubs

	1985 prices (£m)
Factor income (monetary)	
Admission fees	8
Players' subscriptions, match fees etc	357
Hire of facilities to outside groups	24
Sponsorship, advertising	7
Raffles, gaming machines etc	81
Bar	572
Other	87
Subtotal (factor income)	1136
Other income (monetary)	
Grants	29
Interest	21
Employers' subsidies to clubs	292
Total monetary income	1478
Non-monetary income	
Voluntary work	81
Imputed rent for dual use	9
Total income	1568

Source: Henley Centre for Forecasting (1986)

Table 8.6 Estimates of voluntary work contributed to sports clubs

	Number (000)	Average hours per week	Annual hours (million)
Administrators	451	0.9	21
Coaches	122	3.5	22
Referees	20	0.58	0.6

Source: Henley Centre for Forecasting (1986)

Expenditure of the voluntary sector in sport
Table 8.7 shows the expenditure pattern of voluntary clubs in sport. 'Factor expenditure' refers to wages paid out to bar staff, cleaners, ground staff, etc. The item

Table 8.7 Estimates of expenditure by voluntary clubs in sport

	1985 prices (£m)
Current factor expenditure	
Wages etc	345
Travel	22
Ground hire	29
Referee expenses	7
Equipment	12
Ground maintenance	145
Other	806
Subtotal	1366
Current transfer expenditure	
Rates	26
Interest	5
Non-monetary factor expenditure	
Voluntary work	81
Imputed rent	9
Total current expenditure	1487
Capital expenditure	
Investment	14

Source: Henley Centre for Forecasting (1986)

under 'Voluntary work' relates to the value of labour services provided voluntarily; no actual payment is made and the figure simply balances the equivalent item in the income table.

Comment
This example illustrates the real importance of the voluntary sector in leisure. Most of the £81m valuation will not be included in the official estimates of GNP. These figures only relate to one small sector in leisure. It has been estimated that voluntary organisations in leisure have a total membership exceeding 11 million in Britain. No similar exercise has been carried out to estimate the economic valuation of the free labour services provided by such members. This case study gives an indication of just how important such communal production is.

The only indirect evidence on the scale of voluntary sector supply is the membership numbers of voluntary organisations with some kind of leisure role. The main types of organisations with leisure connotations are sports, with over 2 million members; young people's organisations, with over 4 million members; women's organisations, with a million members; and environmental organisations, with 3.8 million members.

One problem with such data on membership in the voluntary sector is the disentanglement of a mixture of demand and supply factors. We do not know what proportion of membership represents demand for the organisation's activities (participants) and how much is concerned with supply (voluntary work). It is the supply of voluntary sector leisure services that we are concerned with here. The question arises, though, why is the voluntary sector supplying leisure services? What are the objectives of the voluntary sector?

If we had an ideal market economy with a benevolent and efficient government intervening to correct for market failure, then the voluntary sector probably would not exist. All consumer needs would be met either by the commercial sector or government. The existence of the voluntary sector has something to do with both market failure and government failure. Government is supposed to correct for market failure but as we have seen it often fails to do this due to lack of adequate information on consumer demands and also due to government officials following their own personal objectives rather than acting on the basis of abstract concepts of allocative efficiency and distributional objectives. The voluntary sector does a similar job to the one that government aims to do, it corrects for market failure, but a particular type of market failure.

Let us consider a good that is similar to a public good but the benefits are limited to a small group of people rather than being pervasive as are the benefits of a public good. In these circumstances the group of people affected might well get together and organise provision themselves. By forming a 'club', it may be possible to restrict provision to its members only and provide a service themselves that both the market and government fails to provide. The market fails because of the difficulty of restricting benefits to non-payers (due to the public good nature of the commodity), the government fails because the group receiving the benefits are not big enough to be politically important: the voluntary sector steps in.

This explanation gives one objective of the voluntary sector: to provide leisure services that members demand but do not feel are adequately supplied by the market or by government. In sport, this is certainly the case. A group of people get together to form a football club because they all enjoy playing football; all members pay a subscription and use the money to hire a pitch and pay league fees to join a league containing similar clubs that also have members that enjoy playing football. Nobody can receive the benefits unless they join the club. If the club becomes popular, and spectators come to watch the games, then the club may charge the spectators to share in the benefits they are providing in the form of a football match. They are then behaving like a commercial firm: charging an entrance fee for a service provided. The motivation for the existence of the club though is the enjoyment of playing football: not maximising spectator revenue (which would be the commercial objective).

If the objective of the voluntary sector in leisure is to provide leisure services for a group of people (its members) not being satisfied by the market, it seems as though the voluntary sector is acting like a mini-government. The difference from government is that voluntary bodies do not have the ability to raise tax revenue and are therefore affected by basic commercial constraints. Thus the voluntary sector has social objectives, like government, but it also has commercial objectives: a voluntary body must at least break-even (ie cover its costs) otherwise it will cease to exist. There are various sources of revenue available to the voluntary sector ranging from sales of goods and services in direct competition with the commercial sector to direct subsidy from government similar to a public agency. Sources of revenue vary from one voluntary sector organisation to another depending on the type of organisation. Some voluntary sector leisure organisations are 'exclusive clubs' only providing benefits to members. Such organisations (such as a sports club) normally will raise revenue mainly through membership fees and from sales (eg bar sales). Other leisure organisations have a wide role providing benefits to a large number of people whether members or not. Such organisations are more similar to government and will raise a significant amount of revenue from either government grants or private sector voluntary donations, or both. The National Trust is an example of such a voluntary sector organisation in leisure.

Thus the voluntary sector is sandwiched in between the public and private sectors, having similarities to both but meeting needs the other two do not.

Consumer needs and the supplier

We have seen above that the rationale of the voluntary sector is in the meeting of consumer needs. It should also be the rationale of the public and commercial sectors. In the public sector, the rationale is often seen as in providing for social needs, but as we pointed out, there is a large element of normal trading in public leisure services. The individual consumer is willing to pay for services and the local authority is quite happy to accept the payment. There may well be some 'social' or 'public' benefits realised as a result of the transaction. Often this arises because the benefit is directed towards a minority group, eg the unemployed. Increasingly though such groups are targeted by the use of selective subsidies. For the majority of local authority leisure facility users the prime benefits are likely to be personal to the individual consumers, in the same way as any commodity provided by the commercial sector.

The commercial firm must cater for consumer demands or it will simply not survive. To a certain extent advertising can 'persuade' consumers to purchase a commodity; but to grow a firm must anticipate changes in consumer demands and adapt supply accordingly. In a similar way a local authority's leisure services will only expand consistently if they show proven success at satisfying consumer demands. This 'proven success' may take the form of very high visitor figures or high revenues, or indeed both; but without such success the political sanction to expand is unlikely to be forthcoming.

Conclusions

Any organisation attempting to supply leisure opportunities is likely to have a range of objectives, and it is probable that there will be considerable overlap between the objectives of public, commercial and voluntary suppliers. At best the objectives will reflect different aspects of service delivery, or compatible targets for individuals in the organisation. At worst, the objectives will conflict with each other and thus reflect internal conflicts within the organisation. It is not unusual for such conflicting objectives to be unwritten, implicit, and non-operational, especially in the public sector.

We have argued above that certain commercial objectives (eg the financial objective, growth, and catering for consumer demands) are common to public, commercial and voluntary suppliers in leisure. The chapters in the rest of this section will therefore deal with aids to decision-making in leisure supply that are relevant in all three sectors.

Further Reading

Collins M 1991 The economics of sport and sports in the economy: some international comparisons, in Cooper CP (ed) *Progress in Tourism, Recreation, and Hospitality Management*, Vol 3. Belhaven Press.

Gratton C and Taylor P 1987 *Leisure industries – an overview*. Comedia.

Gratton C and Taylor P 1991 *Government and the economics of sport*. Longman.

Weisbrod B 1988 *The non-profit economy*. Harvard University Press.

9 Production and costs

No matter what sector suppliers of leisure goods and services are in, public, private or voluntary, they will all be making supply decisions about the same basic things. How much output to supply, how many inputs to use and in what combinations, what to pay for the inputs, what budget to set in order to supply a given output: these are all questions relating to the physical and monetary relationships between inputs and outputs in the production process. Inputs are the factors of production or resources used to make the finished product, such as labour, materials, machinery, equipment, land, buildings, etc. Outputs, of course, are the finished products. The basic relationships between inputs and outputs are at the heart of the supply problem and have consequences for all supply decisions.

Inputs and outputs are related in a variety of ways and it is the intention of this chapter to explore these relationships. They lead to various concepts of performance too, and it is important from the outset to define some of these performance concepts. A study of the use and value of inputs in relation to outputs must underpin any concepts of efficiency, which we examine in more detail in Chapter 12, but which we now define.

Efficiency

First, 'technical efficiency' is achieved when the best possible use of inputs is made in the production process. In other words output is maximised for a given set of inputs. Clearly this chapter is concerned to identify the ways in which technical efficiency can be achieved.

Second, 'economic efficiency' (also termed allocative efficiency) requires that the inputs and outputs are all priced and allocated competitively. This ensures that inputs are allocated properly between suppliers because they are only purchased if they are contributing their maximum potential to the production process. Outputs are likewise allocated properly between consumers such that the maximum total benefit is derived from their consumption. If, for example one man was employed producing more hamburgers than consumers wanted at the current price, then this would not be economically efficient. The excess hamburgers would remain unsold, the man would not be worth employing, so he would be moved to producing something that *was* wanted by consumers, and economic efficiency would be improved.

Clearly economic efficiency concerns such a wide range of management decisions, such as pricing, marketing and investment, that it would be attempting too much to look at all these aspects in this chapter. In fact we confine our attentions for the moment to one side of economic efficiency: the cost side – the monetary measure of inputs. We leave until later chapters the issues of pricing and revenues, although obviously what we have to say about costs, and the way they alter at different output levels, has a direct bearing on pricing and investment decisions.

The third type of efficiency to be considered is '*X-efficiency*', which is concerned with the motivation and organisation of suppliers. Even when all the right technical inputs are present, it is possible for the output to be of inadequate quality, or even not the anticipated quantity. This may be because the motivation to be efficient is not present, as has been said of public sector leisure services, for instance. Or it may be because the organisational structure is too large and lines of communication are too long, so that messages get distorted. Whatever the reason, the problem is one of '*X-inefficiency*', and it causes higher costs per unit of output, so it is part of this chapter's analysis of the costs of providing leisure services.

As well as efficiency, the chapter is relevant to another performance concept, '*economy*', ie the achievement of a given output at minimum cost. But before analysing the nature of costs it is necessary to examine the nature of both outputs and inputs in leisure production.

Leisure outputs

The physical outputs produced by leisure industries are fairly easy to identify in the case of the manufacturing sector. Production of barrels of beer, tennis rackets, or magazines is tangible and easy to measure. However, as we have seen in Chapter 3, most of the leisure sector is concerned with the production of services, and here output is harder to pin down. Commonly, output in leisure services is seen as the quantity of customers dealt with in a given time period. This, though, is a measure of *demand* not supply.

In the manufacturing of magazines, for example, if out of 10,000 magazines that are produced only 8000 are sold, output would not be said to equal just the sold copies. In the same way, an hotel can supply 40 bedrooms and 100 covers for dinner, but if no-one turns up the product is still on offer. It is supplied but is not demanded. The problem in the service sector is that the product is highly perishable. Once a service is provided at any given time, if it is not demanded then it is wasted completely.

So the output of a service is clear in principle. It is the *capacity* which the service provides in a given time period. Combining a measure of this capacity output with visitor figures gives another common performance measure – *capacity utilisation,* or the *load factor.* But it is important to look at the nature of capacity in more detail, since it is not always a straightforward measure of output.

Capacity in leisure facilities

Unfortunately there are a number of ways of defining capacity for leisure facilities. Some are appropriate for certain types of facility, some are practical, but some are misleading. To illustrate with the example of a dance hall, it is possible to define the capacity of this hall by measuring the absolute physical capacity of the hall to hold people. However, this is hardly a practical measure of capacity unless the manager of the hall is interested in an entry in the Guinness Book of Records: it would certainly not allow much dancing to occur!

A more practical way of defining capacity for the hall would be to measure the capabilities of *all* inputs in terms of their ability to cater for certain numbers of customers. In other words, instead of just assessing the extreme capacity of the hall, it is necessary to measure the numbers of customers that could be accommodated by the number of staff employed, the amounts of food and drink in stock, the size of the car park, the maintenance and legal cost implications, etc. The overall capacity of the hall would then be defined by the highest acceptable number of customers according to any one of the inputs concerned.

Yet another definition of capacity could be framed in the context of the perceptions of the customers. Each customer will have their own subjective judgement of when the hall is 'full'. This judgement will be conditioned by such considerations as the demand for dancing space, the demand for seating and standing accommodation, and the queues for the bar, the food and the toilets. Furthermore, different customers will have different perceptions of capacity, according to their individual preferences, patience, bladder capacity, etc! Clearly this form of capacity is very difficult to pin down, and only very careful market research could help to identify it. Managers often have their own perceptions of what a 'comfortable' capacity is for their facilities, which may well be lower than the fixed number of places available.

Already we have three potential measures of capacity for the dance hall, and they will probably yield very different numbers. For certain types of leisure facilities another consideration assumes importance in the measuring of capacity – the environment. In outside facilities such as parks (ranging from urban parks at one extreme to National Parks at the other) the capacity may well be defined with reference to the damage caused to the physical and ecological environment. This *'carrying capacity',* though, while being clear in principle is not so easy to identify in practice.

Environmental damage can vary from slight ecological damage such as the diminution of the populations of insect and plant life, to severe physical erosion of top soil. The problem is where to draw the capacity line, ie what is an acceptable level of damage? Here even the experts often disagree, partly because the physical measurement of damage is uncertain, but more importantly because the environmental damage is nearly always only one of a number of considerations. It may be that the site of environmental damage is one which is very popular with visitors, so any curtailing of these visits by a carrying capacity constraint will cause a cut in revenue and visitors' pleasure.

In economics the concept of capacity is sometimes seen to be the point at which the total costs of a facility begin to exceed the total benefits. In order to identify this capacity usage, it is necessary to identify all the costs of provision on the one hand, including such costs as environmental costs (which are rarely paid for by visitors), and on the other hand all the benefits, which include not only revenues but also any benefits felt by visitors over and above the price they may have paid (such benefits are called consumer surplus). Furthermore, such calculations need to be done at all reasonable levels of use so that the critical point can be identified where costs begin to exceed benefits. Obviously this capacity is only as practical as the measurement of the costs and benefits, and the non-monetary costs and benefits are often extremely difficult to value. A public sector leisure manager may well be interested in such economic capacity, since the public sector provider is commonly concerned for the social benefits of provision. However, a commercial supplier may be more interested in a narrower version of economic capacity, ie where *financial* costs begin to exceed *financial* revenues.

For leisure facilities with a single purpose or a fixed number of accommodation places, the identification and measurement of capacity is fairly straightforward. Such is the case, for instance, in cinemas, theatres, squash courts, hotels, restaurants and aeroplanes. However, problems arise in the identification of capacity in multi-purpose leisure facilities. Take the example of a leisure centre main hall. If this hall is used for aerobics or a disco it is possible to get far more people into the facility than if it is used for such activities as five-a-side, badminton or tennis. But it would be unrealistic to expect the manager of this facility to define capacity for it in terms of the former activities alone. So the only way in which capacity can be meaningfully defined is by reference to existing programmes or feasible, alternative programmes.

Outputs of leisure services, then, should be seen as a capacity level of production. Costs of production are incurred in producing this capacity, not just in catering for the level of demand that happens to occur.

Inputs to leisure production

Inputs are the factors of production used to produce the commodity on offer to the customer. In leisure the most important input is commonly labour, but other inputs typically used include materials, land, energy, and capital. Capital is a general term used in economics to describe the physical, long term assets used in the production process, such as buildings, transport and machinery.

Most analysis of inputs is conducted in terms of the costs of these inputs, but before moving on to consider such costs of production, it is necessary to examine the technical relationships between inputs and outputs. A basic decision facing the leisure manager is how much of each input to employ. This is probably a matter of habit to many suppliers, but such habits might be open to question.

There can be quite a discrepancy between the input profiles of similar facilities under different ownerships. As an example, take the case of the labour input for local authority leisure centres without pools. In 1984/85 employment costs for such facilities represented on average just over half of operational costs (excluding debt charges). But the range for individual leisure centres was between one-fifth and three-quarters of total operational costs taken up by the labour input. This example illustrates that leisure managers should question the automatic adoption of traditional input employment levels. There is obviously a choice to be made about the 'right' input combinations.

Inputs in leisure provision are often largely *'fixed'* in the sense that they do not vary as the number of customers varies. Obviously inputs like buildings and equipment are fixed in this sense, but often so too are inputs that might at first be considered to be variable, such as staff (particularly full-time staff), maintenance, and heating and lighting.

Inputs also differ in divisibility and mobility, which poses management problems. Labour in particular often has full-time employment preferences, and also specific skills and geographical locations which limit the employment options of the manager.

Productivity

One major principle that underlies the employment of any factor of production is that of productivity. Productivity is the output produced in a given time period per unit of the input. A common indicator of labour productivity, for example, is output per staff-hour, and this can be expressed in physical or monetary terms, eg production of so many bottles of whisky per staff-hour or the sales value of whisky produced per staff-hour.

Whereas the physical measurement of productivity is possible in manufacturing industry, it presents great problems in service industries such as leisure, because of the basic difficulties in measuring output as described above. The only physical measure available to monitor productivity is not output as represented by capacity, but instead demand or usage of the service. So the nearest the service industry comes to physical productivity measures is indicators like the number of visitors per staff-hour.

However, the *value* of output, or *'revenue productivity'* is a more important indicator of performance to many suppliers than physical productivity, particularly in the commercial sector. Revenue productivity is expressed in terms of actual revenue attained from selling the product, eg visitor revenue per staff-hour. Expressing it in relation to the capacity number of visits would be a measure of *potential* productivity, as compared to actual.

Ideally, both the employment and payment of inputs should be linked to their contribution to production, ie their productivity. Taking the labour example, it would be uneconomic and inefficient to employ an extra person whose contribution to output either remained unsold or earned a revenue less than the person's wage. This, of course, is the dominant principle on the manager's side of the negotiating table! Other considerations will arise, especially in the payment of labour, but as far as the manager is concerned efficiency requires that input payments are covered by revenue productivity. Case Study 9.1 puts such issues in a broader context for a hotel operation.

Case Study 9.1 Fawlty Towers

Fawlty Towers is a seaside hotel which typifies the production problems of the most apathetic parts of the leisure industry. Management decisions are made according to the crisis of the day, so any thought of making decisions to improve efficiency is condemned to the idle dreaming of the owners, Basil and Sybil Fawlty, in their spare time.

The hotel, which has a restaurant and bar, 'gets by' in terms of profitability, but more by luck than judgement. The owners do not know what separate profit contributions are made by the hotel, the bar, the restaurant, residents or casual visitors. Management policy is determined by what was done last year, and the year before, etc. Costs are tolerable and traditional. Outputs are mostly tolerable and even more traditional.

Inputs are dominated by purchase of food and drink, and by labour. A full-time staff of five, including the owners, is severely stretched at peak times of the year and markedly underutilised at off-peak times. In addition to Basil and Sybil, the full-time staff are the chef, the housekeeper/receptionist/dogsbody Polly, and the head

Table 9.1 Recommendations for Fawlty Towers

a) Retrenchment
Close the hotel at off-peak times.
Offer the chef and Polly temporary, seasonal, employment.
Sack Manuel. Use temporary, part-time local labour at low cost, where necessary.
   Offer placements for students from the local catering college.
As a contingency retrain Sybil or Basil as a chef.
Allocate costs and revenues under the following heads: bed and breakfast; restaurant; bar.

b) Growth
Take out loan/extra mortgage.
Refurbish bedrooms, restaurant and bar areas including 'flexible' furnishing
   arrangements for the next recommendation.
Promote off-peak weekends and business/conference trade.
Set targets for capacity utilisation, eg 55 per cent for next year.
Supplement wages of the chef and Polly with bonuses related to custom of the
   hotel.
Sack Manuel. Employ experienced/trained person at higher wage, with opportunity
   for future bonuses related to custom of the hotel.
Allocate costs and revenues under the following heads:
   i) bed and breakfast; restaurant; bar.
   ii) leisure; business/conference.
Appraise long term investment in:
   i) proper conference facilities
   ii) leisure facilities, eg swimming pool, gym, tennis courts.

waiter Manuel. Both the chef and Polly are felt by the owners to possess skills and other assets that are very difficult to replace, especially on a seasonal basis. So they are kept on at full-time status, despite their off-peak underutilisation. In the case of Manuel, productivity is felt to be extremely poor, but his pay is particularly low to compensate.

The seaside hotel business is of course in long run decline, so the production and cost problems of Fawlty Towers are steadily getting worse. Average capacity utilisation is falling as the peak season shortens perceptively and peak demand is not sustained for the whole of the season. It is now 50 per cent for the year, 90 per cent for the peak season.

Finally, Sybil acts. Conscious that the slide towards extinction is inexorable, she asks a friend who is a management consultant to make some feasible recommendations. He concentrates on production and costs and finds that over time labour costs are assuming a larger proportion of the total operational costs. Both physical and revenue productivity are in decline, the former measured by the number of visitors per staff-hour, the latter by the revenue per £ of staff costs.

The consultant suggests two broad alternative strategies, summarised in Table 9.1. Sybil finally lets Basil in on the act and asks his advice on which strategy to choose. If you were Basil, what would you suggest?

This discussion of inputs and productivity has necessarily swung towards the issue of costs and it is to a more systematic discussion of costs that we now turn.

The costs of leisure production

The cost structure involved in supplying leisure goods and services varies considerably, depending on the type of supplier. Labour costs can be as high as three-quarters of the total operating costs in leisure centres, for example, but in a theatre or hotel they are more typically about a third of the total, in pubs a tenth, and in inclusive tour holiday companies well below a tenth.

Other dominant costs depend on the nature of the business. For theatre companies, materials and buildings feature significantly – up to half of costs in a major company. Liquor supplies dominate operating costs in pubs, of course, accounting for about 70 per cent of the total. Inclusive tour companies pay about a third of their operating costs out in charter air fares, and another third for hotel accommodation.

The costs discussed above are annual costs of production. In the way they are typically presented, in income and expenditure accounts, they are not related in any way to outputs. However, the whole point of the economic analysis of costs is to see how production costs vary with output. This can be examined in the short run and the long run.

In the short run any leisure provider is restricted by the capacity of the service or manufacturing process provided, the capital used is a fixed input. In the long run, however, the capital input can be changed – buildings can be vacated, new premises purchased, new equipment installed. Sometimes such changes in capital do not take a long time, but compared to the potential variability of other inputs capital takes longer to adjust, which is why it is the crucial difference between the two time periods used in economic analysis. Short run and long run is a simplistic split, of course, but again it is necessary to model costs in this way so as to keep the analysis free of unnecessary complications, but retain usefulness for management purposes. Essentially short-run analysis of costs assists pricing and output decisions, whilst long-run analysis helps the investment decision; ie about buying new capital.

Cost analyses use a variety of terms to describe different costs, so we now define the main cost terms:

Average or *unit* cost: total cost divided by output. This is one of the easiest to measure, and as such is used as the basis for many pricing decisions, eg the full cost of each hamburger produced in a fast food restaurant.

Fixed cost: a cost that occurs whatever the amount produced, eg the cost of the oven used to cook the hamburgers. In accounting this is called an *indirect* cost, whilst other terms used are *overheads,* and *secondary* cost. Capital cost is commonly a major part of fixed cost.

Variable cost: a cost that varies with the amount produced, eg the cost of the meat used in the production of hamburgers at the fast food restaurant. In accounting the approximate equivalent is *direct* cost. Another term used is *primary* cost. As long as such primary costs are covered by revenue it is worth continuing production, since a contribution will be made to fixed costs.

Marginal cost: the addition to total costs which results from the production of one extra unit of output, eg the cost of an extra hamburger. The concept of marginal cost is important in economic theory, as we will demonstrate, but in practice it is very difficult to measure, so a more generalised, practical version is *incremental, avoidable* or *attributable* cost. This is the cost incurred (or saved) by a change in production, such as introducing a new production technology, developing a new product, or dropping an old product.

Common costs: where services share costs, such as multi-purpose leisure facilities which are shared by various activities and user types. A very specific version of this is *joint* costs, where provision of one service necessarily provides another – the two are inseparable.

Private costs: those costs that are incurred by the supplier of the product.

External costs: costs imposed by the production or consumption process on parties other than the actual producer or consumer of the product, eg environmental damage, noise, congestion, vandalism.

Short-run costs

It is likely that in the short run, operational costs of many leisure facilities will be dominated by fixed costs. Apart from such overheads as rent, rates, insurance and maintenance of buildings, equipment and transport, even the labour costs are at least partly fixed. This is especially the case for skilled labour, which is normally employed on a full-time, permanent basis, regardless of the level of output required. It is not uncommon for such labour to be 'hoarded' at times when demand is low, in preparation for the time when it will be needed to produce at maximum capability.

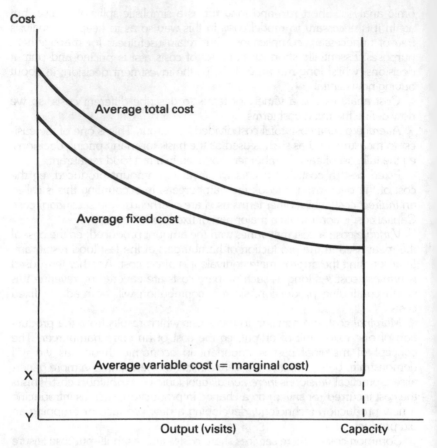

Figure 9.1   Short-run costs for a leisure facility

In leisure services in particular the extent to which extra customers impose extra costs is minimal. So the typical short-run cost structure might be said to look like Figure 9.1.

The average total cost (ie cost per visit) falls steadily up to the point of capacity because it is dominated by fixed costs. As these fixed costs are spread over more and more customers, so the average fixed cost per customer falls. The average variable cost, by comparison, is fairly small: remember these are the costs imposed directly by new customers. In Figure 9.1, because the average variable costs are constant, they are equal to the marginal cost – the cost of catering for an extra customer is always the distance XY on the diagram.

The nature of the cost structure in Figure 9.1 is particularly important for pricing and promotion policies. If the marginal cost of an extra customer is very low then it may make sense to attract the extra customer in by a low price, so that some contribution is made to fixed cost. This will be discussed further in the next chapter.

Cost centering

In leisure facilities it is often the case that a variety of different products are produced by the same resources. This is even the case in facilities that might appear at first to be single purpose – public houses, for example will be interested in the performance of not just drink, but also food, gaming machines and, increasingly, special occasions such as live entertainment, quizzes, or darts matches as opposed to normal business. Such multi-purpose facilities as leisure centres, clubs and hotels make management decisions not just for the whole facility, but also for the individual aspects of operations, ie the different activities. The programming decision is, by its very nature, concerned with the balance between these different activities.

In order to make rational decisions about these different activities and to properly assess their contributions to overall performance, it is necessary to know what costs are involved for each activity. This process is known as *cost centering,* or *functional costing.* A major problem is that many of the costs in leisure services are common to all activities, particularly fixed costs such as management and other labour, buildings, equipment, fittings, fuel, rates, insurance, etc. Such costs need to be allocated to the different activities.

How can such common costs be so allocated? If an area within a leisure facility is used for one purpose only, such as a catering area, then cost centering could simply take the form of allocating fixed costs associated with the facility's space (such as rent, rates, insurance and maintenance), according to the proportion of the total facility's floor space taken by that area. If more than one function takes place in the area, such as catering for ordinary visitors and catering for special events, then the fixed costs allocated to the area can be divided according to the amount of time taken up by these functions. If catering for special events takes up a quarter of the programmed time of the area, then events get allocated a quarter of the common costs for the area.

As regards labour, if individual staff members work in more than one area in the facility it is necessary to estimate the proportion of time spent by each employee in each area or on each function, and allocate the costs of each person accordingly. It is not unusual for labour in local authorities to have to fill in regular 'time budgets' declaring how their time has been apportioned between a variety of functions in a given time period, usually a week. As long as they are completed accurately, such time budgets would enable the cost centering of labour costs.

Obviously the process of cost centering can be more refined than the simple procedures outlined above. Adjustments can be made for obvious inequalities in the distribution of costs between functions or areas, maintenance being a typical example, or activities like swimming and discos that need much more direct supervision. But the main point is that any attempt at cost centering is likely to improve the efficiency of decision making in a multi-purpose leisure facility.

Long-run costs

Because the capital input can be varied in the long run the major questions raised for economic analysis to address are questions of investment – in new products, new technology and possibly a new scale of production. The last of these questions is particularly influenced by the behaviour of average costs as the scale of production increases. If average costs fall as scale increases then there are said to be *economies of scale*. In Figure 9.2 this would mean building facilities at least as big as Q_1, the *minimum efficient scale of production*, to exploit economies of scale.

Such economies are achieved in a variety of ways. Firstly there are technical economies of scale, derived for example from the saving in construction cost per unit of space constructed if larger facilities are built, or by the use of specialist capital equipment. Secondly there are financial savings through bulk purchase discounts, bargaining pressure on contractors, or

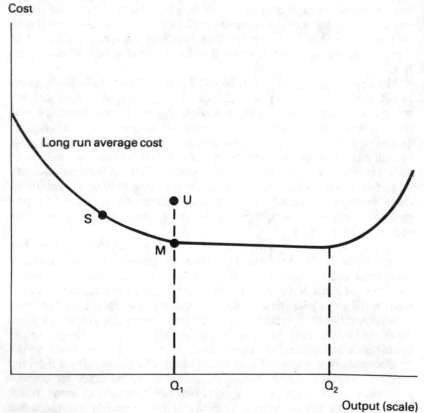

Figure 9.2   Long-run costs for a leisure facility

special arrangements for the financing of large scale projects. Thirdly there are managerial economies, brought about for example by the use of specialist labour for separate management functions such as marketing.

Finally economies of scale may be gained by vertical integration, such that essential supplies and services are drawn into the organisation and their costs are minimised. Such is the case, for example, with holiday companies integrating 'backwards' vertically by taking over or developing their own aircraft companies, and brewing companies integrating 'forwards' vertically to control the retail outlets for their produce, pubs.

If average costs *increase* as scale increases, then there are *diseconomies* of scale. It would be inefficient, for example, to build facilities larger than Q_2 in Figure 9.2, since diseconomies begin to occur. Such diseconomies can be of a technical nature, particularly in manufacturing industry, but in services they are more likely to be the result of control, communication and motivation problems in large enterprises or organisations, ie X-inefficiency. Between Q_1 and Q_2 there are constant returns to scale – any size of facility between these two points has the potential to be efficient.

Of course in leisure services, where it is impossible to store the product, it is important to examine the size of the potential *market* as well as average costs of production. As we have pointed out before, the obvious way to do this is to estimate the average cost per visitor *not just assuming that the facility were going to be fully used,* which is the assumption behind the cost curves in Figure 9.2, but instead using the *actual* number of likely visitors.

Let us take the example of the decision over what scale of facility to build in a new location. Evidence from existing facilities of different scales has to be treated with caution. If such evidence represents points S and M in Figure 9.2 it suggests that there are indeed economies of scale. But if demand in the new location is not strong enough to sustain full utilisation of a larger facility, this evidence supporting points S and M would be misleading. A more appropriate comparison in such a circumstances would be between the costs of a smaller, higher cost facility (point S in Figure 9.2) and a larger, *under-utilised* facility (point U). In management terms it is no good having a facility that has the potential to reach very low average costs per visitor, but never reaching this level of efficiency because demand is insufficient to fill the facility.

On the other hand if the evidence from existing facilities reflects a comparison between points S and U in Figure 9.2, this might cause investment in a new facility to be at the smaller scale since it has lower average cost. However, if market demand were stronger in the proposed location than in the facility from which point U is estimated, it would be worth investing in the larger scale, since point M would be attainable.

The point of this example is to emphasise that in order to assess the right scale of facility, it is necessary to know what *load factors* lie behind any existing evidence of economies of scale, and what load factor is likely in the proposed location. Knowledge of demand is essential to a proper assessment of economies of scale in leisure services.

What is needed of course is statistical evidence of the relationship between scale of production and average costs, for a variety of leisure ser-

E

vices and production processes. Unfortunately such evidence does not exist. Instead there is only fragmentary evidence to suggest that there may be some economies of scale in leisure provision. Furthermore, cost efficiency may be improved by not only scale but also *multi-activity* developments attracting larger numbers of visitors. Modern developments such as the Metro Centre in Newcastle mix multiple leisure and shopping opportunities on a vast scale. It is too early to say, though, whether such developments prove that there are economies of scale in leisure provision.

Conclusions

The moral of this chapter is 'take nothing for granted'! It is too easy to keep making leisure management decisions on the assumption that efficiency, output and costs are OK. But it is necessary to keep asking questions about these important management concepts, and set up systems of information to help answer those questions.

Improving management knowledge on these issues is an important foundation for both decision making and performance monitoring, which we look at in subsequent chapters. With a secure knowledge of the relationships between inputs and outputs, and the behaviour of costs in the short and long run, better decisions can be made on such important issues as production, programming, pricing, investment and manning. Performance, whether it be in terms of financial indicators such as profit, or measures such as technical and economic efficiency, cost effectiveness or economy, will be identified and expressed using indicators relating to outputs, revenues and costs. Although revenues have not been explicitly covered in this chapter, they are central to our discussion of performance appraisal (Chapter 13) and pricing decisions, to which we turn next.

Further reading

Crowson P 1985 *Economics for managers: a professional's guide.* Macmillan.

Gratton C, Taylor P 1985 *Sport and recreation: an economic analysis* E and F N Spon, London.

Livesey F 1983 *Economics for business decisions* Macdonald and Evans, Plymouth.

10 Pricing leisure services

We have already seen in Chapter 4 that prices have a critical role to play in the operation of any markets, acting as a signalling device to the consumers on the one hand and the suppliers on the other. If a price is too high then too much will be supplied and not enough demanded. This will cause the price to fall towards what economists term the equilibrium. If the price is too low then the opposite will happen – excess demand eventually driving the price higher. In this chapter we look more closely at how prices are decided. The simple picture of market forces painted above rather takes for granted that producers will recognise, and indeed be looking for, the signs that tell them what price to set. We consider rational ways of setting prices. We also examine the ways in which prices are set in practice, to identify the scope for improvement in this important managerial decision.

Because leisure provision spans both public and private sectors of the economy, we make comparisons between appropriate pricing criteria in both sectors. We are *not* going to consider in detail, though, what might be the 'right' level of subsidy for leisure services in the public sector. The broad principles of subsidisation are covered in Chapter 4 and it is up to each public sector provider to decide how important these principles are to their particular service. Our main objective in this chapter is to show that economics can provide a set of rational guidelines by which prices can be set, *whatever* the objectives of the supplier. However for reasons that we make clear, price-setting in the public sector is a lot more complicated than for the commercial sector, so of necessity we examine these complications.

Prices have many functions. They ration demand, they bring in revenue, they can even help select certain groups of users for a service. The four most obvious determinants of prices for leisure commodities are the objectives of the suppliers, the costs of production, the nature of demand for the service, and the state of market competition. The objectives determine the balance between the rationing, financial and selecting functions of price. Costs of production underlie the supply of leisure commodities, and need to be covered by the revenue raised from setting prices in the commercial sector, the voluntary sector, and increasingly in parts of the public sector too. The strength of demand determines the amount of revenue to be earned at different prices. The state of competition imposes varying constraints on pricing options facing the leisure manager.

Objectives for pricing leisure

In order to price rationally it is important to know what organisational objectives the price is helping to achieve. This basic requirement may seem so obvious as to be not worth mentioning. However, it is sadly the case that many leisure providers fail to specify their objectives precisely enough to be able to measure achievement, and consequently they fail to monitor what effects decisions like pricing are having on this achievement. Such organisations are more likely to be found in the public sector, and for good reason. Public sector leisure suppliers have a much more complicated set of objectives than their commercial equivalents, which may include such things as providing a variety of leisure opportunities, ensuring access for underprivileged members of society, and encouraging as much participation as possible for the good of the community. The situation regarding the setting of meaningful objectives in public sector leisure services is improving markedly under the influence of preparations for CCT, particularly in contract specification, but it is still far from easy, as we discuss in Chapter 12.

In the private sector the main objective for the organisation as a whole may be to earn a certain level of profit, but other objectives are relevant in both the long and short terms. In the long run the stability of prices, and hence profit margins, is important to suppliers, and also possibly the deterring of potential or actual competitors. In the short run pricing will serve targets for such objectives as revenue, usage and market share for different product lines. Revenue is important for cash flow into the company, and is not necessarily synonymous with profit, since higher revenue may incur even higher costs.

For efficient pricing it is necessary to specify *operational objectives,* ie objectives that have targets and whose achievement can be judged from available information. This is easy for most of the objectives likely to be found in the private commercial sector. In the public sector it is more problematic, especially for the more 'social' objectives. But it is only through operational objectives and targets that managers in local government leisure services can begin to rationally set prices which simultaneously satisfy numerous objectives. The crucial point is that targets help to impose the discipline of having to judge the effectiveness with which pricing helps to achieve objectives.

Some of the main objectives found in public sector are relatively easy to set targets for. Cost recovery targets, similar in principle to profit targets in the commercial sector, require an explicit decision on the level of subsidy to be given to facilities and services, but this decision has to be made when budgets are prepared anyway – few public sector leisure services have 100 per cent subsidies. Moreover, as Chapter 8 demonstrates, local authority leisure services have cut their subsidies over time as they become more conscious of cost recovery as an objective. Competitive tendering will probably continue this trend.

Capacity utilisation is difficult to set targets for in many leisure services, because of the problems discussed in Chapter 9. Capacity utilisation is closely associated with a frequently used indicator of cost efficiency in leisure services – the ratio of cost to the number of visits, ie the cost per visit. Price can be used to improve capacity utilisation, and hence this measure of cost efficiency. A reduction in price will normally cause a rise in the number of visits, whilst costs will not change much because they are largely fixed. It may be, of course, that the price reduction also improves revenue, if demand is price elastic, but that need not be the case.

Price also has an important role to play in achieving social objectives, but these are probably the most difficult objectives to set meaningful targets for. They include equal access to facilities for all citizens and the encouragement of recreationally underrepresented groups, such as the disabled, women with young children and the elderly. One of the easiest ways of promoting such objectives is to keep the price low. Again this may or may not be consistent with the objective of raising revenue – it depends on the price elasticity of demand by the relevant users.

However, it is one thing to suggest the subsidising of consumers for reasons of equity or external benefit; it is another to actually calculate the *value* of such considerations. For this reason subsidies are essentially a matter of value judgement and political debate, and cannot in practice be 'calculated' rationally.

It is important to stress that the public and commercial sectors of leisure provision are moving towards each other in terms of objectives, and this will be reflected in, among other things, their pricing behaviour. The public sector is becoming more commercial in outlook, especially with the spread of competitive tendering in local authority leisure services. As well as bidding for such local authority contracts, commercial sector providers are increasingly involved with explicit partnerships with public authorities in the construction of leisure facilities. They are also keen to reach arrangements with local authorities which satisfy planning permission requirements ('planning gain') – these often involve the provision of social amenities. All these links with local authorities encourage more awareness by commercial providers of social benefits such as local economic impact.

Costs and prices

The single most important consideration on which a pricing decision is commonly made in practice is the cost of provision. In commercial firms it is normally the unit or average total cost of supplying the product that is the basis for price, above which such firms add a net profit margin. This is called *cost-plus pricing* or *full-cost pricing*, an example of which can be found in Case Study 10.1. A close alternative is to calculate the direct (variable) costs of production and add a gross profit margin which contributes to both indirect (fixed) costs and profits. In public sector organisations the recommendation is that price should be based on marginal cost, since this is said to approximate most closely a competitive price for the product. Whatever the appropriate cost is, the principle of a price at least partly based on production costs is clear.

An unfortunate problem in the context of costs and prices is that many leisure organisations, particularly in the public sector, have very uncertain knowledge of what the unit costs of production are – particularly with respect to individual services, as we highlighted in Chapter 9. This may be for good reasons, such as the problem of common costs, but it is extremely important that efforts are made through cost centering to identify the costs of production, since without such estimates the setting of a price is missing one of its essential ingredients.

In Chapter 9 we also discovered that most of the costs of leisure facilities are fixed, in the sense that they do not change much as the number of customers alters. This is important for pricing policies, since attracting more visitors at times when the capacity is underutilised will not incur many extra costs. In economist's terms the *marginal cost* is low, ie the cost of catering for an extra visitor. So on cost grounds there is a clear incentive to reduce prices at such times and aim to maximise capacity utilisation. This spreads the fixed costs over the greatest number of visitors.

However the issue is more complicated than just costs. If, for example, a cinema cuts daytime admission prices by 50 per cent, and this only encourages admissions to increase by 20 per cent, then although costs will not be much different and the cost per visit is lowered, the *revenue* suffers. Before price reductions of this type are made in the commercial sector, therefore, it is necessary to be fairly sure that demand is fairly elastic to price reductions. In the example above demand is inelastic, so a price cut causes a fall in revenue. So although high fixed costs and low marginal costs imply an opportunity for low prices at times of underutilised capacity, it is necessary to check that demand conditions are favourable too before cutting prices. Of course in a public sector facility it may not matter if revenue falls as a result of low off-peak prices, if high utilisation is a more important objective.

In the manufacturing of leisure goods the cost structure is not so likely to be dominated by fixed costs. Even so it is likely that the costs per unit of output (average costs) are lowest near to capacity production, so there is every incentive again to produce at the most efficient, least-cost point. If demand is not appropriate to this level of output, then the manufactured product can be stored in the short run, and manufacturing capacity can be altered in the long run.

Some leisure providers do not charge a direct price at all. One of the principal reasons for this decision is that direct charging for entry is too costly in terms of transaction or collection costs – the costs of collection and administration would outweigh any revenues collected. National Parks in Britain are an example. In other less extreme leisure supply situations, transaction costs may influence the type of pricing structure adopted, as we show at the end of the next section.

Case Study 10.1 Pricing an hotel room

Pricing in hotels has many of the features and problems characterising the leisure industry in general, including the peak-load problem common costs, price discrimination and oligopolistic competition.

Not untypically the basis of many room rates is the cost of provision. This is only a starting point, however, as we shall show. Two common practices illustrate the cost-plus pricing technique. The first is a simple rule-of-thumb whereby after dividing the construction costs (plus maintenance and repair costs for older hotels) for the hotel by the number of rooms, then for every £1000 of building cost per room, an average room rate of £1 per room per night is charged. So a building cost of £50,000 per room would give a room rate of £50 per night. This average is then the basis for different prices for different types of room, customer, time of week, etc. Obviously this is the simplest possible cost basis for the price of a room, making implicit, sweeping assumptions about the relationship between construction costs and operating costs.

The second practice, known as the Hubbard formula, requires the estimation of total operating costs and profit margins for the year. From this figure sales from other areas such as food and liquor are deducted, leaving the cost to be covered by room sales. This residual cost is then divided by the number of room nights expected to be sold, based on estimates of the occupancy rate (ie load factor) for the hotel, to give the average room rate. Again there are usually different prices for different types of customer, especially commercial customers.

Both these methods of cost-plus pricing make no attempt at cost centering. One of the reasons for this is that hotels have many common costs. These include staff costs, variable costs such as cleaning, printing and energy costs, and fixed costs such as insurance, rates and maintenance. Together these account for about three-quarters of the total operating costs, so allocation of common costs would be a big task.

Having arrived at an average room rate based on costs, separate room rates have to be established for different types of room – single double, with or without bath, etc. But the major pricing complications come from moving beyond the simple cost basis, to information and intuition about the state of competition and the state of demand likely to be faced by the hotel. The peak-load problem is one such complication, which causes lower prices to be offered at the weekend, ie weekend or leisure breaks, when demand from commercial customers is absent and, recognising that marginal costs are low, the hotel is seeking any contribution to overheads and hopefully profit, rather than have empty rooms.

There is a seasonal peak-load problem too, as well as weekly one, and this causes seasonal banding of prices, explicitly recognising the different strengths of demand. In Trusthouse Forte's Post House hotels, for example, there are five different seasonal bands of leisure break prices used during the year, with Easter being the highest and December/January being the lowest. This seasonal banding was a group management decision but individual hotel managers have the discretion to choose the actual prices charged.

Price discrimination abounds in hotel room prices, in the form of various discounts. The leisure break market segment is one obvious example, but others include commercial customers, conferences, tours or groups, or special parties. Each of these will normally be given a discount on the advertised room rate. Indeed in many cases such customers expect and even *demand* such a discount. The discounts are always on the price of rooms. This protects the high gross profit margins traditionally earned in other areas of hotel service, eg food and beverage.

An interesting insight into the psychology of price discrimination is provided by the example of commercial customers booking hotel rooms in the Stoke-on-Trent area a year in advance of the National Garden Festival held there in 1986. These customers demanded their normal discounts even though it was obvious that demand would be unusually high during the Festival period. The response of hotels was typically to give the discounts, but also to increase their room rates by a very high proportion for the year of the Festival. So the customers were happy that they received a discount, and the hotels exploited the strength of demand in *all* their prices. The normal practice of offering price reductions to various types of customer has some disadvantages. It clearly discriminates against some customers who pay the standard rate; it is complicated to administer and account for. An alternative pricing strategy recently adopted by THF is one price for all customers with little or no reductions.

Finally, the state of competition is increasingly oligopolistic in the national hotel market and this is also the case in local markets. This has an influence on the setting of room prices, such that there is very much a 'going rate' for each standard of hotel room. The enhanced state of interdependence among suppliers in an oligopolistic market means that there is always the threat of intense price competition. The response of the hotel industry to this threat is to concentrate on non-price competition, through such improvements in service as televisions and refrigerators in rooms, leisure facilities like swimming pools and gymnasia, and other complementary services. Typically these services are included in the price of the room. This is a good example of another composite commodity packaged under one price.

Demand and prices

If there is any rationality in the way prices are set in practice it is that they bear a relationship to costs. The influence of demand factors is more difficult to detect, since they are external to the supplier and so are not of such immediate concern as costs of production, which are internal considerations. Nevertheless, for financial performance both costs and revenues are important and, to restate the obvious, it is the right combination of price and sales that ensures adequate revenue. So a supplier cannot afford to ignore the basic relationship that exists between price and sales, expressed by economists in the demand curve.

The strength of demand for a product, or 'what the market will bear', is evident in the pricing behaviour of many leisure services, particularly in the commercial sector. Case Study 10.1 demonstrates this for the hotel industry. It is a fundamental factor in the profitability of commercial concerns. Table 10.1 shows that within the catering industry it is normal to expect dif-

Table 10.1 Gross profit guidelines for catering organisations

Type of Business	Gross profit (%)	
	Liquor	Food
Public house	40–55	40–60
Restaurant	45–65	50–65
Banqueting	55–70	55–70
Wine bars	45–55	40–50
Self service	45–55	60–70
School meals	—	30–50
Members' clubs	25–45	30–60
Outdoor catering	50–60	50–70
Fast food	—	55–70
Kiosks	—	30

Source: Croner's Caterer, May 1991. Croner Publications Limited

ferent gross profit margins from different types of operation. These differences in profitability are caused partly by the different strengths of demand,
which in turn leads to different prices being set. Other reasons include different costs, such as lower staff costs per visitor in self service restaurants
contributing to high gross margins, and different objectives, like the non-
profit objectives of members' clubs causing low profit margins.

Demand for most leisure services peaks at certain times of the day, week
and year. We noted in Chapter 5 that this peak load problem is likely to be
'firm' in the sense that peak time customers cannot or will not easily switch
to off-peak times. So there is a likely persistent problem of underutilisation
of capacity at off-peak times. This, of course, increases the financial risks
attached to leisure provision, especially if the off-peak period is long and
capacity is high to cover a large peak demand. This is typically the case, for
example, with accommodation and entertainments provision in holiday
resorts.

One logical response is to charge lower prices at off-peak times, to
encourage more visits. This makes sense for both private and public sectors, because, as we have noted above, the costs of provision are likely to
be largely fixed and the marginal costs low. In hotels, as Case Study 10.1
shows, off-peak is normally the weekend, which causes weekend 'bargain
breaks' to be offered at low prices. In some markets off-peak discounts
may, besides attracting new customers, also put off some existing customers if they perceive a fall in the quality of the product on offer. For public sector providers the types of people sought and available at off-peak
times are mostly those who are commonly identified as the socially disadvantaged and recreationally under-represented groups. So low, off-peak
prices are consistent with social objectives commonly found in local authorities.

The peak load problem also means that there is the possibility of dis-
criminating *against* the peak-time user. This is a pricing decision much
more commonly found in private leisure facilities than in those belonging to
the public sector. Imposing 'premium' prices on peak-time users is not a
dirty commercial trick. It demonstrates an important function of prices, that
is to ration excess demand. At peak times many leisure facilities have
excess demand and for some reason public sector managers seem to prefer
the queue as a rationing device. However, a queue can be just as frustrating as a high price and it does not increase revenue, whereas a premium
price exploits the strength of demand to improve financial performance.

Whether a leisure service is provided by a private, commercial supplier
or a local authority, neither can escape the influence of the elasticity of
demand, as we have seen in this and previous chapters. To illustrate the
point, consider the pricing of a new good or service. Two contrasting
approaches to pricing new products have been observed. Firstly, *skimming*
policy charges a high price to exploit price *inelasticity* of demand in certain
market segments – the high prices of videos and compact disc players,
when they first appeared on the market, are examples. Secondly, *penetration pricing* recognises the high price *elasticity* of demand by the mass market – Amstrad personal computers being an obvious example.

It is worth examining the relationship between elasticity of demand, price changes and revenue a little more closely. If the price of a game of squash is increased from £2 to £2.20, a 10 per cent increase, but demand only falls by 5 per cent, then revenue will increase, because the increase in price is proportionately greater than the fall in demand. However, if the fall in demand had been 15 per cent, then this would have outweighed the beneficial effects of the price increase and revenue would have fallen. In the former case demand is said to be price inelastic, and in the latter, it is price elastic. So it is clear that a price increase could lead to either a better or worse cost recovery position, depending on the actual price elasticity of the demand for the service. Similar conclusions apply to a price decrease too – revenue could fall or rise as a result.

What about in the real world? Unfortunately there are few studies of the price elasticity of leisure services. One good example is an experiment with the pricing of local authority leisure centres prompted by the Scottish Sports Council, monitored on their behalf by market research conducted by the Centre for Leisure Research, with economic analysis by the present authors. The general conclusion of this demonstration project is that although people complain about significant price rises, if these are from an already highly subsidised price then there is little fall-off in demand – ie price inelastic demand. There is sufficient value for money in the services, even after such price rises, to maintain the level of demand or in some cases increase demand.

Such evidence is in a particular circumstance – price rises in subsidised local authority leisure centres in Scotland. Other piecemeal evidence tends to suggest that demand for leisure services is price inelastic, but it would be *inappropriate* to *generalise from them*. Price elasticity of demand will vary between different facilities, even in the same locality, and between different activities. It is also likely to vary over time, eg demand may well be more price elastic immediately after a price rise, especially if it is a large rise, compared with a few months later. The point is, though, that only by *experimenting* with price changes can a leisure supplier find out price elasticity of demand for particular facilities and activities.

There are distinct dangers to ignoring elasticity of demand, as many public trading services have found to their cost. The dangers are most sadly illustrated in a downward spiral of increased prices, falling demand, falling revenues and cuts in services. Recent financial pressure exerted by central government on the revenue spending of local authorities has caused a simple 'gut' reaction in some trading services, ie put prices up. This has been particularly likely in leisure services because they are often considered non-essential. The downward spiral is harmful to leisure services – there are few things more depressing to a manager than an underutilised facility.

It is possible that in the face of a falling demand for the product, the appropriate pricing tactic is to *reduce* prices, not increase them. This will increase demand and might even raise revenue, or at least stop the rise in losses. Revenue would improve with price cuts if demand were elastic, because the proportionate increase in demand would more than compensate for the fall in price. The Rank Organisation found this to be the case in

1985, when it cut the entrance prices to its Odeon cinemas and generated a 48 per cent increase in admissions. The increase in sales was as high as 300 per cent at some cinemas. There were other reasons for the increase but Rank management are sure that the response to price cuts was elastic.

Another interesting example of responses to price cuts occurred in Salford. In 1983 Salford City Council's Recreation department cut entrance charges for their leisure centres by an average of 50 per cent. The short-term result was a 100 per cent increase in attendances and a 30 per cent increase in revenue. Moreover in the longer term the improved utilisation and revenue was maintained. For individual facilities the response was mixed; some increased revenue, but others suffered a decline in revenue. An important point to note, though, is that the overall revenue from sport and recreation *activities* did not rise as a result of the drop in entrance charges, but fell slightly. What caused the total revenue to increase was that the increase in the number of visitors caused revenue from *ancillary* facilities, particularly the bars, to rise dramatically. The prices in such ancillary facilities had not been cut, of course.

The Salford example demonstrates that price changes do not just affect the direct product on offer, in this case the demand for activities. The leisure experience is a composite commodity, as we have pointed out before, so that a change in one price has a knock-on effect on the demand for complementary parts of the leisure experience. This will affect the providing organisation if it is supplying these complementary products.

Some leisure organisations 'package' their prices as well as their composite commodities – theme parks charging just one entrance price for example. Such a pricing policy means that any excess demand for individual rides will not be rationed by price, so any opportunity for gaining revenue from strong demand for one part of the leisure package is lost. Instead the excess demand is rationed by the queue, as many visitors hoping to have a go on the big rides at Alton Towers in Staffordshire have found out! Of course there are also arguments in favour of the simple, all-inclusive entrance price: it minimises transaction costs for instance, and it may increase the feeling of value for money by visitors and thus encourage repeat visits.

Competition and prices

In making pricing decisions any supplier of leisure opportunities has to be aware of the state of competition that exists in the relevant markets – particularly competition for the same service or good, but also more general competition for people's leisure time and expenditure.

The state of competition lays down acceptable upper limits within which prices must be set, prices outside these limits are likely to set off an elastic demand reaction as customers switch to competing products. Competition can vary enormously, from highly competitive markets with numerous independent suppliers, such as newsagents, to markets dominated by a few suppliers (oligopolists) who might compete viciously at times, but generally exist in a 'friendly' competitive environment with fairly clear, informal 'norms' concerning decisions such as pricing. Such norms include price leadership and product or market segmentation.

Competition can be reduced not only by such behaviour, but also by replacing price competition with non-price competition, such as advertising and other promotion policies. Case Study 10.1 provides examples in the hotel industry. This is very common in oligopolistic markets and it shelters the suppliers from price competition by building up brand loyalty for their products. Another way in which price competition can be reduced is by setting prices low enough to deter new suppliers from entering the market. This is especially appropriate if existing producers have a cost advantage over new entrants, eg through experience or economies of scale.

Competitive tendering is a specific example of market competition where price plays a vital role. Essentially one customer, the client, is faced with several competing suppliers, and the scale of the tender is commonly very significant to the suppliers. The contract is usually awarded largely on the basis of price (the client normally having restricted the competition to an approved list of contractors), so the pricing decision is crucial. Too high a price and the contract is lost; too low a price and profit margins are in danger of disappearing if unforeseen circumstances occur.

Price discrimination

One of the most common and sensible pricing tactics to be employed by both private and public sector leisure suppliers is price discrimination. Essentially price discrimination means charging different users different prices despite the fact that the cost of providing the service to these users is practically the same. Such discrimination is either to favour some market segments with lower prices, eg for equity reasons, or to exploit other market segments with higher prices, eg for revenue purposes.

The most common form of such discrimination in leisure services, particularly in the public sector, is the lower prices charged to children. The use of price discrimination depends on the objectives of the suppliers. In the case of children the objective for public sector providers may well be to encourage constructive and healthy leisure pursuits, or to capture a future market.

Other objectives can be interpreted in a variety of forms of price discrimination. A recent one which is becoming increasingly popular, even in commercial facilities, is discrimination in favour of the unemployed, which is demonstrated for local authorities by the evidence reproduced in Table 10.2. What is interesting about this evidence is that as this form of policy developed in the early 1980s, it swung away from a simple price concession and increasingly took the form of more sophisticated arrangements such as leadership schemes and special sessions. This may have been at least partly because price concessions were found to be necessary but not sufficient to encourage increases in use by the unemployed. The principle

Table 10.2 Concessions for the unemployed

Type of provision	Percentage of UK local authorities	
	1982[1]	1985[2]
No provision	40	29
Off-peak concessions for all	7	7
Unemployed price concessions	42	33
Organised sessions	0	5
'Passport to Leisure' schemes	5	14
Leadership schemes	5	9
Other	1	3
	100	100

Source: © Pack CM, Kay TA and Glyptis SA, 1986, Targeting the Unemployed, in Mangan JA and Small RB (eds) *Sport Culture and Society: International, historical and sociological perspectives*, E & F N Spon. Used by permission.

Notes: [1]England and Wales only [2]UK

of price discrimination for social reasons matured in many cases into the charging of lower prices to a whole variety of so-called 'recreationally disadvantaged groups' – typically through 'passport to leisure' type schemes.

The capacity utilisation objective can also lead to price discrimination, largely because of the peak load problem as discussed above. The setting of low off-peak prices and high peak-time prices are obvious examples of price discrimination, since operating costs are largely fixed and so they are very similar for both time periods. Peak loading, of course, occurs not only by time of day, but also time of week and time of year, as Case Study 10.1 shows. Holiday companies are good examples of leisure providers who are very conscious of the need to reduce prices and discriminate in favour of low season customers, as any of their brochures will reveal.

If the peak load is a 'firm' one, as is often the case, it means that off-peak usage is not going to be increased by encouraging peak-time users to switch to off-peak times. Instead, the increase in demand must come from new customers. This highlights the need for promotion policies. Many leisure facility managers have found that attempting to deal with the peak load problem by price discrimination alone is not enough, but it needs to be accompanied by effective promotion.

It is vital that promotional policies are targeted to off-peak users and times. The obvious targets are those people who do not suffer from the strict timedating imposed by work schedules, such as the unemployed, housewives, the elderly and in the case of local authority leisure facilities, schools. Promotion of off-peak opportunities is common for the weekend breaks offered by hotels, and winter breaks offered by holiday companies, but less common for the weekday deals offered by many leisure facilities.

Other forms of price discrimination can favour particular activities within facilities, the frequent users (ie by season tickets or memberships), and penalise other groups, such as users from outside the authority in the case of local authority leisure facilities. The message is that this is a powerful, explicit way of putting objectives into practice. In many cases it is possible to satisfy a number of objectives at once. Off-peak prices, for example, improve capacity utilisation, attract users that don't normally attend and may even improve cost recovery if demand is elastic enough.

The main thing to remember about price discrimination is that in order to get it to help in the achievement of objectives the leisure manager must work out as precisely as possible what effects changes in prices for different sub-markets have on the separate demands. At the very least this means monitoring closely the exact effects of any price changes, which helps the manager to identify the nature of demand for his product. In addition it may be appropriate to conduct market research to establish the importance of price in the consumers' decision making and the strength of demand at different times, activities, facilities, etc.

Membership schemes

Rather than set a single price for participation in leisure activities it is not uncommon for price to be split into at least two parts, a membership fee and an entrance or participation fee. This is a common pricing policy in the voluntary sector and is also to be found in the public and commercial sectors. The advantage of *two-part tariffs*, as they are called, is that they encourage *all* participants to make a contribution to fixed costs regardless of their level of participation in the activities of the organisation. So the 'fixed' part of the fee corresponds with the fixed costs of the supplier. In addition the 'variable' part of the fee, the entrance charge, corresponds with the variable costs of actual participation.

Two-part tariffs also make sense in terms of cash flow, particularly in a seasonal activity, since a certain amount of revenue is raised before the activity gets under way. Furthermore, it is possible to exploit the two-part tariff in such a way that revenue, profits and/or visits are increased. Having to pay a membership fee is an incentive for the customer to increase the number of visits made to a leisure facility, particularly if the membership fees are high and the entrance charges are low.

On the other hand it is possible to charge membership fees at such a rate that many customers pay for membership with every *intention* of visiting frequently, but do not actually visit any more frequently than they would have in the absence of such a fee. The two-part tariff is effectively extracting extra revenue from such customers. Moreover, if visits are not in practice as high as members intended, there is a saving on variable costs.

So the balance between membership and participation fees is a delicate one that has effects on visits, revenue and profit. Institutions like the National Trust and many voluntary leisure organisations are well practised at this balancing act, with the added benefit from membership fees that many members pay not just for their potential leisure activities, but also as a charitable contribution. In the case of the National Trust, of course, the customer does not pay both a membership fee and an entrance charge, but instead pays *either* through membership or through casual entrance charges, and the charitable donation is more likely to be made via payment of a membership fee. For this reason National Trust entrance charges have often been set in such a way as to encourage visitors to become members.

Pricing leisure services in practice

In the commercial sector, not surprisingly, the evidence is that prices are based on average unit cost plus a margin for profit. The surprising finding of many studies is that the private sector does not take great account of demand factors when setting prices, although obviously such considerations are more difficult to detect, and there are clear examples such as that of the Odeon cinemas mentioned earlier where demand is a critical factor. Case Study 10.1 gives a good example of how costs may be the *starting* point for calculating a price, but demand factors are then used to set the final prices.

In the public sector the evidence is not very complimentary. Three studies, by the Audit Inspectorate, Coopers and Lybrand Associates, and the Audit Commission, agree on the main features. It would appear from these studies that the most common way in which prices are decided is by reference to the prices of other local authorities. This is easy, quick and uncontroversial. It is also far too simplistic! Looking at the economic logic behind such decision making, it assumes that the costs, the nature of demand and the objectives of the authorities which are being copied are all the same as the deciding authority, which of course, is highly unlikely. It is also an irrelevant comparison if the authorities are not competing with each other for the same customers, which is most typically the case.

Another feature of local authority leisure services pricing is that the decision is rarely made by the facility manager. It is much more likely to be made by a committee, sub-committee, one or more officers who are remote from the facility, or even in a non-leisure department such as the Treasurer's. A consequence of this is that irrational prices may be set, such as common prices for all the facilities of the same type in the local authority. This may appear fair to residents in the authority, but again the economic logic is dubious. It assumes that all the facilities face similar costs and demand characteristics, which even within one authority is unlikely. This practice is also criticised because it offers no incentive to the facility manager to actually take managerial responsibility.

Conclusions

This chapter has demonstrated the role and the determinants of prices. It is clear that in order to set rational prices the leisure manager must have clear information, on the way demand responds to price changes, on the costs of supply, and on the objectives the prices are supposed to be serving. In order to get the first of these pieces of information it is necessary that the manager *experiment* with prices, so as to find out something about the elasticity of demand for different times, facilities, activities, and groups of people.

Only with the right attitude and the right information will price setting become a *positive* management decision. The alternative is that it becomes a sterile, status quo kind of decision whereby prices are put up in line with inflation, or set at a level that seems to be what others are charging. It is also important to note that managers will only make positive decisions if they are given an incentive to do so. In the commercial sector this is automatic, since improved performance is related to pay, promotion prospects and the expansion of the company. In the public sector the incentive needs more careful planning. It does not have to be personal; if as a result of good price decisions the performance of a facility improves, then it should directly benefit that facility, rather than be swallowed up in the general pot. This would give the managers in that facility an incentive to continue with sound, sensible, and above all positive pricing decisions.

Further reading

Audit Commission 1989 *Sport for whom?* HMSO.

Audit Inspectorate 1983 *Development and operation of leisure centres; selected case studies.* HMSO.

Bovaird AG, Tricker MJ, Stoakes R 1984 *Recreation Management and Pricing.* Gower.

Coopers and Lybrand Associates 1981 *Service provision and pricing in local government.* HMSO.

Glyptis S, Pack C 1988 *Local authority sports provision for the unemployed.* Sports Council Study 31, Sports Council.

Gratton C, Taylor P 1985 *Sport and recreation: an economic analysis.* E and FN Spon.

Scottish Sports Council 1992 (forthcoming) *Differential charges.* Scottish Sports Council.

Walsh RG 1986 *Recreation economic decisions: comparing benefits and costs.* Venture publishing, Pennsylvania, USA (UK distributors E and FN Spon).

11 Project appraisal

Sometimes the management of leisure services is to an extent doomed well before the first customer crosses the threshold of a facility. This is because the planning of the service is inadequate. The location of a facility, for example, may be simply in the wrong place for its most likely market, so that its penetration of that market will never achieve full potential. Many local authority leisure service facilities are located not at the best possible site, but at the site which was the cheapest at the time of conception, which in many cases was on land already owned by the local authority. This has a certain short term logic, but does not represent sensible long term planning. Neither does the provision of facilities on a rota basis, ie 'Whose ward is next for something?' Facilities are usually built to last, so the poor manager has to live with the consequences of bad planning for a long time.

In Chapter 7 we identified the necessary conditions for planning – basically a systematic approach to acquiring and processing relevant information, particularly about the social, economic and spatial characteristics of the market that the service is intended to serve. We now take this approach one stage further to investigate the techniques that are available to assess the viability of individual leisure projects. Viability in the commercial sector of course means an investment that will make a healthy rate of return. For the public sector, though, viability can mean a lot more than just a financial return; indeed it can mean a project going ahead even if it is forecasted to make a financial loss. Economics can offer safeguards in the planning of new facilities. In principle, project appraisal techniques enable those making capital investment decisions to have a bedrock of information on which to debate the options. However, evidence suggests that investment appraisal techniques in practice can often be rudimentary, or even non-existent! This chapter will show a less risky way of assessing proposed projects.

Public and private sector projects

It is nearly always the case that project appraisal in the public sector is more difficult than in the private commercial sector, for reasons similar to those affecting pricing decisions, which we noted in Chapter 10. Objectives in the public sector are complicated by a whole range of 'social' purposes that the commercial firm does not need to consider, such as employment and prosperity in the local area.

It is important to emphasise, though, that many commercial firms will be conscious of social objectives, as we have suggested a number of times already in this book. Especially in urban areas, partnerships in development between public and private developers and 'planning gain' conditions for planning approval both offer incentives for commercial developers to appraise social benefits, an example of which can be seen in Case Study 11.1.

Social objectives, however, can cloud the judgement of a project appraisal, because they are rarely quantified and therefore their incorporation into the appraisal is more impressionistic. Because they are much more difficult to quantify, there is a greater danger of misrepresenting them. Such misrepresentation can take the form, at one extreme, of implicit or explicit bias against leisure projects for not creating 'real jobs', which of course is a nonsense. At the other extreme, an uninformed debate can concentrate too much on social benefits arising from the provision of leisure facilities, especially if the facilities are for under-represented groups or deprived areas. Whereas it is right and proper that such equity considerations are debated as part of project appraisal in the public sector, they are rarely the only factors to consider.

The role of a formal, systematic project appraisal before the project enters the board room or the debating chamber is to ensure that the managerial or political debate is as *informed* as possible. This is done by information from specific techniques, and it is to such techniques that we now turn. Most of these techniques are relevant to the commercial sector as well as certain parts of public and voluntary leisure provision – all sectors should be interested in getting the best out of capital investments.

Pay-back

In the private sector a common and simple method of project appraisal is pay-back. This at its simplest requires the calculation of the time it takes for a project to pay back its initial capital costs. The calculation requires accurate estimation of not only the capital costs of the project but also the financial returns, so demand forecasting is critical in this, the simplest of project appraisal techniques. Three to five years is a typical pay-back period necessary for a private firm to invest in a project. This would apply to most standard scale leisure projects, such as a cinema, a dance hall or a fitness gym.

For smaller investments such as a particular piece of equipment the pay-back period would commonly be a year or less. Of course for very large scale projects, eg theme parks, the time needed to pay back initial costs will be quite long. In the case of the massive satellite television investment made by British Satellite Broadcasting, the project was not forecasted to break even until ten years after its 1991 launch, which given the demise of

BSB demonstrates not only the long term nature of such investment but also the risk.

Clearly, this is a convenient method of project appraisal for an organisation concerned primarily with financial objectives. It might also be appropriate for some parts of public sector leisure service provision, since there are sections of such services that can and arguably should endeavour to meet normal commercial objectives.

However, although it is the simplest technique, even in the narrow context of financial objectives the pay-back method is not the best one. It does not, for instance, cater for comparisons between projects with different lifetimes or different time profiles to their costs and benefits. It could easily reject projects with a healthy financial return over a longer time period. If, for example, a theatre was forecasted to make losses for the first three years of its life and was thereafter forecasted to make profits, it would not pass a simple three year pay-back criterion. Yet obviously theatres, like most leisure facilities, last a long time.

Pay-back in fact is a very conservative way of appraising projects, and the use of it will cause many worthwhile projects to stay on the drawing boards. It is appropriate for organisations which are as concerned with their short run liquidity as their profitability, focussing as it does on the point at which breakeven occurs. In Case Study 11.1, for example, project A gives the quickest breakeven and would therefore be chosen by the pay-back method.

Pay-back, because it only looks to such a short time into the future, does not take account of the fact that money changes value over time. Capital investment is, after all, the management decision with probably the longest duration of consequences, so time should be a critical element in the project appraisal. There is, for example, something intuitively wrong with ranking projects B and C equally in Case Study 11.1, as pay-back would. There is also something odd about recommending project A just because it pays back the initial capital cost the quickest, in preference to other projects which yield larger returns over longer periods. The better alternative, taking account of all the defects of pay-back, is the discounting method.

Case Study 11.1 Investment appraisal: an example

A leisure supplier is faced with the choice of spending £500,000 extending equipment and facilities in one of four ways – projects A, B, C and D. Each investment is

Table 11.1 Investment Appraisal: an example

Project	Years					
	0 (–now) Capital cost	1	2 Revenues net of operating costs (all figures in £m)	3	4	5
A	–0.5	0.5	0.1			
B	–0.5	0.25	0.25	0.1		
C	–0.5	0.3	0.2	0.1	0.1	0.1
D	–0.5	0.1	0.2	0.2	0.3	0.3

Table 11.2　Discounting calculations

Project A	= (0.5 × 0.91) + (0.1 × 0.83) − 0.5
	= 0.455 + 0.083 − 0.5
	= 0.038
Project B	= (0.25 × 0.91) + (0.25 × 0.83) + (0.1 × 0.75) − 0.5
	= 0.2275 + 0.2075 + 0.075 − 0.5
	= 0.01
Project C	= (0.3 × 0.91) + (0.2 × 0.83) + (0.1 × 0.75) + (0.1 × 0.68) + (0.1 × 0.62) − 0.5
	= 0.273 + 0.166 + 0.075 + 0.068 + 0.062 − 0.5
	= 0.144
Project D	= (0.1 × 0.91) + (0.2 × 0.83) + (0.2 × 0.75) + (0.3 × 0.68) + (0.3 × 0.62) − 0.5
	= 0.091 + 0.166 + 0.15 + 0.204 + 0.186 − 0.5
	= 0.297

estimated to yield a different profile of returns. These revenues, net of operating costs, are shown alongside the capital cost in Table 11.1.

According to the pay-back criterion, A appears the best project, since it breaks even after just one year, whereas projects B, C and D pay back after two or three years. If the leisure manager were desperate for a quick return on the investment, cash flow being the main priority, then project A would be the choice.

However, the manager is also interested in the overall profitability of the projects under consideration, so discounting calculations are employed. These are shown in Table 11.2. A 10 per cent discount rate is used, giving discount factors of 0.91 for year 1, 0.83 for year 2, 0.75 for year 3, 0.68 for year 4, and 0.62 for year 5. So, for example, for project A the net revenue of £0.5m in one year's time is multiplied by the first year discount factor, 0.91, to give a present value of this revenue of £0.455m. The second year's net revenue, £0.1m, is multiplied by the second year's discount factor, 0.83, to give a present value of this revenue of £0.083m. After deducting the capital cost of the project, £0.5m (which is already at present values since it is incurred now), from these discounted revenues, the net present value of the project is £0.038m. In other words, after accounting for the fact that money changes value at an assumed rate of 10 per cent a year, project A earns a return of £38,000 in present day values.

So the Net Present Values of the projects (ie the present value of the returns net of capital and other costs) are:

A = £38,000
B = £10,000
C = £144,000
D = £297,000

The manager, not being desperate for a quick breakeven, goes for the project with the highest overall return, project D.

Discounting

This method converts all estimated costs and benefits over the lifetime of the project to values equivalent to a moment in time, usually the present day. Discounting does this by the use of an interest rate. Just as an interest rate can be used to find the future value of a present sum of money, so if it is used 'in reverse' it will give the present value of any sum of money occurring in the future. For example assuming a 10 per cent of interest, £110 occurring in a year's time is worth £100 *now*. When an interest rate is used in this way it is called a discount rate. In fact it is more usually presented in the form of discount factors for each year in the future, by which future costs and revenues are multiplied.

The discounting method is fairly straightforward. Costs and revenues relevant to each proposed project are aggregated. But instead of using the cash values regardless of when they occur, the *discounted* values are estimated. So, in Case Study 11.1, where a 10 per cent discount rate is used, any values occurring one year after the reference date (which is usually the present day) are multiplied by a discount factor of 0.91, any values occurring in the second year are multiplied by a discount factor of 0.83, etc. Appropriate discount factors for different discount rates and years can be found in accounting tables.

Case Study 11.1 includes discounting calculations for the projects on offer which demonstrate that the pay-back selection, project A, is not the best investment when more, relevant information is considered. Project D emerges as that with the highest net present value, and is therefore the best investment in this simple example.

The discounting method has the same fundamental requirements as pay-back of measuring accurately all the costs and revenues of a project, but it considers these over the lifetime of the project and it discounts them to present values. This way alternative project options with different lifetimes or different growth patterns can be compared. It is likely that any leisure organisation will have a whole range of options on how to spend a limited capital budget. Discounting therefore offers a rational way of deciding between a variety of options.

Cost escalation

The use of pay-back or discounting will only be as good as the quality of the estimates of financial costs and returns which these techniques use. If these estimates come back from 'back of the envelope' type calculations then the techniques will not improve the quality of the project appraisal, or its likelihood of success. An essential requirement for the successful use of the techniques, therefore, is that the costs and returns are calculated as accurately as possible. This is no easy task. Returns can only be estimated with the help of accurate demand forecasts, and there is evidence that such demand forecasting is not a common feature of leisure project appraisals, particularly in local authorities. Capital costs, too, are difficult to estimate because of such factors as inflation, unforeseen technical problems and deliberate underbidding by building contractors to gain the contract. Evidence suggests that cost escalation of up to 50 per cent is not unusual in either local authorities or private, commercial sector projects.

It is worth illustrating the point by reference to a notorious example in a service very similar to leisure services, the Harrogate Conference Centre. Initial estimates put the cost at £7.4m, but the eventual cost was £28m. It was initially planned to be completed in 1975, but it was finally completed in 1982. The financial consequences for taxpayers in Harrogate were not, of course, confined to the period of construction – they have to help pay for debt charges of about £3m a year.

However, the Harrogate Conference Centre was a difficult case for project appraisal, because of its size and complexity. Experience of dealing with leisure projects, either by the organisation concerned or by consultants employed to help with the appraisal, will suggest a likely cost escalation factor. If the cost estimates were to be modified by this factor, this would be better than ignoring the problem or hoping that it will not occur.

Cost-benefit analysis

In the public sector, of course, the estimates of costs and returns are more complicated. In principle they have to include all relevant social considerations as well as the normal financial ones. For leisure projects this might include some valuation of the beneficial effects of reducing vandalism or petty crime by youths, or the benefits of a more rewarding leisure lifestyle for such groups as the unemployed, the elderly, the handicapped and women with young children. Valuing such benefits is difficult but not impossible. The costs of clearing up the effects of vandalism and crime are well known to such people as the police, insurance companies, and maintenance companies. The benefits of an improved leisure lifestyle can be valued by the individuals who are directly affected and by other people with whom they are in regular contact, eg social workers, family, friends etc. Surveys would reveal the nature and extent of social benefits derived from improved leisure opportunities.

Cost-benefit analysis, then, attempts to value not only the direct financial costs and returns of a proposed project, but also other costs and benefits that are not normally measured or felt in financial terms. Furthermore, these 'external' costs and benefits will affect people other than the immediate users and providers of the leisure facility. For example, the external benefits of reduced vandalism, brought about by the construction of a leisure facility for youths, will be felt by people other than those directly involved with the facility. If values for external costs and benefits cannot be derived from the people concerned via surveys, there are other alternative valuation methods such as examining the value of property around a facility relative to other similar property elsewhere.

When all the appropriate costs and benefits have been estimated as best as possible for the lifetime of the project, cost-benefit analysis then applies the discounting method to obtain a present value for the net worth of the project, much in the same manner that a private concern would appraise the financial value of a project.

Economic impact

In addition to the social costs and benefits of projects, which are measured in cost-benefit analysis, it is now almost obligatory in the case of large scale projects, be they funded by either the private, commercial sector or the public sector, for an assessment to be made of the full consequences for the local economy. These economic impact studies attempt to identify the *full* impact of a project on local expenditure, income and jobs; not just the immediate expenditure and jobs at the project site. They are often the main reasons for large scale investments in leisure facilities by local authorities – there is often little chance of financial profits being made. In the case of private sector or partnership projects, evidence of economic impact can help to secure planning permission and possibly financial assistance from government agencies such as the Urban Programme or Development agencies. Case Study 11.2 is just such a case.

Case Study 11.2 Appraisal of the G-MEX Exhibition and Events Centre

G-MEX is a transformed railway station which is one of the most stylish buildings in the centre of Manchester. It is the result of a partnership in investment between the Greater Manchester Council (GMC) and Commercial Union Assurance, together with a large central government grant and a European Social Fund grant.

In planning this development GMC and Commercial Union set up a joint venture study. Table 11.3 shows the breadth of research which was contracted out to service this venture study – all completed within a year. The reasons for such extensive project appraisal were that GMC had to be assured of a significant economic impact, Commercial Union had to be convinced that there was a reasonable financial return on any investment they made, and if it turned out that substantial assistance was necessary from the central government, then they too had to be convinced that the project was worthwhile.

Having considered six options for the use of the site the study group decided on an exhibition centre, the most important factor being that it would provide a catalytic function for the regeneration of the area as a whole. This is the economic impact argument in its broadest sense, including not only the impact of the centre, but also the likelihood of other developments that would follow as a result.

The total development cost was estimated at just over £14m. The eventual cost was £22m, which is partly because of inflation but also because of unforeseen structural work – the cost escalation factor. One important condition arose from the development plan. It was necessary to have over half the capital cost of the project paid by the government, in order for the project to be viable for the private partner, Commercial Union. In 1981 this grant, £7.25m, was approved under the Urban Programme – the largest single grant given in the scheme.

Table 11.3 Special studies for the planning of G-MEX

1) Structural Surveys	a) Train hall
	b) Warehouse
	c) Railway arches
2) Costs and Finances	a) Costing alternative developments
	b) Financial analysis
3) Market research	a) Exhibition centre
	b) Leisure proposals
	c) Hotel
4) Impact Analyses	a) Economic Impact
	b) Traffic and transport

Source: Joint Venture Study Group (1981)

Table 11.4   G-MEX economic impact study, summary of results

	Short run (3rd year)	Long run (Full potential)
Direct expenditure (£m)		
Visitors	7.402	10.89
Exhibitors	4.8	8.57
Total	12.202	19.461
Direct employment		
from visitors spending	290	480
from exhibitors spending	216	387
Total	506	867
Multiplier effects		
Rise in income (£m)	4.7	8
Additional jobs	240	420
Total employment creation ie Direct plus multiplier effects	746	1287

Source: Joint Unit for Research on the Urban Environment (1981)

Of particular importance to both central and local government interests was the forecasted economic impact of G-MEX on the region. This was the subject for one of the specialist studies, conducted by the Joint Unit for Research on the Urban Environment. The main results of this research are presented in Table 11.4. Two forecast periods were taken, short run and long run. The short run was represented by estimated effects in the third year of operation of G-MEX, when use was anticipated to be about 193 days in the year for exhibitions and events. The long run was represented by estimates of the impact if and when G-MEX reached its full potential in terms of usage, which was seen to be 250 days use a year. Any more use in an exhibition hall is unlikely because of 'setting up' and 'breaking down' time.

With limited resources of time and money it was not possible to conduct original surveys in Manchester for the purposes of assessing economic impact. So estimates of the expenditure, income and employment created by the G-MEX centre were calculated by adapting data from the National Exhibition Centre (NEC) at Birmingham, and borrowing key calculations from other studies.

First, expenditure at the NEC provided the means by which expenditure at G-MEX could be estimated. Second, these expenditure figures were converted into direct income and employment effects, by using typical ratios of turnover to income and turnover to jobs, for such sectors as stand contracting, catering and transport. In hotels, for instance, it has been calculated that every £4 of expenditure creates £1 of direct income, and in 1981 it took £10,000 of new turnover to create one new job.

The third stage was to estimate the spin-off effects for local businesses as the increases in expenditure and income from G-MEX stimulate further increases in spending, income and jobs. This is the multiplier effect which we encountered in Chapter 3. The multipliers used for the G-MEX impact study were again borrowed from other studies. For hotels, for example, it is estimated that the employment multiplier is 1.165, which means that *total* employment created in the local hotel sector by a new project is equal to the newly created *direct* employment multiplied by 1.165. For transport employment the multiplier is estimated to be 1.5. The size of the multiplier depends on how much of the original expenditure is retained in the local economy. Most of it drains out of the local economy in the form of purchases from other parts of the country, or imports. It is only the fraction that circulates around the local economy that has an impact in the form of a multiplier effect.

The standard approach to assessing economic impact involves estimating the three ways in which expenditure and jobs are increased by a project, which we introduced in Chapter 3: ie direct, indirect and induced effects. These elements will be permanent benefits for the local economy. In addition there are temporary benefits arising from the construction of the project.

In estimating the local economic impact of a project, it is important to distinguish between the expenditure of local residents and the expenditure of visitors from outside the local area. The latter is likely to dominate the economic impact, since it represents a net *addition* to economic activity in the local area. Most of the spending by local residents at the project will not add anything to local economic activity, it is merely a transfer from one local outlet to another. This is called 'deadweight' expenditure. However, to the extent that local residents' expenditure on the project either replaces expenditure on similar facilities out of the locality, or is extra to normal expenditure in the locality, it legitimately contributes to the economic impact of the project.

The net economic impact of the project is normally calculated in the form of three indicators: additional expenditure in the local economy, additional local income, and additional jobs created by the project. An economic impact study does not attempt to cover *all* the economic benefits of a project. It does not, for instance, attempt to identify the social benefits which cost-benefit analysis aspires to measure. Nor does it attempt to identify any of the costs of the project. Instead, it simply yields results that show how important the project is for the local economy. So economic impact studies are important for 'selling' the idea of the project to the local community and politicians. They are not, though, full appraisals of the net value of the project, because of the things they omit to calculate.

Sensitivity analysis

Many project appraisals end up with a neat financial answer to the question 'is it worth investing in this project?' This 'answer', however, is often an illusion of certainty. We have already indicated that both cost and benefit estimates for a proposed project are riddled with uncertainties, particularly in the public sector. Given this uncertainty it is not appropriate to end up with a definitive, single answer. Neither is it really necessary. A more accurate reflection of the situation would be to present a range of feasible outcomes for a variety of possible future scenarios. This is typically the requirement of major project appraisals in the private, commercial sector. This range can be calculated by means of a sensitivity analysis.

The idea of sensitivity analysis is to feed into the project appraisal a variety of reasonable estimates for key variables, such as future demand, prices, capital and maintenance costs, appropriate discount rates, and, if relevant, values for external costs and benefits. The resulting range of possible outcomes would be a more difficult set of information for policy makers to decide on, but it would also be far more realistic. By looking at the whole range of possible outcomes the organisation would be able to judge how risky a project is by seeing how sensitive its net worth is to the way costs and revenues were estimated. If for example one project's showing in an appraisal is insensitive to the variety of cost and revenue estimates, whilst another project only looks good under average or optimistic assumptions, then this is an important part of the comparison between the two projects that would be missing without a sensitivity analysis.

Practical problems

Unfortunately there is a formidable list of reasons why project appraisal techniques such as those reviewed above are not very widely practised, especially in the public sector. For a start, the numeracy of decision makers and their skills of interpreting financial information are sometimes limited, simply through a lack of training. This is especially likely with elected members, but it is also probable in leisure management generally, given the diverse and non-managerial training of many managers.

Without the appropriate skills there is much more danger of decision makers being influenced by such things as fashion and managerial hunch. The classic example here of course is skateboard parks, which rapidly turned into 'white elephants'. You would think that the lesson would have been learned, but the problem is likely to arise whenever a rational project appraisal system is missing. BMX tracks represent another example – although the capital costs for these facilities are not very high there was still an apparent 'emotional' provision of sites which quickly fell into disuse as the fashion faded. Leisure preferences are sometimes very volatile, as we have noted elsewhere, so the time profile of benefits has to be carefully assessed.

Another problem is that decision makers are often not able to be objective about a proposed new scheme, particularly if it is fairly prestigious. It is sadly the case that the techniques above can be manipulated to produce a favourable outcome if that is the wish of those in charge of the appraisal. When this happens the data is used as a public relations exercise or smokescreen, rather than for an objective, rational, project appraisal.

Furthermore, in the public sector there is a built-in incentive to make a project look favourable, if much of the finance for the capital expenditure involved comes from outside the organisation concerned, eg from the Department of Environment, the Urban Programme, etc. Another problem with this sectionalisation of public sector interests is that it is all too easy to see the capital expenditure decision as a separate one from annual revenue budget decisions, and therefore ignore or not fully explore the revenue budget consequences of a project. This has led more than one authority into the embarrassing position of having a new facility built, but not being able to finance the running costs! As emphasised above, a proper project appraisal should consider all costs and benefits for as much of the lifetime of the project as is feasible.

Conclusions

The techniques demonstrated above help to avoid expensive mistakes. They also help leisure suppliers to provide cost effective and/or socially worthwhile leisure services. It seems a pity then that many leisure facilities are built without rational planning and project appraisal. There are obvious constraints to the wider adoption of such techniques, but really there is no excuse for putting the success of a capital investment project at risk just for the want of a bit of foresight.

Further reading

Bates J, Parkinson JR 1982 *Business economics*. Basil Blackwell, Oxford.

Barker P, Button K 1975 *Case studies in cost benefit analysis*. Heinemann, London.

Gratton C, Taylor PD 1985 *Sport and recreation: an economic analysis*. E and FN Spon, London.

Hawkins CJ, Pearce DW 1971 *Capital investment appraisal*. Macmillan, London.

Joint Venture Study Group 1981 *Central Station: proposals for regeneration*.

Joint Unit for Research on the Urban Environment 1981 *The economic impact of an exhibition centre at Manchester Central Station*.

Vaughan DR, Wilkes K 1986 *An economic impact study of tourist and associated arts developments in Merseyside*. Merseyside Tourism Board, Liverpool.

Vaughan DR 1986 *Estimating the level of tourism-related employment: an assessment of two non-survey techniques*. British Tourist Authority, London.

Plus any good introductory management accounting textbook which includes 'capital budgeting'.

12 Contracting leisure management

In previous chapters we have implied that the boundary between public and private sector leisure management is distinctly blurred. Public sector leisure organisations can be seen taking relatively commercial decisions in order to satisfy financial objectives, while private sector leisure companies are increasingly conscious of the wider social benefits attached to their leisure investments, such as economic impact. One of the most significant changes in the management of public leisure services in Britain in recent years continues this development of pulling private and public sector leisure management closer together — this is compulsory competitive tendering (CCT).

By opening up the possibility of private commercial leisure management firms bidding for contracts and managing local authority leisure facilities, this legislation is requiring local authorities to work, if necessary, alongside commercial firms in the provision of their leisure services. It also requires any commercial firm interested in bidding for such a contract not just to take seriously but also *actively to pursue* local authority objectives, which will almost certainly include social objectives.

Under CCT legislation the management of many local authority built sports facilities (except those specifically exempted on the grounds of small size, high schools' use, dominant non-sport purpose, sports development work, or one or two other exceptional reasons) must be subject to a contracting process. This means that management contracts must be specified; suitable contractors then bid for the contract and, normally, the lowest cost bid is accepted. Because these facilities normally make a loss, each contractors' bid is the fee or subsidy they require to operate the facilities. Two principal types of contractor organisations have emerged. First the existing in-house local authority leisure management team almost always bid, in effect, for their own jobs. If they win the contract they are relabelled a Direct Service Organisation (DSO) and they have a new contractural relationship with the local authority but they will remain employees of the local authority. Second, specialist commercial firms have emerged to compete for the contracts to manage local authorities' leisure facilities.

In this chapter we use economic analysis to examine the advantages and disadvantages of such contracting as a means by which local authority leisure facility management is organised. As a direct consequence of this analysis some clear advice emerges concerning the ways in which CCT is conducted by the client local authorities.

Definitions and misconceptions

Many commentators have described CCT as 'privatisation', but this is *not* the case because privatisation involves selling the assets to the private sector. The local authority assets for which management is to be contracted, ie the leisure facilities, remain firmly in local authority ownership. It is unlikely that privatisation will occur in the foreseeable future for the simple reason that many of these leisure facilities are nowhere near a profit-making situation. CCT is also not 'liberalisation', since this involves breaking up monopolistic government businesses by allowing direct private sector competition to occur. CCT has often been called 'contracting out', but even this is inaccurate because it is only *contracting out* if a private contractor wins the bid. In fact all the evidence is that a large majority of the first round of leisure management contracts will be awarded to the existing in-house team, ie 'contracting in'.

CCT is quite simply a process of 'contracting'. It opens up one point of competition between the local authority in-house team and private management companies at the time of bidding for the contract. After the successful bid has been identified the competition disappears until the next point of bidding, which normally occurs at the end of the contract period in four to six years' time (earlier if the contract is terminated early).

There is no imperative under CCT legislation for the subsidies given by local authorities to their facilities to be cut. Even though the local authority is obliged under the legislation normally to accept the lowest bid, the objectives of the local authority as reflected in the contract specification will determine the extent to which subsidies are required. For example, a specification which stipulates considerable entry price concessions for a wide range of customers, and extensive programming requirements for recreationally or socially disadvantaged groups will almost certainly attract bids which require a high level of subsidisation.

It is a fairly safe prediction that local authority leisure facilities subject to CCT will continue to be subsidised by local authorities and also, therefore, by central government through the Revenue Support Grant. Any pressure to reduce the subsidies to such facilities comes not from the implementation of CCT but rather from the way in which central government is squeezing the financing of local authorities. In particular the percentage of local government spending which central government is prepared to finance through grants (principally the Revenue Support Grant) has been steadily cut since the 1970s, and the threat or implementation of 'capping' local authorities' own taxes (ie rates, poll tax and council tax) has inhibited local authorities' spending plans.

Implicit and explicit contracts

Contracting is nothing new. All organisations run according to contracts. Some of these contracts are explicit and involve direct market payments, such as employment contracts, purchasing contracts and sales contracts. But most contracts, particularly in local government services until recently, have been implicit – that is, unwritten, informal and largely unaccountable in the sense of having to conform to a set of written objectives. Even employment contracts are largely implicit, given that they rarely set measurable achievements for staff to work to and by which they may be judged, disciplined and rewarded.

Regarding the management of public sector leisure facilities, until CCT there had been unwritten management contracts in the main. The managers of local authority facilities, whether they were managers on-site or officers off-site in leisure departments, had largely set their own management agendas, with only loose monitoring by fellow officers or members. CCT is designed to change these implicit contracts into explicit contracts, the main objectives being to inject competition into the awarding of contracts and accountability into the administration of contracts. For this to improve value for money in the management of leisure facilities, however, several hurdles have to be overcome, which we discuss below.

Transactions costs

All transactions cost money. Implicit contracts are costly because they are so informal that they do not ensure cost-effective delivery of the service. We have reviewed many of the criticisms of government supply and management decision-making in local authorities, in Chapters 4, 7, 10 and 11 particularly. Such criticisms are rooted in problems normally associated with bureaucracies – eg lack of competition and motivation, inadequate management objectives and information. If contracts are implicit there is no obvious direct line of accountability for decisions made, because there is no written contract to hold managers to. The costs of resulting inefficiencies are difficult to quantify but are indicated very clearly in recent Audit Commission value for money reviews for local government services in sport, entertainment, arts, museums and art galleries (*see* Chapter 13).

Explicit contracts, such as those created by CCT, create a new set of costs, however. The contracts have to be specified, awarded, monitored and, sooner or later, re-contracted – all of which creates new expenditure for local authorities. If for any reason a contract variation is required, for example if a new investment is made by either the client or the contractor, then negotiation of each variation is necessary, or possibly renegotiation of the whole contract. Such variation is likely given the rapid changes that can occur in leisure markets, eg demands, fashions and technology. Any contract variation will increase transactions costs.

If experienced, skilled labour is used to administer the contracting process, this can be expensive not only in terms of the one-off costs of specifying contracts and selecting contractors, but also in the continuing process of monitoring the contractors' performance and negotiating variations. If economies in these transactions costs are sought by employing cheaper labour to administer the contract process, then any deficiencies in the contracting administration will add to transactions costs. For example, if the contract is not specific enough about the pricing and programming of a facility, then the subsidies may end up in practice benefiting people for whom they were not intended, which is an unnecessary cost.

The 'bottom line' of CCT is that the new transactions costs arising from explicit contracting must not be greater than the old inefficiency costs of implicit contracting. Otherwise moving from implicit to explicit contracts is a waste of time and money. CCT explicit contracts must cause net operational costs to fall, and/or they must improve the service provided through their increased accountability.

Bounded rationality

Explicit contracts have very stringent information requirements. They need to specify what the job is about in such a way that all potential contractors know what is expected of them. They must also enable the client authority to monitor accurately whether or not the contract is being adhered to and the authority's objectives are being achieved. Any shortage of the information necessary for the contract to work properly will cause transactions costs, either tangible ones in the form of time taken to correct for the deficiencies, or intangible costs associated with inefficiency.

When information is limited it is termed a 'bounded rationality' problem in economics, since any decisions taken will only be informed by a limited amount of the required information. Consumers and producers *typically* operate in circumstances of bounded rationality, ie missing at least some of the information they would like to make the decisions they are making. There are limits, for example, to the amount of research an average consumer can undertake before deciding what hi-fi equipment to purchase. Even with the help of specialist magazines and knowledgeable salespeople, it is likely that the consumer will be short of essential information – eg how will each of a number of alternative systems sound in the home environment where the hi-fi will be located? The consumer will eventually have to limit the amount of information sought to assist the purchasing decision and make as rational a decision as possible in the light of this limited information: ie bounded rationality.

In the same way, the rationality of decisions made concerning the specification and awarding of leisure management contracts is bounded by information constraints. The ideal specification is one which identifies precisely what is to be achieved from the contract. Whereas this is reasonably straightforward for technical contracts such as building or refuse collection, it is very difficult in leisure services management. The fundamental outputs of leisure services involve such achievements as higher quality of life, health benefits and reductions in crime and vandalism. Such 'social' outputs are difficult enough to measure in their own right, let alone trying to identify to what extent they are achieved by local authority leisure services. Yet they are important reasons for the continued public ownership of leisure facilities and the public subsidies given for their operation. So straight away there is a vital piece of missing information in the specification of leisure management contracts.

The information used to specify leisure management contracts, therefore, is likely to concern at best 'intermediate outputs' and at worst not outputs at all but inputs. Intermediate outputs are usually throughput indicators, such as usage and utilisation. They are intermediate because it is not necessarily the case that if you have more 'bums on seats' the real, social objective of the local authority will be achieved, ie if they are the wrong bums . . .

Instead of outputs it is highly likely that many leisure management contracts will concentrate on inputs, ie technical issues such as pool and air temperature, staffing, prices, opening hours and programming. Such input specifications are based on the assumption that if you can get the contractor on the right track, then they will reach the local authority's objective, even if it is almost impossible to identify if and when this happens! This is highly speculative since the relationship between inputs such as expenditure on staffing, decisions on pricing, etc, on the one hand and outputs like quality of life and better health on the other is very complicated, not least because leisure management inputs are only one factor determining such outputs.

Thus, bounded rationality is an inescapable backcloth to the process of contracting. The more difficult it is to get information relevant to the contract specification, the less likely it is that explicit contracts will enable cost effective achievement of the local authority's objectives. The problem would be worse if it were not just a lack of information but rather an *imbalance* in information between the client and potential contractors. Many local authorities are quite openly favouring their in-house bid for the contract, not necessarily by biased selection, which is against the law, but rather by giving the in-house bid every assistance in its preparation. One way of doing this is by volunteering the in-house DSO more information about the operations of the facilities than external bidders are likely to ask for.

Adverse selection

If it is impossible to specify properly the outputs expected from leisure management contracts, and consequently specifications concentrating on determining the inputs that the contractor must use, then one consequence is that the selection of contractors will be dominated by economy, the saving of money. Indeed, the legislation requires that the lowest bid should be accepted unless there are good reasons for not doing so – again encouraging the client authority and the potential contractor to think in terms of inputs rather than outputs. Because of this, it might well be that some potentially good contractors will not even bid for the contracts. They will be put off by the concentration on specifying inputs, because in effect many of the important managerial decisions are taken out of their hands. Pricing, programming and opening hours, for example, are decisions that under the legislation remain the local authority's decision.

Even if 'good' contractors do bid for the contract, they may lose out to other bidders who concentrate on cost cutting, simply because of the bounded rationality problem – if local authorities cannot specify social objectives accurately, how can they judge the respective social merits of different bids? Even if one contractor was aware of the output requirements and fully costed these in the bid, if this made the contractor more expensive than another contractor who had not fully thought through the output requirements, there is a danger that the latter contractor wins the contract and the former loses out.

This problem is one of 'adverse selection', whereby the contract specification favours the 'wrong' type of bid, from what might be termed 'respectable cowboys' – approved contractors with an emphasis on cost cutting. These are not just from the commercial sector; many in-house bids being assembled are concentrating on cost-cutting, because that is what the process of CCT and contractor selection is inviting.

Moral hazard and opportunism

If the contract is poorly specified, in terms of not specifying desired outputs, then it opens the door for any contractor to distort operations to fit their own objectives – this is the problem of 'moral hazard'. If the contractor has more facility-specific information than the client this increases the risk of moral hazard. The problem is an inevitable consequence of poor specification. The contractor organisation will have its own set of objectives and if the contract specification allows the contractor too much slack then the temptation to pursue contractor rather than contract objectives is obvious. One fear in local authority client organisations is that a commercial contractor can remain within a technical, input-orientated specification of the contract but still steer a leisure facility away from social objectives (because they are not specified accurately enough) and towards commercial, even 'profiteering' objectives.

This behaviour is 'opportunism', because the opportunity to pursue the contractor's objectives is increased by poor client information and contract specification. It is not just a potential problem with commercial contractors, either. Another form of opportunism is said to have occurred under the old system of implicit contracts with existing in-house operations. This type has been rather cruelly labelled 'shirking' and is summed up in its most extreme form by such attitudes as 'the customer is a nuisance', 'more than my job's worth', etc. In the case of implicit contracts, poorly specified in terms of objectives and outputs, it allowed employees the opportunity to shirk with little or no recrimination. This form of opportunism is still a danger with DSOs, because they are used to the old system and the poorer the contract specification the greater the opportunity to return to the old ways.

F

Contractors are not to be blamed for having their own objectives; this would be a ridiculous criticism. Commercial contractors, like any other private commercial business, have to make a profit to survive and grow. At the other extreme the shirking in-house operation cannot be blamed for its lax attitude if it is given no measurable objectives, little management decision making powers, no incentives to pursue objectives, and is accountable only in the sense of having to keep to its budget! It is important for client organisations to consider what in the CCT process is going to curtail the opportunistic behaviour of *any* type of contractor. The discussion of incentives on page 157 is particularly relevant to this issue.

One irony in the implementation of CCT is that many local authorities and many leisure departments are not sympathetic with the change in legislation. Consequently, some local authorities also demonstrate moral hazard by exploiting any weaknesses in the legislation to favour the in-house bid. In other words they have an incentive to pursue their own objectives in preference to those of central government. Under the legislation this is termed 'anti-competitive behaviour', but it is very difficult to define and monitor, so the scope for opportunism by local authority client organisations is considerable.

Anti-competitive behaviour by client authorities is recognised as a serious threat to the competitive intentions of CCT legislation. This behaviour includes not awarding the contract to the lowest bidder without good reason, packaging facilities together to make unattractive contracts by being too small, too big or an odd 'exotic' mix, onerous pre-tender vetting of potential commercial contractors, and unrealistically demanding performance specifications in the contract. Monitoring this and other possible anti-competitive behaviour is at best an extensive and difficult task. The government and its watchdog for this legislation, the Audit Commission, are to an extent reliant on appeals from losing bidders to uncover such behaviour. Appeals procedures can be very involved, which adds to the transactions costs involved in implementing CCT.

Investment and asset specificity

The driving force for efficiency in any free market economy is competition. One of the purposes of explicit contracting is to introduce competition into the supply of public sector leisure services where there was no competition before. However, one constraint to such efforts to encourage competition is in the leisure-specific nature of both physical assets (buildings, equipment, etc) and human assets (management, coaches, technical specialists) in leisure services.

Such 'asset specificity' restricts the ability of the market to compete for the use of these assets and without such competition there is less pressure to use the assets efficiently. Poor use of a leisure centre or a sports coach, for example, even though it is signalled in the market place by poor returns and poor pay, would not cause non-leisure businesses to compete for these assets. So the lack of full market competition for these resources increases the chances of their continued inefficient use. This would not matter if there was sufficient information to specify contracts in such a way that efficiency could be closely monitored. Nor would it matter if there was no opportunism, since contractors could be relied on to adhere strictly to the client organisation's objectives. However, asset specificity in combination with bounded rationality and opportunism means that there is a lack of control over the efficiency of an explicit contract arrangement.

Another investment problem is that of reinvestment in both physical assets, through capital expenditure, and human assets, through training. Continued investment in both types of asset is essential in any industry for improved productivity, profitability and growth. But explicit contracting complicates the process of reinvestment. The responsibility for new investment in physical assets (and its appraisal) lies with the client authority, but the contractor has a strong vested interest in such development. The client has to assess carefully the distribution of returns, financial or non-financial, to themselves and to the contractor, as part of the appraisal.

In the early years of the contract the contractor may well be prepared to finance new investments, so long as they have a reasonably quick payback. However, with leisure management contracts typically lasting between four and six years, there is little incentive for contractors to pay for investments in the latter half of the contract period. Contractors and clients will have to negotiate for variations in the contract and possibly even recontract when further investment in physical assets is required – adding to the transactions costs of the contracting process.

The overall effect of CCT on investment in public leisure services is difficult to predict. On the one hand the legislation encourages commercial firms to invest as partners in the public leisure infrastructure. Any investment of this type can be negotiated with the client authority to ensure the contractors a reasonable return. On the other hand few commercial firms are bidding for contracts and even if they do win and invest, the response by some local authorities might be to see it as an opportunity to reduce their capital spending on leisure. When DSOs win contracts investment will be as before, purely a public sector matter, since DSOs do not have the capability of investing in new capital.

As regards investment in human assets, explicit contracts lasting only four to six years again give little incentive for any contracting organisation to invest in long term training programmes. This comes on top of a more fundamental problem in service industries such as leisure, which is that labour productivity is difficult to measure, let alone relate to changes in training, so training is always difficult to justify quantitatively. This problem is rooted, of course, in the difficulty of measuring output in service industries such as leisure, as discussed in Chapter 9.

Imperfect markets v imperfect government

The principles outlined above amount to an imposing set of constraints to the effectiveness and efficiency of contracting local authorities' leisure management. It would be wrong, though, to infer from such problems that CCT is necessarily a mistake. It is obvious that there were elements of 'government failure' in the old way of organising public sector leisure in the form of local government monopolies, as suggested by an impressive catalogue of publications, most notably Coopers and Lybrand (1981) and the Audit Commission (1989 & 1990). The move from government monopoly to contracting serves to remind us that markets 'fail' too; that is why public sector provision was organised in the first place.

The market failure which contracting is in danger of rejuvenating will be mainly apparent when private, profit-seeking firms win contracts. If it occurs, it will take a form closely related to that associated with purely private commercial sector suppliers. Rather than ignoring any social objectives completely, the contractor has every financial incentive to rank social objectives below the profit making objective, where this does not break the terms of the contract.

Even if the in-house DSO wins the contract, efficiency problems may still occur. The relationship between the DSO and the local authority has changed to a contractor/client relationship. The possible outcomes of this changed relationship are various, but include the chance that when 'the dust has settled' operations continue much as before, ie government failure. Such problems may be worse if the DSO workforce consider that they have been conned into an 'all that fuss for nothing' situation. On the other hand contracting may lessen government failure even if DSOs win a substantial proportion of the contracts, simply because the process has increased the accountability of the in-house workforce to the client authority.

So the dilemma is which is the lesser of two problems, the risks of market failure brought about by private contractors, or the risks of continued government failure from DSOs? Since the dimensions of both market and government failure are very difficult to measure, this is an impossible question to answer. Contracting is a form of compromise which retains government ownership, social objectives and subsidies but allows some competition and the possibility of more commercial management practice. Contracting, though, brings a new set of problems, reviewed above, as well as the benefits of compromise between commercial and social values. The process of CCT therefore needs to minimise such problems and two issues within the control of local authorities will help in this respect: information and incentives.

Information

The key resource in any contract is information. Information is needed to specify the contract in a meaningful way. Although the outputs of public leisure services are difficult to quantify, it is not necessary to revert totally to input specification. It is possible to identify and set targets for 'intermediate outputs' in leisure provision, such as usage by certain target groups, either as a proportion of total facility/service usage or in relation to their importance in the local population. Financial targets can relate to social objectives too, such as requiring per capita subsidies at specified levels for different programmes or user groups. Cost centering would be necessary to set such financial/social targets. Such performance appraisal issues are covered in detail in Chapter 13.

In the case of intermediate output specification it is necessary to generate accurate information to make the contractor accountable to the specification. Some of this information, such as use by target groups and user satisfaction, can only be achieved by regular market research. Management information is not only the key to successful contract specification, but it also reduces the likelihood of adverse selection and moral hazard. If contractors had clearer output targets, this allows the client to give the contractor more freedom to make managerial decisions rather than trying to tie the contractor down by specifying in detail the decisions themselves.

Incentives

To control opportunism, the key issue in administering contracts is offering incentives such that the contractor is interested in following the client's objectives as well as, and ideally in preference to, their own. Financial incentives are most effective the nearer they are to the individual. A great temptation to local authorities distrustful of commercial contractors is to concentrate on negative 'incentives' such as penalties for failure to conform to specified inputs. Although it is necessary to have legal safeguards for failure to fulfil contract specifications, an undue emphasis on policing and contract penalties is hardly likely to foster a cooperative and developmental client–contractor relationship.

A cooperative client–contractor relationship is also necessary to promote partnership investments by commercial contractors. Incentives here are easy to devise, eg guaranteed shares of profit or income even if the firm loses the contract in the future. The main difficulty is in ensuring that private commercial investments do not subtly change the operation of a leisure facility away from the client authority's objectives. Commercial investments, after all, require a commercial rate of return.

The problem of an in-house DSO continuing in the same operational culture as before CCT, or even in a *worse* state of motivation, is all too probable in many leisure contracts. This is particularly the case where in order to put in what is perceived as a competitive bid the workforce agree to a pay cut, only to find out that they would have won the bid without such a pay deal! This is happening in some authorities because either the DSO bid is the only one or the DSO bid is far cheaper than competing bids. Clearly incentives are needed to keep up the momentum of positive change in the efficiency of public leisure services.

To offer workforces direct incentives to improve performance (or simply to meet targets) is a relatively new concept in local authority leisure services. One reform that is riding on the back of many preparations for CCT is the introduction of performance related pay. This is a direct incentive to follow the objectives specified by the client authority, the success of which depends on the accuracy with which objectives can be monitored and the targeting of incentives. Social objectives will be the most problematic in this respect, being difficult to monitor and therefore hard to attach incentives to.

Conclusions

Contracting can work. It is nothing new, even to local authorities. In leisure management, though, a positive approach to specification and administration of contracts is necessary if the whole process of CCT is not to degenerate into another expensive change in bureaucratic procedure, with at best no change in the cost effectiveness of public leisure services.

The effectiveness and efficiency of *any* leisure service, regardless of the way management is organised, is dependent on information and incentives. So the issue might not be so much 'should leisure management be by an in-house operation, a DSO or a private commercial contractor?'. Instead it is possibly 'have the management got sufficient information, motivation and accountability to ensure an efficient service?'

As yet little empirical evidence exists to judge what effects CCT has had on the management of public leisure services. One limited but interesting report, from Leisure Futures Ltd, finds little difference between the quality of service offered by traditional in-house local authority management organisations and private commercial firms contracted to manage local authority facilities. In this report, management type is not nearly as important for the quality of services as the age and size of the facility, which takes the debate back to the issue of investment.

Further reading

Audit Commission 1989 *Sport for whom?* HMSO.
Audit Commission 1990 *Local authority support for sport: a management handbook*. HMSO.
Coopers and Lybrand 1981 *Service provision and pricing in local government services*. HMSO.
Gratton C, Taylor P 1991 *Government and the economics of sport*. Longman.
Hebden R 1991 *Guide to good practice in leisure management*. Longman.
Leisure Futures 1991 *Do private contractors provide better quality services?*. Leisure Futures Ltd.
Sports Council 1991 *Facilities factfile: recreation management*. The Sports Council.
Walsh K 1988 The consequences of competition in Benington J, White J *The future of leisure services*. Longman.

13 Performance appraisal for leisure

An underlying theme to this supply section of the book has been the objectives of suppliers. This is brought out in the explanation of the structure of leisure supply in Chapter 8, it is a basis for key management decisions examined in Chapters 9, 10 and 11, and it is an essential prerequisite for successful contracting of leisure management as discussed in Chapter 12. However, it is one thing to recognise that different suppliers have different objectives and therefore make decisions in different ways, but it is an entirely different matter to monitor whether these objectives are being realised, as the previous chapter demonstrates.

The purpose of this final chapter is therefore to concentrate on this process of monitoring and review. It does not concern any management decisions as such. Rather it discusses essential information that should underpin any decisions made by management, the simple principle being that if you don't know where you are now, or where exactly you want to be, how can you decide which direction to go?!

Why measure performance?

Performance for a leisure supplier can mean any number of things, depending, as we have suggested, on objectives. In Chapter 8 we identified a large array of possible objectives for leisure managers. Furthermore, it is apparent that there is no simple split in such objectives according to ownership. For example, a public sector supplier is likely to be interested in financial objectives, even if profit is unlikely; and a private sector supplier will be interested in serving the community's needs, not least because this is seen as consumer demand and is the source of revenue and growth for the supplier.

Only by *targeting* supplier objectives is it possible accurately to judge whether the leisure provider is achieving them. The main message of this chapter is that it is important to set up and use systems of management information to provide regular, quantitative information on performance. What would such information be used for? One problem identified in

Chapter 8, particularly for the public sector, is that with a variety of objectives relevant to any one supplier, there is a potential problem of inconsistency between different objectives. If the objectives are monitored quantitatively it helps to reveal any trade-offs between them.

Measurement also enables early identification of problems or under-achievement, which can be translated into management priorities. Evidence from some industry-watchers has suggested that 'crisis management' is often the norm – ie only reacting to a problem when it reaches crisis proportions. It is very likely that the reason this happens is because until the crisis occurs the managers are not aware that a problem is brewing, or at least are not aware of the full dimensions of the problem. With regular monitoring of performance there would be an early warning system. Ideally this system should be brought into the regular management processes.

Performance appraisal is important in bidding for funds and credibility too. This applies to a private firm raising money for investment, or persuading shareholders that the company is on the right course. It is also relevant to a public leisure service competing for funds and credibility within a local authority or from central government. Many a local authority leisure service faces a 'credibility gap' in the eyes of some political members and administrative officers (especially in Treasurers' departments!), because they are not considered to be 'essential' services. It is also the case in the public sector that taxpayers and customers need to be convinced that the service they are paying for is good value for money. Competitive tendering, too, requires more accountability, either from the in-house service or the private contractor. So the purposes of performance appraisal stretch far beyond normal management decisions.

We have already seen a version of performance appraisal in Chapter 11. Project appraisal yields information about the forecasted performance of individual capital projects, which assists the decision about whether or not to invest in them. But such appraisals only happen when a potential project is being considered, and they are *forecasts*. It is necessary to complement such appraisals with monitoring of what *actually* happens in practice. This should be done on two broad levels. First, the planning level concerns decisions about the medium and long term direction of the organisation – decisions which affect performance in a year or more's time. This level then involves '*strategic appraisals*'. Second, there is a need for information which is directly relevant to decisions and performance *now*, or next week, or next month. This we call '*operational appraisals*'.

What is performance?

Performance, of course means different things to different organisations. But it is possible to generalise about the nature of performance, and do so in the context of *any* types of supplier. So before going on to look at specific performance indicators it is important to identify the different aspects of performance that leisure providers will be interested in.

First, the most common type of performance found in the private sector is *financial* performance. This is often simplified in economics to mean profit, but in fact financial performance means much more than this. Revenue, costs, debts, liquidity (the ability of the firm to turn its assets into cash), security, all these are different aspects of financial performance. They might all ultimately be related to changes in profitability, of course, which is why economics simplifies the commercial firm conceptually down to a profit maximising organisation. But for both operational and strategic appraisal purposes it is necessary to examine the different strands, as accountancy does.

Effectiveness is a second type of performance measure, which is concerned solely with the achievement of output targets. It does not, therefore, consider the costs of achieving the output targets. Effectiveness is an important performance aspect in public sector leisure services, since they are concerned with specific social objectives. These objectives include education, with such services as swimming and other activity classes, and educational use, in its widest sense, of leisure facilities such as museums and libraries. They also include catering for particular, disadvantaged, target groups. Furthermore, although public sector providers have the discipline of their budgets, this is not as demanding as having to make a profit, so the costs of provision have not, historically, been a major consideration.

Efficiency has already been identified in Chapter 9 as having technical and allocative dimensions. However, common to both of these is the objective of achieving objectives and targets at minimum cost. So efficiency considers the best possible relationships between inputs and outputs. It is sometimes given the terms 'cost effectiveness' or 'cost efficiency', and is also what is meant by the term 'value for money'.

Economy is solely concerned with the input side of the production process. Economy is achieved if inputs are acquired at minimum cost, but it does not consider the output consequences of this achievement. There is, then, always the danger of 'false economy' if economy is the only performance considered in an organisation. A more appropriate version of economy is minimising cost of inputs *for a given quantity and quality of output*, but of course qualitative output is difficult to judge. This broader definition of economy is very close to the concept of efficiency.

Sometimes a fourth 'e' is added to this list of performance dimensions, particularly in public sector organisations. This is *equity*, which implies fairness in the treatment of all customers. This has a variety of interpretations, such as equality of access regardless of ability to pay, giving priority to the most socioeconomically disadvantaged members of society, or even service benefits distributed according to how much tax people have paid to support the service. Whatever the form of equity being considered though, it can be argued that equity is a particular form of effectiveness, since it is a measure of output with no reference to inputs.

There are other concepts which are related to performance in leisure organisations, but in many cases they are only partly related to performance. They are, though, all too often used by suppliers as their only measures of performance, which is better than nothing but not really the best form of performance monitoring. Throughput, workload or sales is one such measure, such as the number of visitors in a given time period. Such a measure has also been termed an 'intermediate output', since if throughput is changed then it is likely that the end product, eg health, quality of life, will have changed in a fairly predictable way. Throughput may be a measure of how much demand there has been for a service, but it does not really indicate how effectively the demand has been satisfied and it does not say anything about the economy or efficiency with which the sales have been achieved.

In the public sector it is often the case that performance is 'measured' by expenditure on inputs, ie increased spending is taken automatically to mean an increase in service output. But of course this is no measure of performance at all. It says nothing of the actual outputs of the service, which could be highly ineffective, inefficient and wasteful of resources despite the rising expenditure.

Performance indicators

Ideally, indicators of performance should have certain qualities or properties to make them suitable for management purposes. These qualities are worth stating from the outset. Briefly, a set of performance indicators should have the following attributes. They should reflect all the objectives of the leisure service *accurately*. They should cover different facets of performance, such as effectiveness and efficiency. Preferably, indicators should be capable of being measured for separate parts of the service, since it is likely that different objectives and different targets are applicable to different parts of the service, even within one facility. Indicators should be administratively manageable, easily understood and, for comparisons, it is important that they are consistent over time and between service elements or organisations.

Having stated these requirements, however, it is necessary to stress that any set of indicators is unlikely to fulfil all of these properties. This is simply because these qualities are difficult to achieve – all indicators have their good points and their bad points.

Private, commercial sector

For a private, commercial supplier of leisure, issues of performance are largely documented in financial terms, although there are other important considerations. Business accounting ratios are designed principally for planning purposes (strategic appraisal) and control purposes (operational appraisal). The ratios are sometimes expressed as percentages. They are concerned not just with profit, but also with liquidity, asset utilisation, capital structure and investment potential. A sample of such ratios is given in Table 13.1.

Liquidity will be of interest not only to managers, but also to potential traders with a company and to creditors. Asset utilisation relates directly to management consideration of efficiency and productivity, as discussed in Chapter 9. Capital structure is important for security from takeover and to

Table 13.1   Some performance ratios for commercial firms

Profitability	
$\dfrac{\text{Either gross or net profit}}{\text{Sales}}$	No rules of thumb. It varies widely between industries and firms.
$\dfrac{\text{Net profit after tax}}{\text{Total assets}}$	'Return on capital employed'. No standard definitions, so care is needed in making comparisons between firms and industries.
Liquidity	
$\dfrac{\text{Current assets}}{\text{Current liabilities}}$	'Current ratio'. Rule of thumb = 2:1.
$\dfrac{\text{Current assets} - \text{Inventories}}{\text{Current liabilities}}$	'Acid test', 'quick' or 'liquidity' ratio. A more discriminating test of ability to pay debts.
$\dfrac{\text{Balance sheet trade debtors} \times 365}{\text{Total credit sales}}$	Average collection period of trade debts, ie average number of days before accounts are paid.
Asset utilisation	
$\dfrac{\text{Sales}}{\text{Fixed assets}}$	Indicates the effectiveness in using fixed plant to generate sales.
$\dfrac{\text{Cost of goods sold}}{\text{Inventories}}$	'Stock turnover'. Varies a lot between industries.
$\dfrac{\text{Sales}}{\text{Number of employees}}$	Indicates revenue productivity of labour.
Capital structure	
$\dfrac{\text{Net worth}}{\text{Total assets}}$	Indicates shareholders' interest in the business. (Net worth is ordinary shares + preference shares + reserves.)
$\dfrac{\text{Borrowing}}{\text{Net worth}}$	'Gearing'. An indication of the riskiness of the capital structure.
Investment	
$\dfrac{\text{Dividend per share}}{\text{Market price per share}}$	'Dividend yield'. Indicates rates of return on investment in shares.
$\dfrac{\text{Net profit} - \text{preference share dividend}}{\text{Number of ordinary shares}}$	Earnings per ordinary share.
$\dfrac{\text{Market price per share}}{\text{Earnings per share}}$	'Price/earnings ratio'. Indicates the market's evaluation of a share.

Details of the use of these ratios can be found in any good accounting text

shareholders interested in risk, whilst investment ratios are important to potential shareholders and bidders.

These ratios, and many more, are detailed for individual companies and industry sectors by commercial publications such as ICC Business Ratio Reports. By such means performance is put in the context of other similar companies, ie cross-section comparisons. But in the context of time series comparisons within companies the strength of ratios is that they put performance in a consistent perspective. For instance it is one thing to declare £30,000 profit, but this figure only really takes on a meaning if it is put in the context of turnover, or capital, as rate of return figures do. Because the ratios commonly involve two monetary sums, such as the ratio of a firm's debt to its equity, they enable financial comparisons to be made over time, without having to worry about adjusting for inflation. They also allow disclosure of potentially sensitive or confidential information in a disguised form – eg labour costs expressed as a percentage of total costs, or turnover.

It is important to stress, however, that ratios have to be treated very carefully. Many are more appropriate for comparing a single firm's performance over time than comparing this firm with another, particularly if the other is in a different industry. Some ratios involve estimates which can be done in various ways, so comparing like with like is a potential problem – for example, valuing inventories and intangible assets. Another problem of estimation is that some values are annual averages, so getting the information from balance sheets is unreliable, merely averaging the beginning and end of the year situations, when more observations during the year are really required – this is particularly a problem with liquidity ratios, for example.

Private firms are also interested in other aspects of performance. *Market share* is an important objective that is normally measurable, even at the local or regional level. It is, of course, a piece of strategic appraisal information, since it is only capable of change in the medium to long term. But market share is indicative of another major concern for strategic appraisal besides financial indicators – the *demand* for the product. The second part of this book identifies major changes in demand for leisure commodities and the factors that influence such changes. It is vital for any provider, private or public, to be informed about changes in demand for the products they are supplying, and this is the primary function of market research.

Most large private leisure organisations have marketing departments, with market research sections. As well as continual monitoring of demand for their products by this means, they regularly employ outside market research agencies or consultancies to conduct specialist market research, usually in the population at large rather than existing consumers of their products. Some of these agencies and consultancies produce regular reports with market research information alongside financial data for different leisure industries, examples being *Mintel, Euromonitor,* and *Key Note.*

Public sector

Public sector leisure providers are slowly waking up to the functions of market research and marketing in general, functions that private commercial

Table 13.2   Some performance indicators for public sector leisure
suppliers

Effectiveness

$\dfrac{\text{Gross operating expenditure}}{\text{Local authority population}}$	Gross expenditure per capita. This can be disaggregated into different service elements. An imperfect effectiveness measure, since high spending does not ensure a good service.
$\dfrac{\text{Visits by the elderly}}{\text{Total visits}}$	Indicator of effectiveness in catering for one target group. Other targets can be similarly measured.
$\dfrac{\text{Users}}{\text{Local authority population}}$	'Participation rate' eg for facilities. Better still if disaggregated into different types of user.
$\dfrac{\text{Bookings}}{\text{Total bookings available}}$	An aspect of capacity utilisation.
$\dfrac{\text{Market expenditure}}{\text{Total visits}}$	Assumes a relationship between two! Needs to be very carefully interpreted.

Efficiency

$\dfrac{\text{Net operating expenditure}}{\text{Local authority population}}$	'Per capita subsidy'. An imperfect indicator, since a high subsidy does not necessarily mean an inefficient service.
$\dfrac{\text{Gross operating expenditure}}{\text{Total visits}}$	'Cost per visit'. An imperfect indicator of efficiency (see text p. 166)
$\dfrac{\text{Net operating expenditure}}{\text{Total visits}}$	'Subsidy per visit'. An important equity indicator. Better still if it is disaggregated into different types of user and/or activity.
$\dfrac{\text{Direct income (from fees and charges)}}{\text{Gross operating expenditure}}$	'Cost recovery'. This can be disaggregated into different service elements. A very imperfect indicator of efficiency, since it may be an authority's intention to provide a highly subsidised, effective service.
$\dfrac{\text{Direct income}}{\text{Staff or staff-hours}}$	Revenue productivity of labour. Similar indicators can be calculated for other major inputs.
$\dfrac{\text{Total visits}}{\text{Staff or staff-hours}}$	Physical productivity of labour.

Economy

$\dfrac{\text{Staff costs}}{\text{Gross operating expenditure}}$	Economy on staff. Such a ratio could be used for any other cost element, eg energy, administration.
$\dfrac{\text{Cleaning expenditure}}{\text{Floor space}}$	This indicates nothing about the cleanliness of the facility! Like all economy indicators it ignores the quantity and quality of output.

providers have long recognised as essential to their success. There are now good examples of leisure market research specific to local authority areas, such as that done by the London Borough of Waltham Forest featured in Chapter 7. They provide authorities with strategic performance appraisals which not only identify the successes and failures of the past but point the way to management decisions of the future.

Some public sector performance indicators are listed in Table 13.2. This is an illustrative rather than a definitive list. The ratios in this table are designed to cover effectiveness, efficiency and economy. However, as with the commercial indicators in Table 13.1, it is important to stress that these ratios only capture performance imperfectly and there are often inaccuracies or inconsistencies in the measurement of the required data.

Cost per visit, or its reciprocal, visits per pound of costs, is an indicator commonly used for public sector performance, but it is really a reflection of capacity utilisation more than financial performance. If, for example, the price of entry is reduced and a conventional demand response occurs, ie demand increases, then because costs are unlikely to rise much (remember most costs are likely to be fixed) the cost per visit will fall. Clearly, this indicator reflects the primary concern of the public sector with usage rather than finances.

Whether financial performance improves in the example used here depends on the elasticity of demand. If demand is inelastic the increase in demand will not compensate for the fall in price, so that although cost per visit has decreased, the profitability or cost recovery of the service will deteriorate. Alternatively, if demand is elastic then not only will the cost per visit fall but also the cost recovery will rise. So this is a good illustration that an indicator for one thing is not necessarily a good indicator for another. Ideally if cost per visit is going to be monitored, then so should cost recovery.

It is really up to each organisation to choose a manageable array of indicators to reflect the performance priorities, or objectives of the organisation. For a local authority this may include throughput indicators for particular groups of clients, such as women, the elderly, the unemployed, and beginners, since this would monitor the effectiveness of the organisation in dealing with target groups. It may also include very conventional indicators of financial performance such as those relevant to the private supplier in Table 13.1, particularly for parts of the service which have no particular 'social service' function, such as the bar, cafe, vending machines and other merchandise sales. In addition any organisation should be interested in efficiency, as suggested in Chapter 9, so some measures of productivity in physical and revenue terms will be desirable, such as sales per manhour.

Each different type of public sector leisure service will have a different list of appropriate performance indicators. The Audit Commission's recent value for money reviews (1989, 1991) give excellent examples of performance indicators for sports facilities, entertainments and arts venues, museums and art galleries.

Quantity, frequency and new technology

Obviously there is a limit to the amount of information that a manager can reasonably cope with in operational and strategic decision-making. So it is important that a representative number of performance appraisal indicators be systematically monitored. This helps managers get used to interpreting the indicators and building this interpretation into decision making. The question does arise though, how often should the performance indicators be produced? There is no easy answer to this. Appraisal for a business strategy will probably only be needed on an annual basis.

In fact it is most common for performance indicators to be calculated on an annual average basis. However, there are good reasons for wanting *operational* performance appraisal indicators to be available on a far more regular basis. Decisions about promotion, programming, manning and purchasing arrangements may be modified at any time, so a regular flow of up-to-date information assists such decisions. Furthermore, there is a need for performance appraisal to be not just average, but also *marginal* or *incremental*. This would show the consequences for performance of any change in operations.

There is a direct analogy here with the information produced by the government for the management of the national economy. Strategic indicators such as public expenditure estimates are produced annually, in the Autumn statement for example. Other data, such as inflation, unemployment and balance of payments, are produced monthly, because policy changes do not just occur once a year on budget day! Moreover, some data for management purposes (not usually published) are marginal or incremental in nature, such as the financial effects of recent or proposed changes in policy.

With today's choice of new technology, of course, there is really no excuse for not generating regular management information on perform ance. Modern tills can record a lot of useful information, which can be linked to microcomputers with software designed to produce as many performance indicators as are required, and *on demand* rather than at set times of the year. Here is not the place to review the technological options that are available. Suffice it to say that new technology is an essential prerequisite for a comprehensive management information system.

External comparisons of performance

So far we have been discussing performance appraisal in the context of the internal management of a leisure organisation. However, it is also likely that the organisation will want comparisons to be made with other similar organisations. External yardsticks for performance are important because they give a competitive impetus to the organisation, and they enable other bodies to assess the relative performance of each organisation. This is particularly important in the public sector where the central government, through such bodies as the Audit Commission, is very interested in monitoring the relative performance of individual local authorities, not least because it directly funds half these services!

Comparative performance information is available in published form in both the private sector and the public sector, with the former costing far more than the latter (surprise, surprise!). In the private sector, market reviews are published on a regular basis. Some, such as *Retail Business*, published by the *Economist Intelligence Unit*, confine their analysis to the market as a whole. Others, such as *Business Ratio Reports*, and *Jordans*, publish very specific information about individual firms as well as market averages. A typical list of ratios used in Business Ratio Reports is given in Table 13.3.

Table 13.3   Performance ratios used by ICC's Business Ratio Reports

Return on capital	Profit before tax expressed as a percentage of capital employed.
Return on assets	Profit before tax expressed as a percentage of total assets.
Profit margin	Profit before tax expressed as a percentage of sales.
Asset utilisation	Sales expressed as a ratio of total assets.
Sales to fixed assets	Sales expressed as a ratio of fixed assets.
Stock turnover	Sales divided by stocks. The number of times stocks are turned over in a year.
Credit period	Debtors divided by sales, multiplied by 365. The average number of days taken before accounts are paid.
Export ratio	Exports expressed as a percentage of sales.
Current ratio	Current assets including quoted investments expressed as a ratio of current liabilities.
Quick ratio	The sum of debtors and other current assets divided by total current liabilities.
Borrowing ratio	Total debt expressed as a ratio of net worth.
Equity gearing	Shareholders' funds expressed as a ratio of total liabilities.
Income gearing	Gross interest paid as a percentage of pre-interest, pre-tax profit.
Average employee remuneration	Total employee remuneration divided by the number of employees.
Profit per employee	Profit before tax divided by the number of employees.
Sales per employee	Sales divided by the number of employees.
Capital employed per employee	Capital employed divided by the number of employees.
Fixed assets per employee	Fixed assets divided by the number of employees.
Return on shareholders' funds	Profit before tax expressed as a percentage of shareholders' funds.
Return on investment	Pre-interest profit expressed as a percentage of capital employed plus short term loans.

Source: ICC's Business Ratio Reports, ICC Information Group

Table 13.4 Audit Commission/CIPFA indicators of performance in public sector leisure provision

---

Per capita expenditure for each local authority and its 'family' average, with the following categories:
  Parks and open spaces
  Outdoor sport and recreation
  Indoor sport and recreation, including:
    Sports halls, leisure centres and swimming pools
    Community centres and halls
  Cultural facilities, including:
    Arts centres, threatres and entertainment
    Art galleries and museums
    Grants
  Other, including:
    Grants for recreation
    Promotion of tourism
    Catering
    Other
  Administration, including:
    Recreation departments
    Central departments

Per capita running costs for the same categories as above.

Per capita debt charges for the same categories as above.

Per capita income for the same categories as above.

Cost of difference, ie the total cost of the difference between the local authority's net expenditure and that of the 'family' average, for the same categories as above.

Cost recovery for parks, outdoor sport, sports halls, and community centres.

Source: Audit Commission (1988)

In the public sector there are two main sources of comparative information for local authority leisure services. One is not published but is available to each local authority. It is prepared by the Audit Commission, and contains per capita expenditure comparisons between the local authority and the averages for a 'family' of similar local authorities. Each 'family' has been calculated to represent similarities in socio-economic and demographic characteristics (Craig 1986). So comparisons are as much as possible 'like with like' with respect to the demand side of the market. However, 'families' may not be similar with respect to *supply* conditions. The ideal comparison would be with an authority facing not only similar demand conditions but also similar supply conditions

The current set of Audit Commission indicators is presented in Table 13.4. Comparing this table with Table 13.2, it is apparent that the Audit Commission's indicators do not represent a comprehensive set for performance appraisal purposes. They need to be supplemented, mainly by facility-specific information on usage.

The emphasis in Table 13.4 is very much on economy, especially with the calculation, for each service element, of the total expenditure difference between the authority concerned and the family average. To take an extreme position, an authority would be spending much less than the family average if it provided no service at all – very economical but hardly effective! To be fair to the Audit Commission, though, they do stress that the statistics are limited and that the indicators are designed 'to identify the questions to be asked. They do not imply any answers' (Audit Commission guidance notes 1983). Moreover, it is to their credit that they are attempting to assist local authorities in making performance comparisons with each other. Even so, the direct questions raised by the information in Table 13.4 are ones of economy, whilst questions of efficiency and effectiveness are raised in the recent value for money reviews published by the Commission.

In fact the performance indicators in the Audit Commission tables are calculated entirely from data published by the second public sector source, the Chartered Institute of Public Finance and Accountancy (CIPFA). Two annual publications are relevant, one on Leisure and Recreation Statistics Estimates and the other on Local Government Comparative Statistics. The latter, because it contains information on all local government services, does not have many indicators of leisure service performance. The former is the primary source of information, but even here the data gathered for CIPFA are of necessity restricted in scope to financial statistics, and they are estimates rather than outturns. Furthermore, CIPFA does not group the data for comparative purposes, so care needs to be taken in selecting authorities with which to compare.

CIPFA leisure estimates data, then, offers no clue as to what comparisons are valid, whilst the Audit Commission uses demand characteristics to identify families of similar local authorities within which comparisons may be made. An example of comparisons where there are similar supply characteristics, SASH sports centres, is given in Case Study 13.1. The problem here, of course, is that identical sports centres will not necessarily be serving similar markets, so performance will vary simply because of differing demand conditions.

Case Study 13.1 Performance in SASH sports centres

The Standardised Approach to Sports Halls, SASH, is a concept devised by the Sports Council, the winning design for which is constructed by Bovis. SASH centres are meant to be low cost (ie not just capital but also operational costs), good value for money, high quality facilities. Twenty-three SASH centres now exist in Britain. To assess the success of the design in practice, the Sports Council commissioned a two year study of the performance of nine of the first SASH centres (ECOTEC 1987). This study examined four aspects of operating performance: management, design, energy use and environmental performance. Comments here will be confined to the management findings.

The Sports Council had basic objectives for the SASH centres, so any performance evaluation has to be made with respect to these objectives.

They can be summarised as follows:

(1) The centres were designed to serve a 'neighbourhood' catchment of between 15,000 and 25,000 people.

(2) Usage targets, taken from evidence for similar designs, were set at 90,000 visits a year for single provision SASH centres and 70,000 visits a year for joint provision SASH centres.

(3) The centres should prove capable of catering for the normal Sports Council target groups, eg women, unemployed, the young, women with children, the disabled.

(4) The centres should prove flexible in use, catering for a wide variety of activities, sporting and non-sporting.

(5) Four full-time staff and five part-time staff should be effective in operating the centre, excluding catering staff.

(6) If the management have appropriate policies, the SASH should be capable of breaking even on operational costs, excluding debt charges.

The advantage of a performance comparison of the type undertaken in this study is that the supply characteristics are identical, ie the same SASH halls. However, it must be said that some of the SASH halls in the study sample had added other facilities, such as squash courts and floodlit outside areas. So in this sense the comparison was not 'like with like', even on the supply side. In addition, of course, the nine SASH centres, all being in different regions of the country, faced very different market demand conditions. Furthermore, it was *not* the case that management objectives in the nine sample SASH centres were the same. Therefore, it is to be expected that performance in the nine centres would differ considerably, despite the identical design of the sports halls.

The results of the performance comparison demonstrated that SASH sports halls are capable of fulfilling most of the objectives specified by the Sports Council. The halls served much larger catchment populations than anticipated – as high as 282,000 people in one case. Despite this, though, usage was generally below the targets set. The combination of high catchment population and low usage numbers implies a low participation rate at the SASH halls, but no obvious reasons for this emerge in the study. It could simply be that the usage targets were too ambitious, for example. There was no appreciable difference in usage numbers between single and joint provision centres. The main implication of this finding is that single provision SASH centres suffered from severe peak load problems with chronic underutilisation during the weekday daytime.

The centres achieved good representation in usage by target groups and a variety of different activities. This performance was recorded by indicators drawn from market research which showed the proportion of visits accounted for by each group or activity.

Staffing was generally higher than the minimum specified in objective (5) above, averaging five full-time and six part-time. This may be accounted for by the fact that most of the sample SASH halls had supplementary facilities attached, although the ones that did not have such supplementary facilities did not have noticeably lower staffing. There is also no apparent relationship between the level of usage and the level of staffing, even though we might have expected the former to determine the latter.

As for the financial performance of the sample of SASH centres, the potential to break even on operational costs was realised by one centre, with 99 per cent cost recovery. The range of cost recovery stretched down to 29 per cent at the bottom end, but it is important to stress that 29 per cent cost recovery is not necessarily a sign of poor performance – 29 per cent may be *expected*, because of management objectives and demand characteristics. Generally, cost recovery was high in the nine sample SASH centres, averaging 66 per cent in single provision centres and 83 per cent in joint provision centres (this compares with a national average for all sports centres of 47 per cent at the same time).

In comparisons between local authority leisure services, gross and net expenditures per 1000 population are commonly cited indicators of performance. However, these fall into the category of input measures rather than output or performance measures. Their use can in fact be misleading. Take the example of two local authorities, both with low net expenditure. One could be low because it does not provide much service, the other could be low because although it provides a vast array of good leisure services, it also brings in a lot of revenue. So a superficial scan of differences in a single indicator is not a valid comparison. The message is again clear. For a valid comparison of different organisations supplying leisure commodities it is necessary to make a careful, balanced selection of both the indicators and organisations with which to make comparisons.

Public sector performance appraisal and accountability is undergoing a fundamental review in the 1990s with the advent of The Citizen's Charter. This will require every local authority to report its annual performance using indicators which will be stipulated by the Audit Commission in 1993, after a consultation process. It is anticipated that about twenty indicators will relate to local authority provision of leisure services, including sport, the arts, museums, parks, open spaces and play.

Budgeting implications

Conventionally, budgets are prepared and presented in what is termed a 'line item' style, whereby the structure is determined by the separate inputs, eg staff, supplies, transport, fuel, etc. Such budgets may be good for financial control, but they are not good for assisting management decision making, since they offer little information on effectiveness or efficiency. Budgeting is a formal opportunity to set in motion performance appraisal, since it systematically records essential management information.

In this and other chapters we have stressed the importance of identifying service objectives in a *functional* sense, and therefore making decisions for the individual functions and recording management information for the individual functions. It is clear that if budgeting was to accord with this way of doing things then it should not be structured according to inputs. Instead budgets should be prepared for each functional element of the service, ie *programme budgeting*. A major problem with such a method of organising budgets is allocating costs and revenues to the programmes – the cost centering problem which we have discussed in Chapter 9.

Another required element of programme budgets is that they should not only include details of expenditure and income, but also outputs, so that effectiveness and efficiency targets can be specified as well as economy targets. In the commercial sector this is not such a problem, since financial measures of performance tend to dominate considerations. In the public sector, however, there is a more pressing problem of how to measure outputs. But even if such measures were confined to the number or proportions of users from specified target groups, this could be related to income and expenditure estimates such that a more effective and efficient service delivery can be designed.

Conclusions

Good management of the provision of leisure goods and services requires more than intuitive management. It needs a system of management information so that decisions are taken in the best possible knowledge of the circumstances, the objectives of the organisations, the degree of achievement of these objectives and the effects of past decisions. Putting together a system of information acquisition and presentation needs a lot of work, such as market research and cost centering, which will not necessarily yield an immediate return. But the point of such a system is to improve future decision making and performance. Fortunately, the operating costs of running a good management information system are now quite low, if a suitable investment is made in new technology.

As with most systems of quantitative information, however, it is necessary to add words of warning about the quality of the data used. Many of the performance indicators in common use, or of feasible use, have to be interpreted with care. They are all imperfect in the story they portray. It is necessary, therefore, to put a lot of thought into the design of management information systems, to avoid the 'rubbish in – rubbish out' problem. Equally bad, however is a situation of 'nothing in – nothing out', whereby it is all too easy to think that the pitfalls of performance appraisal are best avoided by not doing any! Our view is quite unambiguous – a performance appraisal system is essential to good management.

Further reading

Audit Commission 1989 *Sport for whom? Clarifying the local authority role in sport and recreation.* HMSO.

Audit Commission 1990 *Local authority support for sport: a management handbook.* HMSO.

Audit Commission 1991 *Local authorities, entertainment and the arts.* HMSO.

Audit Commission 1991 *The road to Wigan Pier? Managing local authority museums and art galleries.* HMSO.

Butt H, Palmer B 1985 *Value for money in the public sector: the decision-makers guide.* Basil Blackwell, Oxford.

CIPFA *Leisure and recreation statistics estimates*, annual.

Craig J 1986 A *socioeconomic classification of local and health authorities of Great Britain.* HMSO.

ECOTEC 1988 *SASH centres in use 2: management and design performance.* The Sports Council, London.

Gratton C, Taylor P 1985 *Sport and recreation: an economic analysis.* E and FN Spon, London.

Hespe C, Sillitoe A, Thorpe, J 1988 Measuring performance, *Management papers. Issue 1*. Sports Council, Greater London and South East Region, April.

Holmes G, Sugden A 1986 *Interpreting company reports and accounts*. Woodhead-Faulkner, Cambridge.

ICC Information Group Ltd *Business ratio reports*, regular reports for many different markets.

Reid W, Myddelton DR 1982 *The meaning of company accounts*. Gower, Aldershot.

Plus any good introductory management accounting text which includes 'ratio analysis'.

Index

182 *Index*

Urban Programme   101–2, 143, 146

vertical integration   121
visibles   23
visit rates   93–4
voluntary sector   104–9, 124, 134

Waltham Forest   89–90
welfare   11, 34, 39, 42, 43
working practices   51
Wynarczyk   42, 45

X-efficiency   111, 121